The Great American Meat Book

ALSO BY MERLE ELLIS

Cutting Up in the Kitchen

THE GREAT AMERICAN MEAT BOOK

≈ by ≈

MERLE ELLIS

Alfred A. Knopf New York 1996

THIS IS A BORZOI BOOK
PUBLISHED BY ALFRED A. KNOPF, INC.

Published in the United States by Alfred A. Knopf, Inc., New York, and simultaneously in Canada by Random House of Canada Limited, Toronto. Distributed by Random House, Inc., New York.

http://www.randomhouse.com/

Grateful acknowledgment is made to the following for permission to reprint previously published material:

Chronicle Features: Recipes and other material from syndicated columns "The Butcher" and "Cooking Around the Country" by Merle Ellis. Reprinted by permission of Chronicle Features, San Francisco, California. *Cole Publishing Group, Inc.*: Recipe "Brain Fritters" from *Innards and Other Variety Meats* by Jana Allen and Margaret Gin, copyright © 1974. Reprinted by permission of the publisher, Cole Publishing Group, Inc. *Contemporary Books, Inc.*: Recipe "New Yorker's Steak" from *Honest American Fare* by Bert Greene, copyright © 1981 by Bert Greene. Reprinted by permission of Contemporary Books, Inc., Chicago. *Dutton Signet*: Barley recipe from *The James Beard Cookbook* by James Beard, copyright © 1959 by James A. Beard. Reprinted by permission of Dutton Signet, a division of Penguin Books USA Inc. *HarperCollins Publishers, Inc.*: Recipe "Roast Loin of Veal" from *Veal Cookery* by Craig Claiborne and Pierre Franey, copyright © 1978 by Craig Claiborne and Pierre Franey. Reprinted by permission of HarperCollins Publishers, Inc. *William Morrow & Company, Inc.*: Recipe "Lemon Veal Roast with Rosemary" from *The Splendid Table* by Lynne Rosetto Kasper, copyright © 1992 by Lynne Rosetto Kasper. Reprinted by permission of William Morrow & Company, Inc.

Library of Congress Cataloging-in-Publication Data
Ellis, Merle, [date]
The great American meat book / by Merle Ellis.
p. cm. — (Knopf cooks American ; 15)
Includes index.
ISBN 0-394-58835-5 (alk. paper)
1. Cookery (Meat) I. Title. II. Series.
TX749.E42 1996
641.6′6—dc20 96-4117 CIP

Manufactured in the United States of America
First Edition

ILLUSTRATION CREDITS

The photographs and illustrations reproduced in this book were provided with the permission and courtesy of the following:

The National Provisioner magazine and Stagnito Publishing, Northbrook, Illinois: pages x, 7, 67, 77, 142, 150, 304
The Bettmann Archive: page 14
Culver Pictures: pages 85, 99, 157, 229
Marc Kehoe: page 92
American Sheep Industry Association and American Lamb Council: pages 204, 205
Karl Stuecklen: pages 10, 94, 152, 210, 239, 266
Gourmet magazine, Condé Nast Publications, Inc., New York, New York: page 283

Contents

≈

Dedication

≈

I had a mentor—his name was Mike. He was the best butcher I have ever worked with, and I have worked with many.

I first worked with Mike at a Council Oak store in Sioux City, Iowa. I was a "clean-up boy." I came into the market after school and cleaned the place. It was a good job for a kid of thirteen, but it was not an easy job. Working for Mike was never easy. He demanded a great deal from all of his men, and even though I was thirteen, he treated me like one of them; I loved him for that and gladly worked my tail off for him. All of his men did.

Every afternoon for years, I washed the greens—those strips of plastic greenery that separate the meat trays in an old-fashioned meat case. In most markets they got washed—if at all—once or twice a month. Every afternoon the sawdust on the floor of the cooler and behind the counter got changed. In most markets that's a once-a-week operation. When you worked for Mike, it was once a day. Why? "It gives the market a nice fresh smell, and anything worth doing is worth doing right."

When I first began working with a knife, trimming chops, cutting stew, making ground beef, doing some of the simple things that apprentices start doing when they begin learning the trade, I was given the simple guideline by which every cut was made when you worked for Mike: "Do it the way you'd want it done." When you trim a chop or steak, trim it just the way you would if you were taking it home yourself. Don't put anything in the hamburger trimmings that you wouldn't want ground in your own hamburger. The worst reprimand any apprentice butcher could possibly experience was to have Mike bring back a steak or chop that you had cut or trimmed and quietly say, "Would you want to take this home?"

I have worked with countless butchers over the years and have learned something from every one of them—some little trick or method that made doing something easier or resulted in a better finished product. But the man who taught me the business, who taught me to love the smell of a clean market with fresh sawdust on the floor, who gave dignity to what some would consider dirty work, the man who made me proud to be what I am, was Mike. He was the best butcher I ever knew, and one that I have always tried to emulate. He was my mentor and my friend. He was my father. This book is dedicated to him.

Introduction

≈

We are a nation of meat eaters. In spite of the animal-rights activists, healthy hypochondriacs, and vocal vegetarians, we will continue to be a nation of meat eaters. Preferences for one meat over another may shift (they always have), but Americans love meat.

Pork became popular early in our history—pigs were the perfect choice for our forebears. Pigs are easy to raise—they'll eat most anything. They have large litters and produce quantities of lard and meat that takes well to smoking, pickling, and "puttin' down" for the winter. Beef began its rise in popularity following the Civil War, when Texans learned there was a market in the North for the millions of Texas Longhorns running wild on the state's southern plains. Longhorns were to be had for the taking. The cattle drives, the cattle trails, and the cowboys that followed have become not only American history but American legend. The beef that reached American tables as a result of those cattle drives, and the industry that grew following them, have made us beef eaters for the best part of the past hundred years. Pork is still popular; but it's changed a lot. Pigs today are much, much leaner, and perhaps because of that, pork has been regaining some of the popularity that it lost to beef for so many years.

It is impossible to predict what will be the favorite meat of tomorrow—we are so fickle when it comes to our food. Perhaps lamb, which has been much ignored in parts of America for far too long, will gain its rightful place on our table. Now that we have quality veal available, maybe it will become the meat of tomorrow. Whatever the choice, we will continue to be meat eaters.

We don't eat as much meat today as once we did. We don't need to. My grandfather had a good-sized steak, half a pound of bacon, and six eggs most every morning for breakfast. But he was up at 4 a.m. every day milking cows, pitching hay, cleaning the horse stalls, and "sloppin' the hogs." You can get hungry doing chores like that, and you burn up a lot of calories. Most of us don't work so hard these days. Nevertheless, meat remains an important part of our diet.

We passed through a period in recent years when "meat" became a dirty word. The concern over fat and cholesterol has caused most of us to change our habits a bit. Not many of us eat a sixteen-ounce steak very often, yet we still seem to want a steak on occasion. Steak houses like Morton's of Chicago, Ruth Chris, and others are some of the most successful restaurants of the day. Meat is making a comeback! New studies keep appearing that indicate that meat in moderation is indeed good for us; even fat is no longer a four-letter word. According to the USDA handbook, pure pork fat contains less than half the amount of cholesterol in butter and, if it has not been hydrogenated, is low in saturated fat.

The nutrition experts seem now to have settled on some sensible advice when it comes to eating right: "Eat a well-balanced diet, use some good common sense and moderation, and exercise." That's not much different from what my grandma used to say—"Eat your spinach and go do your chores!"

If I had known that I would one day write this book, I couldn't have found a better place to grow up in than Sioux City, Iowa, one of the great meat-packing cities of the country. And I couldn't have grown up at a better time than the 1930s and '40s. The great cattle drives were over, but not by many years. The hog was still "the gent that paid the rent" on the farms of many of my kinfolk in Iowa, Nebraska, and southern Minnesota. As I indicated in my dedication of this book, my father was a butcher. I learned the trade from him, starting as a kid. All my grandparents lived on farms across the Missouri River, in eastern Nebraska. Grandpa Simpkins, my mother's father, ran a small feedlot for "Old Man Davie," just outside Ponca, Nebraska. He fed a couple hundred head of Black Angus cattle, fattening them up so they'd grade Prime or Choice when they went to the stockyards and then to the slaughterhouse in Sioux City.

Grandpa Ellis raised corn about twenty miles away on "The Home Place," a 160-acre farm just outside Allen, Nebraska. Dad had four brothers and three sisters, which meant I had lots of aunts and uncles and cousins, most all of whom were somehow involved in the meat industry, one way or another. Aunt Evelyn's husband, Uncle Virg, a state brand inspector, raised Simmental cattle on a ranch out by O'Neill, in the sandhills of Nebraska. Aunt Norma's husband, Uncle Red, ran a farm-implement dealership out on the highway, by the feedlot. Uncle Lester raised corn, and Uncle Armand raised a few sheep, and everybody kept a few pigs and lots of chickens on the "place."

Researching this book has put me back in touch with some of my heritage, a heritage that was, almost without my knowing it, slipping away. We have all, I believe, forgotten where much of our food comes from and how it gets to our tables—particularly when it comes to meat. The generation growing up today knows only pork chops that come in plastic packages. They need to know that pork comes from hogs—live animals that are raised for food, slaughtered, and processed by men and women who do for us today what Grandpa and Grandma used to do. We need to remember that.

Meat in America has provided us with a rich and colorful heritage as well as lots of good food. Enjoy it!

The Great American Meat Book

Beef

≈

The Great American Meat Story begins with beef because this meat has contributed most to the stories and history that are part of America's heritage.

Certain historians argue that Norsemen brought cattle to America several hundred years before Columbus' voyages, but there is no record of it. The only evidence we have is that beef came to America with the Spanish.

Columbus—on his second voyage, in 1493—carried cattle on his ship and brought them to Santo Domingo; Cortés, in 1519, imported long-horned Andalusian cattle to Mexico. In 1540, Coronado brought cattle to what is now the United States in his search for El Dorado, the "Seven Cities of Gold." In the early 1600s, Spanish padres started their chain of missions throughout the Southwest and in California, and raised cattle. Wherever the Spanish went they took cattle and horses with them, and they never castrated the male cattle. As a result, many animals that were lost in travel or through Indian raids, or were just left behind when the group moved on, were fertile to breed. And breed they did. The famed Texas Longhorn was the result.

Longhorns were driven out of Texas to market before the Civil War. As early as 1779, fifteen thousand head were being trailed annually from San Antonio to markets in the Louisiana Territory, mostly for hides and tallow and as beasts of burden to pull covered wagons on the long trail west. It was after the War Between the States, however, that the Texas Longhorn made its mark on the history and legend of America.

During the short period from the end of the Civil War in 1865 until 1895, more than ten million Longhorns were driven out of Texas over the long trails north. The men who drove them, the American cowboys, the stuff of legend and romance, in reality helped make the mid-continent a unified whole. They brought the North and South together following the War Between the States. In days when most Americans rarely traveled more than one hundred miles from home, it was the cowboy who knew the country from the Gulf of Mexico to Canada. The Long Trails started a number of cities on the road to prosperity: San Antonio, Austin, Houston, Waco, Fort Worth, Dallas, Tulsa, Dodge City, Abilene, and Kansas City. The main cattle trails ran from south to north, from Texas to the cow towns of Kansas, and through New Mexico all the way to Colorado. All the trails began in or around San Antonio, and more cattle were added to the herd as they moved north through Texas. The Western Trail led to the railhead at Dodge City, Kansas; the Chisholm Trail to Ellsworth, Kansas; and the Sedalia Trail led to Sedalia, Missouri, a town on the rail line midway between Kansas City and St. Louis.

In 1866, pioneer cattlemen Charles Goodnight and Oliver Loving moved Longhorns west across Texas to Denver, the end of the Goodnight-Loving Trail. They knew there was plenty of free grass on the high plains where they could graze and fatten the cattle after the long trail north, so they could then move them to Eastern markets in peak condition when the selling price was at its best.

The Chuck Wagon

Charlie Goodnight is credited with inventing the chuck wagon, a broad-beamed, sturdily built wagon that carried everything ten or twelve cowboys would need on a dusty cattle trail for four or five months.

On a cattle drive the chuck wagon and the cook in charge (always called Cookie) were almost as important to a cowboy as a good horse. What the cookie said was law around the camp, and there were some very strict laws of chuck-wagon etiquette. You did not, for example, ride into camp at full gallop. You'd be shot! Nobody likes dust in his stew. You never took the last piece of beef or scoop of beans unless you were sure that everyone had his share. Someone might be rounding up strays, and there'd be hell to pay if all the food was gone. Most important, you never dared lift a lid on a simmering pot until the cookie yelled, "Come and git it!" Gabby Hayes, playing the camp cook in those Roy Rogers westerns, may have been the most accurately portrayed character of the Old West to appear on the silver screen. He stood for no nonsense, and evidently that was the way it really was.

Cookie was cranky, cantankerous, foul-mouthed, and usually mean. But he had a right to be. What other cooks have had to endure what a cook on the long trail had to put up with? Dust and dirt, and for fuel often

nothing more than the dried droppings of cattle or buffalo, known as "prairie coal." Aside from beef, beans were about all he had to cook, along with biscuits and coffee. There was salt pork, while it lasted, and in some outfits—the richer ones—some dried apricots or prunes. Makin' a meal from them fixin's in the dust or mud, rain or shine, for months on end, for a bunch of smelly cowpokes—many of whom were drifters and outlaws with a past as shady as a campsite under the cottonwoods—that's enough to make any cook cranky!

THE ENGLISH BREEDS

Long before the Longhorns had disappeared from the plains of Texas, the "English breeds," as they came to be called, made their appearance in Middle America. Other European breeds had come before: three heifers and a bull arrived in Jamestown, Virginia, in 1624 on a ship from England. But these and their descendants were dairy cattle and beasts of burden and played no role in making America the nation that produces the finest beef in the world. That honor goes to the "English breeds"—the Shorthorn, the Hereford, and the Aberdeen Angus.

Shorthorn

The Shorthorns, or Durhams, were the first on the scene, in Virginia in 1783. No record has been preserved, however, as to how they came from England, or how many cattle were involved. A few years later, in 1791, Shorthorns were brought into New York State, but nothing is known of the disposition of these cattle. The 1812 records show that an Englishman named Cox had a Shorthorn bull and two cows from his native country, but apparently the first registered Shorthorn bulls imported to the United States were brought into the Genesee Valley of New York in 1817 by Samuel M. Hopkins.

Hereford

That same year, 1817, the first Herefords of record to arrive in the United States came from Herefordshire, England, imported to Kentucky by the statesman Henry Clay. Herefords can thrive under the worst of conditions: surviving the severe winters of 1881, 1886, and 1887, which killed thousands of cattle on the Great Plains, they proved their superiority. The "white face," as the breed is called (they have white faces on a red body), mature early and fatten readily in feedlots. The meat is excellent, with a high yield of rib and loin, the source of the most tender steaks and roasts.

Angus

The third English breed came not from England but Scotland. George Grant, of Ellis County, Kansas, imported a few bulls from Aberdeenshire in 1873. These solid black animals are known as Black Angus or simply "Blacks." The breed naturally has no horns. Black Angus are smaller than Shorthorns or Herefords and

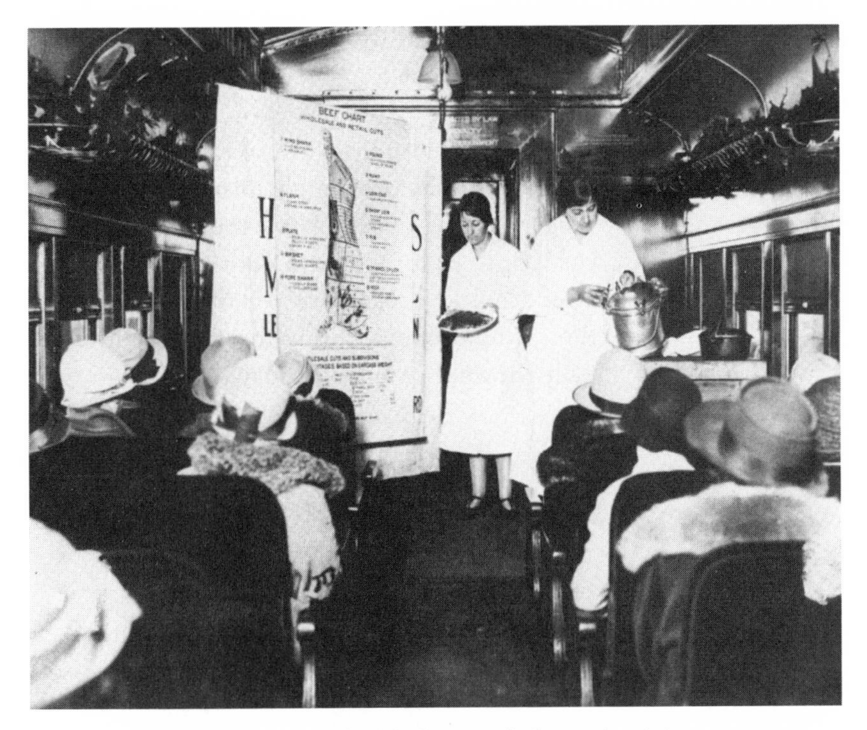

Railroads cooperated with the meat industry in giving meat demonstrations to passengers.

do not thrive as well on desert or sparse rangeland. However, where there is good pasture, such as in the Midwest and the Pacific Northwest, the Angus excels. As for the quality of the beef they provide, there is none better.

As beneficiaries of great beef, we in America owe the most to the English breeds. They made us a nation of beef eaters, and they dominated the market for nearly a hundred years.

THE EXOTICS

In the mid-1960s, cattlemen began importing breeding stock—cattle that have come to be called collectively "the exotics"—from all over Europe: the Simmental from Switzerland, the Limousin and Charolais from France, and the Chianina from Italy, to name but a few. The reason for the importation: grain prices were high and cattlemen were looking for ways to produce cattle that reached market weight sooner and consumed less grain in the process. Exotics are big, and they grow fast. Ranchers began crossing these exotics with the traditional English breeds. The result is that we now have a national cattle herd made up largely of mongrels, born of much crossbreeding between nearly a hundred different breeds of cattle.

The beef of today that has resulted from all this crossbreeding is leaner, comes to the market younger, and is therefore more tender than the beef of yesterday. But because it is young and lean, it doesn't have the flavor that beef once had. Nor can it be cooked as it once was. Stews and pot roasts from beef today need not cook all day to be tender, and steaks need help to be flavorful.

In the recipes that follow, I have tried to bring together the great taste of yesterday's beef with the reality of what's available today.

Beef Inspection and Grading

All beef—indeed, all meat—offered for sale in this country is inspected for wholesomeness by the United States Department of Agriculture. Inspection is a mandatory program paid for by the government to ensure the cleanliness and safety of our meat supply. All negative investigative reporting done by *Prime Time, 60 Minutes,* and *20/20* aside, we have in this country the safest meat supply of any nation in the world.

Grading for quality is a different story. Grading is a voluntary program whose price is paid by the packer but ultimately passed on to the consumer, designed to provide some indication of the quality—tenderness, juiciness, and flavor—of the meat we buy. At one point in our history, grading was mandatory. During World War II, and again during the Korean conflict, all beef sold in this country was graded for quality, and the American public came to rely on the system.

Over the years, the grading standards have been reduced several times to allow leaner and leaner cattle to qualify for the top grades of Prime and Choice. Two and a half percent of the beef graded today makes the top Prime grade, and when you want a really great steak, that's what you should look for. You're apt to find it only in a good steak house, since most Prime beef goes to the restaurant trade.

If really lean beef is what you're looking for, look for USDA Select, the grade below Choice. Thirty percent of the beef graded today grades Select.

Most of the beef in today's supermarket meat cases—67.5 percent—is USDA Choice. Indeed, since the quality standards were lowered in 1976, the range of quality within that grade is now so wide that it has become all but useless as a quality indicator for the consumer. When most beef is Choice, what choice do you have?

In 1978, the American Angus Association began the Certified Angus Beef program to help consumers identify Angus beef in the supermarkets and restaurants of America. Because of the wide variation in quality within the USDA Choice grade, Angus breeders felt there was a real need for a certification program that would take more of the guesswork out of shopping for top-quality beef.

It may cost a bit more at the market, but if you want top-quality beef that you can count on time after time, it may well be worth the price to look for Certified Angus Beef.

STEW, POT ROASTS, AND SUCH

The beef our forefathers ate was for the most part pretty tough stuff. The Texas Longhorns that sated the country's appetite for beef after the Civil War were old and tough by the time they reached market. In the earlier days, most cattle were too valuable to eat; the male animals pulled the wagon west, and the females provided milk, cream, and cheese. You didn't kill critters like these until they had served their purpose, and by then the meat was dry and stringy.

This meat needed special handling: the tenderizing that comes from long, slow cooking. Most of the beef dishes that became traditional on the plains and prairies of the West and Midwest, and ultimately the "comfort food" many of us speak so fondly of today, trace their origins to ranch cookhouses and the farmhouses that sprang up on the Great Plains after the cattle drives. The country was becoming settled. More than a few cowboys met the farmer's daughter, homesteaded the 160 acres the government allowed each settler, and started farming.

The recipes in this section will fill the kitchen with the marvelous aromas that memories, as well as great meals, are made of.

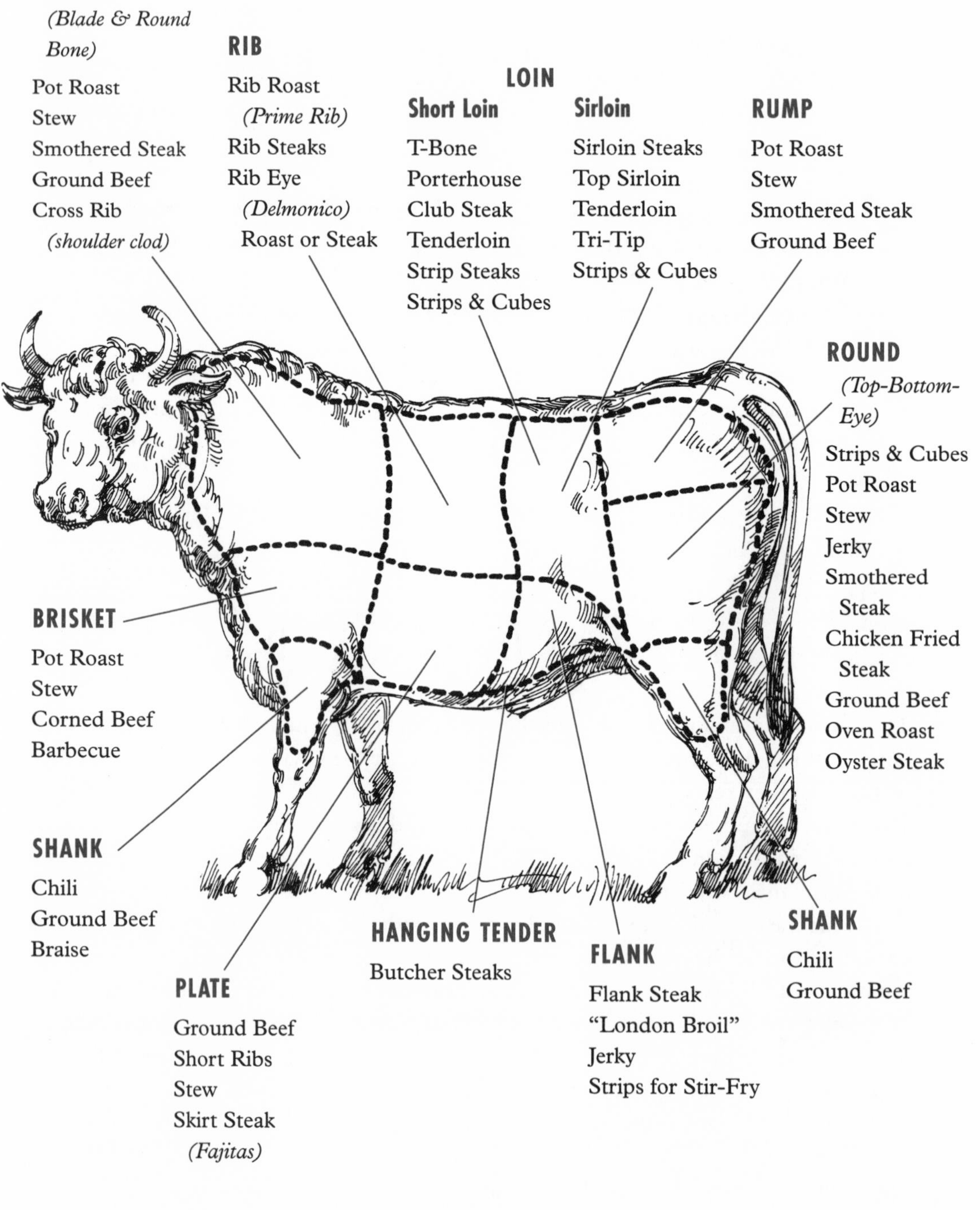
CHUCK
(Blade & Round Bone)
Pot Roast
Stew
Smothered Steak
Ground Beef
Cross Rib
(shoulder clod)
RIB
Rib Roast
(Prime Rib)
Rib Steaks
Rib Eye
(Delmonico)
Roast or Steak
LOIN
Short Loin
T-Bone
Porterhouse
Club Steak
Tenderloin
Strip Steaks
Strips & Cubes
Sirloin
Sirloin Steaks
Top Sirloin
Tenderloin
Tri-Tip
Strips & Cubes
RUMP
Pot Roast
Stew
Smothered Steak
Ground Beef
ROUND
(Top-Bottom-Eye)
Strips & Cubes
Pot Roast
Stew
Jerky
Smothered Steak
Chicken Fried Steak
Ground Beef
Oven Roast
Oyster Steak
BRISKET
Pot Roast
Stew
Corned Beef
Barbecue
SHANK
Chili
Ground Beef
Braise
PLATE
Ground Beef
Short Ribs
Stew
Skirt Steak
(Fajitas)
HANGING TENDER
Butcher Steaks
FLANK
Flank Steak
"London Broil"
Jerky
Strips for Stir-Fry
SHANK
Chili
Ground Beef

Stay Away from Stew Meat

The meat labeled "stew meat" in the meat case is often not the best cut for stew. In most markets "beef stew" consists of scraps from all parts of the carcass that are too small to call steaks. The quality of the cubes of meat in a package of stew meat can be very inconsistent. You'll get more uniformity and very likely save money if you buy a pot roast and cut your own stew. Here are some good cuts to look for.

Rump makes excellent pot roast, and cutting up a boneless rump roast for stew is about as difficult as slicing a hot dog.

Cross rib or *shoulder clod* is another boneless cut, great for pot roasting and simple to cut up for stew.

Chuck roast is a flavorful choice, with a bit more fat and therefore a lot more flavor.

Bottom round is another good choice, particularly if you're looking for lean. There is almost no fat in a bottom round.

The bottom line is to go for what's *cheap*—stewing tenderizes any meat. Even a thirteen-year-old Texas Longhorn would be tender if you stewed it long enough!

Tips for Moist-Heat Cooking

There is, to my mind, heart, body, and soul, no more satisfying meal than a good hearty stew, pot roast, smothered steak, or any braised meat dish simmered long and slow in a rich sauce (Grandma called it gravy) and served up with heaping piles of mashed potatoes and fresh or home-canned corn. That was my soul food, the kind that was always Sunday supper when I was a kid. It's not complicated or fancy, just simple country fare, and I still crave it above everything else. I think a lot of people do. It's the kind of food most of us over forty grew up on.

Unfortunately, few people cook these dishes today. They think they don't have time. If a recipe requires more than thirty minutes to prepare, most home cooks just don't bother, which rules out most traditional recipes for stews, pot roasts, and braised dishes requiring long, slow

Tips for Moist-Heat Cooking (continued)

moist-heat cooking of one and one-half to three hours of cooking time. That's the way Grandma did it, and the recipes haven't changed. However, meat has changed. These days you can make delicious moist-cooked dishes in far less time than the recipes in many cookbooks indicate. Today's beef is younger, so it cooks to tenderness relatively quickly. And you don't have to be there while it cooks. Once you get the stew or pot roast into the pot, leave it alone. Go play tennis, watch the "soaps," work on your computer. The meat will simmer to perfection without you, and fill the house with a wonderful aroma. The kids will come home and think you've been cooking all day.

Here are a few tips that may help you make good old-fashioned country cookin' even a little faster, to be more in keeping with today's fast-paced life styles:

• Dust the meat with seasoned flour and brown it well in a little hot fat before adding any liquid. It only takes a few minutes to get a nice brown crust on a pot roast or cubes for stew. The browning begins the cooking process, so that the "long, slow" simmering needn't be so long. It does, however, need to be slow! *Never* let a stew, pot roast, or braised dish boil; always cook at a gentle simmer. Turning up the heat won't speed up the cooking process, but it will, for sure, toughen the meat.

• While the meat is browning, heat whatever liquid you plan to use. Meat may be braised—that is, moist-cooked—in water, stock, dry wine, beer, or a combination of these liquids. Heating the liquid to the boiling point before adding it to the browned meat not only saves time (you don't cool down the meat and have to wait for it to reheat), but also makes for a smoother sauce or gravy.

• Most moist-cooked meat improves with age. Both texture and flavor are better developed when the dish is reheated the next day or even later, having spent some time in the refrigerator. So cook a stew while you watch TV tonight and serve it for dinner tomorrow. When you're ready to eat, remove the solidified fat that has risen to the surface, then heat the pot on top of the stove or in the oven. If you want to add vegetables, this would be the ideal time to do so. Now you can enjoy a great meal that really didn't take all that much time.

Basic Beef Stew

Basic, simple stews like this could be found in black iron pots over campfires and on wood-burning stoves all over the West and Midwest in the early part of this century. The addition of oregano is, of course, a modern touch.

- 1 teaspoon salt
- 2 tablespoons flour
- 1½ pounds chuck, shoulder clod, or rump, cut into 1-inch cubes
- 1 tablespoon vegetable shortening or oil
- 1½ cups strong black coffee
- 2 tablespoons molasses
- 1 clove garlic, minced
- 1 teaspoon Worcestershire sauce
- ½ teaspoon crumbled dried oregano
- ¼ teaspoon hot red pepper (cayenne)
- 1½ cups water
- 4 carrots, cut into ½-inch slices
- 2 small onions, quartered
- 3 medium potatoes, peeled and cut into 2-inch chunks
- ½ cup cold water mixed with 3 tablespoons all-purpose flour

≈

1. On a sheet of waxed paper or a plate, mix the salt and the flour together. Roll the cubes of beef until lightly coated on all sides.

2. In a large Dutch oven or heavy stew pot, melt the shortening. Over moderately high heat, quickly brown the beef cubes, turning frequently, until crusty. Brown a few at a time; do not crowd the pan, or the cubes will steam rather than brown. Remove them as they are finished, and set aside. Drain the fat from the pan and discard.

3. Return the meat to the pan and add the coffee, molasses, garlic, Worcestershire sauce, oregano, and cayenne.

4. Cover the pan and bring the mixture to a boil. Lower the heat and let the stew simmer until the meat is almost tender, 45 minutes to an hour.

5. Add 1½ cups cold water and the carrots, onions, and potatoes. Cover and cook gently until the vegetables are tender, about 30 minutes. Stir in the flour-water mixture to thicken the sauce. Cook until the sauce is thick and bubbling. Serve in deep bowls.

Serves 4 to 6 generously. Leftovers can be refrigerated or frozen.

VARIATIONS

There are as many variations to a basic stew as there were black iron kettles in cattle country. Here are but a few:

Beef Burgundy Stew with a French flair. Use a red wine instead of the coffee, eliminate the molasses, and use beef broth in place of the water. Instead of carrots and potatoes, use 12 small white onions that have been trimmed and peeled and ½ pound mushrooms cut in quarters. Sauté the onions and mushrooms gently in a tablespoon or two of butter before adding them to the stew.

Belgian Beef and Beer Stew The Belgians drink more beer than any other people in the world. They also cook with it a lot. I must be part Belgian! Proceed as for Beef Burgundy, substituting beer for the red wine. In place of Worcestershire sauce, oregano, and red pepper, use 2 tablespoons red-wine vinegar, 1 teaspoon brown sugar, and a couple of bay leaves. Slice the onions into ¼-inch rings before sautéing, and forget the mushrooms.

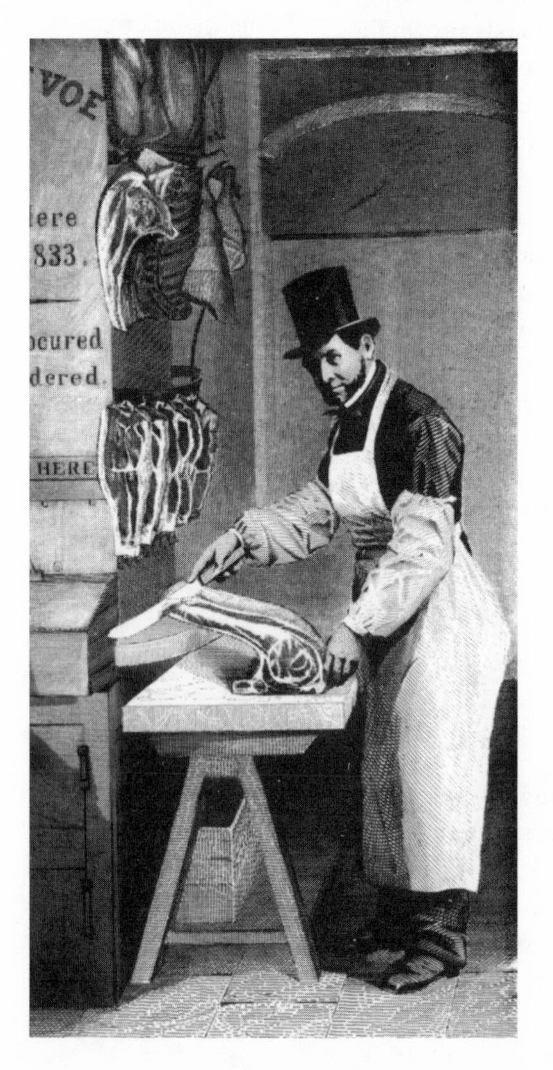

Oriental Beef Stew Cut the beef into 2-by-¼-inch thin strips instead of into cubes. Use 1 green pepper, 1 red pepper, 2 stalks of celery, and a good-sized onion, all cut into thin strips. Sauté the vegetables in the pan after the meat has been browned, then add a 5-ounce can of water chestnuts drained and sliced; return the meat to the pan and add 1½ cups beef broth. Mix 3 tablespoons soy sauce with 2 tablespoons cornstarch and use to thicken the sauce.

Son-of-a-Gun Stew

Unless you kill your own calf, marrow gut is hard to come by. Here is a modern version of SOB stew (page 16), courtesy of Joe Propps, who has been cooking for roundups at the Four Sixes Ranch in Guthrie, Texas, for twenty-six years.

- 2 tablespoons all-purpose flour*
- ¼ teaspoon freshly ground black pepper
- 2 teaspoons salt
- 1 pound beef chuck or bottom round, cut into 2-inch cubes
- 1 veal heart, about ¾ pound, membranes and fat removed, cut into 2-inch cubes
- ¼ pound salt pork, cut into slivers
- 1 large carrot, sliced thin
- 2 medium onions, sliced thin
- 1½ cups tomato juice
- 1½ cups beef broth
- 1 large clove garlic, minced
- 1 bay leaf
- 1 veal brain, about ½ pound
- 1 pair veal sweetbreads, about 1 pound

* Unless otherwise indicated, all the recipes herein that call for flour use all-purpose flour.

≈

1. Mix the flour, pepper, and salt together, and sprinkle the mixture over the cubes of beef and heart.
2. In a large Dutch oven, brown the salt pork over moderately high heat until lightly browned. Add the beef and heart cubes and brown quickly, turning the cubes to brown evenly. Add the carrot and onions, and cook, stirring, for several minutes.
3. Pour the tomato juice and beef broth into the pot, and add the garlic and bay leaf. Cover and bring to a boil.
4. Reduce the heat to low and let the mixture simmer, partially covered, for 1 hour. Check often to see that the mixture does not boil.
5. Meanwhile, soak the brain in salted water to cover for 10 minutes. Simmer the sweetbreads in salted water to cover in a covered pot for 10 minutes; add the brain and simmer 5 minutes longer. Drain the sweetbreads and the brain. Under cold running water, slip off the membrane covering the brain and remove any connecting tissue. Cut both meats into 2-inch cubes.
6. After 1 hour, the meat in the Dutch oven should be tender. Skim off any excess fat. If the sauce is thin, remove the meat and vegetables, raise the heat, and boil rapidly for several minutes to reduce the liquid, stirring constantly. Return the meat and vegetables to the pot, discarding the bay leaf.
7. Reduce the heat to let the stew simmer. Add the sweetbreads and brain cubes and heat through. Serve over rice or noodles.

Serves 4 to 6 generously. Leftovers are even better the next day.

Son-of-a-Bitch Stew

Some claim this dish got its name from an early cowboy who tasted it and said, "Son-of-a-bitch! That's good!"

Back in the early roundup days, cowboys went to work in the spring. Calves had to be branded and castrated, cattle were worked, and cowboys signed on for the season. A good cook always attracted the best ranch hands, and to show off his talent, every cook would make Son-of-a-Bitch Stew when the first calf was killed.

Recipes for this great cowboy treat differ (some call for tongue and liver as well as brains and heart), but the indispensable ingredient is the "marrow gut," the tube connecting two of the calf's stomachs, containing partly digested milk. Only a young animal has a marrow gut; the tube dissolves when the calf is weaned.

According to an old saying: "A son-of-a-bitch may have no brains and no heart and still be a son-of-a-bitch. But if it don't have no guts, it's no son-of-a-bitch."

Chili

The first chili, say some historians of the subject, dates to 1890, when a man named Myers made it in his café on the square in McKinney, Texas. It was an instant success; Jesse James often stopped at Myers' café to eat the stew. Some people pin chili down to San Antonio. "Chili Queens" sold bowls of it from stands in front of the Alamo right up to 1943, when somebody decided the stands weren't sanitary. It is also reported that cowboys on the cattle trails north would choose towns to raise hell in based on the quality of the "jailhouse" chili.

The very best meat to use for chili, according to 98 percent of the old-time experts I've ever talked to, is without question a thirteen-to-fifteen-year-old lean Longhorn bull. But those are a little hard to come by. The second best is beef shank meat. The shank is the lower part of the leg, right next to the ground. No muscle in the critter does more work and gets any tougher than the shank, and that's the stuff good chili is made of. You need something that can stand up under the long simmering that any good chili has got to have. Beef shank is loaded with connective tissue, which is not to be confused with gristle. Gristle is as tough as the seat of a trail cook's saddle, and it stays that way no matter what you do to it, but connective tissue is another story. With long, slow simmering, the connective tissue in beef shank virtually dissolves and makes a rich beefy pot liquor that is the very essence of a good pot of chili.

Ask the butcher for a center section of a beef fore or hind shank. You want the part with the little round marrowbone, not the knuckle. It's the same cut you have probably often bought cut into one-inch-thick slices for soup, but it's much easier to work with when you're using it for chili if you buy it all in one big piece. You'll need about four pounds of meat after you've removed the shank bone, so be sure to get plenty—at least two whole shanks. There's no sense making anything less than a *big* pot of chili.

When you get your shank home, first take the bone out (you might want to save the bone to add to the chili pot, because the marrow imparts a rich flavor). Then trim the fat and gristle off the outside of the shank meat. The outside membrane that covers the shank is tough, like the cook's saddle, and it stays that way, so remove it. The connective tissue is mixed in with the lean meat—don't worry about that—that's what makes a good pot of chili.

Once you've got the meat all trimmed up, cut it into cubes about the size of your thumb. *Do not grind it!* It is as near impossible to make a good pot of chili with a meat grinder as it is with a can opener!

Second-Best Chili

I don't pretend to be any kind of an expert on the subject of chili—to do so would be presumptuous of me in most places and downright dangerous in Texas—but I do love the stuff and make a pretty fair pot, if I do say so. I call mine "Second Best"—not because I think it is, but because it's made with the second-best meat, beef shank rather than a thirteen-year-old Longhorn. It also keeps me out of trouble in Texas.

≈

4 pounds beef shank meat (boneless)
¼ cup vegetable oil
1 medium onion, chopped
2 or 3 cloves garlic, minced
1 15-ounce can tomato sauce
1 12-ounce bottle beer
4 to 6 tablespoons chili powder (depending

1. Cut the meat into cubes about the size of your thumb. Heat the oil in a good-size heavy pot and dump in

(recipe continues)

Second-Best Chili *(cont.)*

upon how hot you like chili)
1 tablespoon ground cumin
2 teaspoons dried oregano
1 teaspoon salt
¼ teaspoon black pepper
¼ teaspoon cayenne pepper—more if you're brave, none if you're chicken
½ teaspoon sugar
2 tablespoons masa harina* or 1 tablespoon flour mixed with 1 tablespoon cornmeal
Chopped onion (1 tablespoon or more per serving) as garnish

* Masa harina is the traditional dough used to make corn tortillas. It is available in Hispanic markets, but should you be unable to find it, you can use a mixture of flour and cornmeal.

the meat; stir with a long wooden spoon so the oil coats the meat. Let cook over low heat, stirring once in a while, until the beef turns gray. Don't let it brown.

2. Add the onion and garlic; cover and simmer for 10 minutes. Add the tomato sauce and beer, put the cover back on, and simmer for another 10 minutes.

3. As the mixture simmers, mix all the remaining ingredients *except the masa* in a small bowl. You may want to use only 4 tablespoons of chili powder to start and add more at the end if needed. Dump the spices into the pot, stir it up a bit, put the lid back on, keep the heat low, and let it cook for an hour or so, until the meat is tender but not mushy.

4. Stir once in a while to prevent sticking, but keep the lid on as much as you can, so all that good rich "pot likker" stays inside.

5. Just before serving, taste the chili and add more chili powder or other seasonings to your liking. Mix the masa or the flour and cornmeal with enough cold water to make a thin paste. Stir it into the chili to thicken the consistency. Serve topped with chopped onions and accompany with cold beer.

Serves 6 to 8.

Pot Roast

In Nebraska, when the days became cold and crisp, my grandma called that "pot-roast weather." She'd send my grandpa into town to pick a pot roast out of the locker box where they stored their meat.

The meat might be a piece of beef chuck one time, a piece of bottom round another. It didn't much matter. They were all "pot roast," and they were delicious the way Grandma fixed them—always a little differently as winter wore on. In early winter there might be carrots and turnips from the autumn harvest, and then, later, when there was nothing left in the storm cellar but potatoes, that's what we had with pot roast. Sometimes pot roast was cooked with a good rich gravy, served over homemade egg noodles or dumplings. However it was fixed, pot roast was one of my favorite meals. It still is.

Since today's cattle come to the meat case younger, leaner, and more tender, pot roast now will cook in half the time called for in old recipes. Nevertheless, it's a good idea to plan ahead. For ultimate flavor, pot roast is best prepared a day or so before you serve it.

A variety of cuts work wonderfully well: bottom round, eye of round, cross rib with or without a bone. The best cut is the chuck, which is a cut from the front shoulder of the beef animal. Chuck with the bone is found in forms called blade chuck, seven-bone chuck, center cut, or arm cut. Boneless chuck is sold as underblade chuck, shoulder clod, and, of course, boneless chuck. The brisket is a cut that works well for pot roasting, but it is such a versatile cut that it deserves special attention (see page 23).

Basic Pot Roast

My preference for a pot roast is a seven-bone chuck, cut at least two inches thick. I still like to brown the meat in lard, although I know it's frowned on these days by some folks.

When the pot roast was tender, Grandma would put it on the porch by the cream separator. The fat rose to the surface and solidified, and was lifted off before the vegetables or thickening was added. Nowadays we just let the roast cool and refrigerate it overnight.

≈

1. Mix the flour, salt, and pepper together, and dust the roast on all sides with the seasoned flour. In a large cast-iron Dutch oven or heavy casserole, heat the fat until it sizzles. Brown the meat well on all sides, turning it as needed. Pour off any excess fat and discard.

3 tablespoons flour
1½ teaspoons salt
1 teaspoon fresh-ground black pepper
A 5-to-6-pound pot roast (see choices above)
3 tablespoons lard or a combination of vegetable oil and butter
3 large onions, sliced
Herb packet: 2 sprigs parsley, 6 black peppercorns, 2 bay

(recipe continues)

Basic Pot Roast *(cont.)*

leaves, 1 teaspoon dried thyme, all tied together in cheesecloth
3 cups beef stock, homemade or canned
2 tablespoons arrowroot or cornstarch, dissolved in 3 tablespoons cold water or stock (optional)

2. Add the onions, the herb packet, and the beef stock. Bring the liquid to a boil, then lower the heat so the liquid barely simmers.

3. Cook the pot roast, covered, on top of the stove, or in a preheated 325-degree oven for 1½ hours, turning it over at the halfway point. Check frequently; do not let the liquid boil.

4. When the roast is tender, let it cool and refrigerate, uncovered, until the fat solidifies. Lift off the fat and discard. Remove the herb packet and add any of the vegetables or seasonings listed in the variations below. If desired, thicken the cooking liquid with cornstarch or arrowroot dissolved in cold water.

Serves 6 to 8.

VARIATIONS

Next-Day Pot Roast Parboil potatoes, carrots, turnips, and celery stalks, all cut into good-size chunks, until almost tender. Add them to the pot. As the dish reheats, the vegetables will finish cooking.

Beef Bourguignon Replace half the beef stock with dry red wine. Add 1 pound fresh mushrooms to the dish as it reheats.

Italian Pot Roast Replace half of the beef stock with 1½ cups canned crushed tomatoes.

Hungarian Pot Roast Blend 1 tablespoon imported sweet or hot paprika into 1 cup sour cream. Add to the dish as it reheats. Serve over noodles.

Russian Pot Roast Mix together 1 teaspoon brown sugar, 2 teaspoons cider vinegar, 1 tablespoon catsup, and ⅓ cup raisins. Add to the roast as it reheats. Serve with Barley Pilaf (page 193) or mashed potatoes.

Sauerbraten

A memorable holiday dinner my family has often enjoyed over the years is a German pot roast, Sauerbraten, always served with Potato Pancakes. It takes planning ahead, because the beef must marinate for four days. Now, marinating—despite what you may have heard—doesn't really do too much in terms of tenderizing, but, oh, can it add flavor!

Use either top or bottom round; I prefer the bottom round, because it is more compact and thus easier to slice.

MARINADE

- 2 cups white-wine vinegar
- 3 cups dry white wine
- 1 cup water
- 2 medium onions, sliced
- 6 carrots, peeled and sliced
- 8 black peppercorns
- 8 whole cloves
- 1 tablespoon salt
- 1 teaspoon mustard seeds
- 6 sprigs parsley
- A 5-pound beef roast (top or bottom round)

COOKING INGREDIENTS

- ¼ cup plus 3 tablespoons flour
- 2 teaspoons salt
- ⅓ cup vegetable oil
- 1 large onion, sliced
- 1 bay leaf
- 2 tablespoons unsalted butter
- 2 tablespoons sugar
- ⅓ cup gingersnap crumbs

≈

1. In a large saucepan, place all the marinade ingredients except the roast, and bring to a boil. Lower the heat and let the mixture simmer for 5 minutes. Let cool.

2. Place the meat in a large bowl. Pour the marinade over it, cover, and refrigerate for 4 days. Turn the meat once a day so that it is evenly marinated.

3. After 4 days, remove the meat and pat it as dry as you can with paper towels. Strain the liquid, pressing down on the vegetables. Discard the solids in the sieve and reserve the liquid.

4. Mix the ¼ cup flour and the salt and dust the meat with the mixture. In a large Dutch oven, heat the oil until sizzling. Brown the meat well over moderate heat for about 20 minutes, turning it as needed. Remove the meat and pour out the oil.

5. Return the roast to the pot. Add the onion, bay leaf, and 3 cups of the marinade. Bring to a boil, lower the heat, and simmer the Sauerbraten until the meat is almost tender, about 3 hours. Remove the meat and strain the marinade. Return the meat and strained marinade to the pot.

6. In a small skillet, melt the butter. Stir in the 3 tablespoons flour and sugar and stir until the mixture turns light brown. Stir this mixture into the liquid in the pot to

Sauerbraten *(cont.)*

thicken it, cover, and continue cooking until the meat is very tender, about 1 hour longer.

7. Place the meat on a carving board. Sprinkle the gingersnap crumbs into the gravy and cook, stirring with a whisk, for 2 to 3 minutes, until the gravy is smooth. Taste, adding more salt and pepper if needed. Slice the meat, not too thin, and arrange in overlapping slices on a heated platter. Ladle on some of the gravy. Pass the rest of the gravy in a gravy boat. Serve with Potato Pancakes.

Serves 8 to 10.

Potato Pancakes

12 medium potatoes
3 onions
4 eggs
1 cup flour
½ teaspoon baking powder
1 teaspoon salt
2 cups vegetable oil or solid shortening

These are a *must* with Sauerbraten. Serve with bowls of applesauce and sour cream. Make the pancakes at the last minute before the meal.

≈

1. Peel the potatoes and soak them overnight to eliminate some of the starch, so that they cook crisper. Drain them, grate coarsely, and squeeze out as much liquid as you can with your hands. Spread the shreds on paper towels so more liquid is absorbed.

2. Grate the onions. Mix them with the potatoes in a large bowl. Stir in the eggs, flour, baking powder, and salt. Place the mixture in the refrigerator until you are ready to cook the pancakes.

3. Heat ½ inch of oil or shortening in a large skillet over moderately high heat. Drop ¼ cup of the pancake mixture into the hot oil, flattening with a spatula into a 3-inch patty. Turn to brown on both sides. Cook several at once, but do not overcrowd the pan. Add more oil as needed.

4. When the pancakes are puffed and brown, place them on baking sheets lined with brown paper or paper towels. Place the finished pancakes in a preheated 200-degree oven while you make the rest.

Serves 8 to 10.

Brisket of Beef—A Regional Roundup

Few cuts of meat have so wide a range of cooking variations as the brisket of beef. Prime-rib roasts served in New York are pretty much like those in New Mexico. A pot roast is a pot roast; flavoring changes, but the cooking method is straightforward. Leg of lamb, almost always roasted, remains the same across America. Not so brisket.

In New England, brisket is simmered with cabbage, carrots, and turnips for a hearty boiled dinner; the same cut is slowly smoked over a wood fire for the traditional Texas barbecue. It is a favorite cut for pot roast in many Jewish homes. Brisket is sold smoked in the Southwest, fresh in the Northeast; in some parts of the country, you seldom see one that hasn't been corned. It's a versatile cut of beef.

The brisket is the breast portion of the beef animal and is usually divided into two separate parts. The "flat cut" portion is the leaner and usually the more expensive of the two, but for my money the somewhat fattier "point cut" has the best flavor. For the best of both, buy both—the whole brisket.

New England Boiled Brisket

- A 4-to-6-pound beef brisket, flat or point cut
- 3 cloves garlic, crushed
- 1 tablespoon salt
- 1 teaspoon freshly ground black pepper
- Water to cover
- 1 onion, peeled and stuck with 2 or 3 cloves
- 2 large carrots, peeled and trimmed
- 1 large stalk celery
- 2 bay leaves
- 4 sprigs parsley
- 8 potatoes, peeled
- 8 medium carrots, peeled and trimmed
- 8 small onions
- 8 medium turnips, peeled
- 1 large or 2 small cabbages, cut into quarters and cored (optional)

A traditional New England boiled dinner is made with corned-beef brisket, but it can be equally delicious—albeit different—with fresh brisket. Serve the strained broth as a first course, or save it for another time.

≈

1. Trim excess fat from the brisket, and, in a heavy Dutch oven over medium heat, melt enough of the fat to yield about 2 tablespoons. Remove any solid pieces of fat and discard. Raise the heat and, when the fat sizzles, brown the brisket, turning it often. When it is nicely browned, pour off most of the fat. Add the garlic and cook over low heat, stirring, for 1 minute.

2. Sprinkle the brisket with some of the salt and pepper. Return to the pot and cover with water. Bring slowly to a boil, and skim off the froth that rises. Add the clove-studded onion, the 2 large carrots, celery, bay leaves, parsley, and the remaining salt and pepper. Reduce the heat, cover, and simmer for 2 hours, until the meat is tender.

3. Add the potatoes, the 8 medium carrots, the 8 small onions, and turnips and cook approximately 45 minutes. Add the cabbage and cook for 25 to 30 minutes.

4. If you want broth as a first course, remove the whole potatoes, trimmed carrots, small onions, turnips, and cabbage, and set aside. Strain the broth through a large sieve, pushing down on the flavoring vegetables that cooked with the brisket from the beginning. Discard the solids. Save the rich broth and keep warm if you are planning to serve it as a first course, or save and freeze for another meal. You can also thicken the broth and serve it as a gravy with the brisket.

5. Slice the meat thinly across the grain and serve with the boiled vegetables, plenty of good mustard, horseradish, and crusty bread. I like my brisket with a cold beer.

Serves 6 to 8.

VARIATION

Crumbed Beef Brisket with Onion Sauce

≈

A 4-to-6-pound beef brisket
Onion Sauce (below)
1 egg, slightly beaten
1 cup fine dry bread crumbs

ONION SAUCE

2 tablespoons sugar
1 tablespoon reserved browning fat
2 medium onions, sliced
1 tablespoon flour
1 cup reserved brisket broth
1 teaspoon white-wine vinegar
½ teaspoon salt

1. Cook the brisket until tender, following the master recipe through step 2. Reserve 2 tablespoons of the browning fat.

2. Remove the meat and place it in a shallow casserole or baking dish. Strain the broth and reserve 1 cup for the Onion Sauce.

3. Make the Onion Sauce. In a large skillet, stir the sugar into the reserved fat, and cook, stirring, until brown. Add the onions and cook, stirring, for about 7 minutes, until tender. Stir in the flour and cook 1 minute. Add the broth, vinegar, and salt. Bring to a boil, lower the heat, and cook about 5 minutes, or until smooth. Keep warm while you finish the rest.

4. Brush the beaten egg over the meat. Pat with bread crumbs, and bake in a preheated 350-degree oven until the crumbs are browned, about 15 minutes. Slice thinly across the grain and serve with the hot Onion Sauce.

Serves 6 to 8.

Brands

The branding of cattle to document ownership was a custom practiced long before the first cow came to America. Four-thousand-year-old tomb paintings depict Egyptians branding their cattle. Hernán Cortés burned crosses on the hides of the small herd he brought with him to Mexico. The Mexican *vaqueros* passed the custom on to the American cowboys, who developed and refined their own cowhide calligraphy.

Brands are registered with state or county governments to show ownership of animals, much as—in today's world—an automobile is licensed. Many brands have been passed down from generation to generation and from ranch owner to ranch owner without modification. Some of the brands that appear on the side, hip, or shoulder of cattle today are the same as they were during the trail drives of the Old West. The "Running W" brand of the famous King Ranch in Texas (the largest ranch in the country) was registered in Nueces County, Texas, in 1869. It is still in use.

It didn't take much money to get into the cattle business following the Civil War. All you needed was a horse, a saddle, a rope, and a branding iron. Not just in Texas but all over the South, Longhorn cattle roamed wild with no owner to claim them.

In those days, there were three unbranded calves for every branded one; whoever put a brand on one first was the owner. The unbranded animals came to be called "mavericks" after a fellow named Sam Maverick who didn't believe in branding. He went out of business in less than a year.

Many a cowboy in the early days of the beef industry in America got his start as a rancher rounding up and putting his mark—brand—on unbranded cattle—mavericks; and more than a few unscrupulous would-be ranchers (they called them rustlers in the old days) got strung up for altering brands on another man's cattle.

Reading a brand is something of an art, one that the greenest cowhand of the nineteenth century quickly mastered, but that this twentieth-century would-be cowboy has not yet quite got a handle on, and I've tried. My Uncle Virgil was a brand inspector for the state of Nebraska when I was a kid. He was the man responsible, at the cattle sale, for makin' sure the man sellin' the cattle was the man that owned the cattle. Uncle Virg and Aunt Ev had a ranch just out of O'Neill, in the sandhills of north-central Nebraska, where they raised Simmentals. Visiting the ranch—riding horses, playing cowboy with cousins—was one of the joys of my childhood. On occasion Uncle Virg would get out the brand book and let us kids try our hand at reading brands. We learned to read the components of a brand in the correct order: from left to right, from top to bottom, or from outside in (a T inside a diamond translates as "Diamond T," not "T Diamond"). Letters and numbers may be easily discernible or they may be "lazy," "open," "running," "flying," "leaning," "hanging," "backward," or "reversed."

Here are a few brands from Uncle Virgil's book. Try your hand at brand reading. There will be a test!

6666 The Four Sixes	Lazy Jay S
J Two-Eyed Jay	W Cross
R R Bar	Y Lazy T
Backward B J	Quarter Circle 3
M7 M Hanging 7	Seven Bar Eleven
AV Open A V	Circle L M

Now that you've studied a little brand reading, you're ready to take the little test Uncle Virg used to give incoming cousins to the brand-reading class. How would you decipher 2NP ? Uncle Virg was a character!

South Texas Brisket

- 1 10-ounce bottle Worcestershire sauce
- 1 2-ounce bottle Tabasco sauce
- ½ cup unsalted butter
- 1 tablespoon black pepper
- 2 teaspoons red-pepper flakes
- 1 tablespoon salt
- 2 cups cider vinegar
- A 5-to-7-pound brisket

Brisket is the cut of beef used in the traditional Texas barbecue. It is usually cooked long and slow, often over twenty-four hours, with mesquite smoke in a cooker that keeps the heat far away from the meat. That kind of brisket cookery is a whole other story, far too complex to cover here; if you want more information, I recommend *The Only Texas Cookbook* by Linda West Eckhardt. The following might best be called not barbecued brisket but "bar-b-sauce" brisket, but it is good and it's *hot!*

≈

1. Combine all the ingredients except the brisket in a saucepan and bring to a boil. Lower the heat and simmer for 10 minutes, stirring occasionally.
2. Line a large roasting pan with aluminum foil and place the meat in it. Pour the sauce over the meat and fold the foil over. Marinate about 4 hours.
3. Bake the meat in foil in a preheated 325-degree oven for 4 to 6 hours, or until very tender.
4. For the last hour, fold the foil down and allow the meat to brown and soak up as much of the sauce as possible. Serve the extra sauce on the side.

Serves 8 to 10.

JERKY

Beef jerky was something of a staple on the trail drives of the Old West. Cowboys carried it in their saddlebags to sustain themselves on the long haul home after riding with a herd to Dodge or Abilene. They learned to make jerky from the Indians, who had been drying buffalo meat as a means of preservation long before cattle and cowboys came on the scene.

Jerky has become a popular snack food and is available at the checkout stands of most supermarkets. It's a great energy boost to have in your backpack when you go hiking or biking. But that stuff at the checkout stand is expensive. You can quite easily make your own jerky at home and save money.

Making jerky like the cowboys and Indians of the Great Plains is a bit impractical if not impossible these days. They used the best meat they could find, usually old bull buffalo or Texas Longhorn, and these are hard to find today. The best meat you can find in the "Great Plains" of today's supermarket is the worst meat you can find. The qualities you look for in a good steak—tenderness, marbling—are best avoided when you're looking for meat to make jerky. Whatever you do, don't buy Prime or Choice beef. Look for a lower grade. There's too much marbling in the better grades for a good chewy jerky. Besides, the fat tends to go rancid if kept too long. Bottom round works well, or eye of the round, but perhaps the best alternative to bull or buffalo is flank steak. Flank has an elongated grain that makes for good jerky if you cut it with the grain rather than across the grain.

Here is a simple recipe for turning a pound and a half or so of flank steak into beef jerky at a cost considerably less than that of buying those little plastic packages at the supermarket. You can vary the seasonings to suit your taste, add a bit of liquid-smoke flavoring if you like, and eliminate the soy sauce. In the original recipe the only seasoning was sunshine, but my family likes the following recipe.

Beef Jerky

1½ to 2 pounds beef flank steak
⅓ cup soy sauce
2 cloves garlic, crushed
¼ teaspoon salt
¼ teaspoon black pepper

1. Slice the flank steak lengthwise, with the grain, into ¼-inch-thick strips.
2. Combine the soy sauce, garlic, salt, pepper, and brown sugar. Mix with the meat strips and let stand 15 to 20 minutes.
3. Drain the meat and arrange it in a single layer on a rack in a shallow baking pan. Bake in a preheated 150-degree oven overnight or for 12 hours, until dried. Cut into 1-inch pieces. Store in a tightly covered container.

Makes ¾ to 1 pound jerky strips.

SWISS, SMOTHERED, AND CHICKEN-FRIED STEAK

For most of us who grew up in this steak nation's heartland, "smothered" or "Swiss" steak has a special spot on the tables of our memories. A slab of beef round steak was dipped in flour, pounded with the edge of a heavy plate to beat it into tenderness, browned quickly in lard in a heavy black iron skillet, then simmered in gravy till you could cut it with a fork. That's how my Aunt Gert did it (everybody's aunt or mother had her own way). The good cooks in Iowa, Nebraska, Kansas, and Missouri may have used a tomato or mushroom rather than a cream gravy, but the similarities far outnumber the differences. Smothering and Swissing were wonderful ways of turning a tough steak tender.

Almost any cut of meat can be cooked tender in under an hour, using one of the following recipes. Top round is my favorite cut, but bottom round or chuck can also be used.

Basic Smothered Steak with Onions

½ cup flour
1 teaspoon salt
1 teaspoon freshly ground black pepper
2 pounds top round, bottom round, or chuck steak, cut ¾ inch thick
1 tablespoon lard or vegetable oil
3 large yellow onions, thinly sliced

Smothered and Swiss steaks are cooked by both moist and dry heat. Any of the next-to-tender cuts (page 41) work well with this method.

≈

1. Mix the flour, salt, and pepper together. With the edge of a heavy plate, pound the mixture well into the meat. Cut the meat into 4 to 6 serving pieces.

2. Heat the lard or vegetable oil in a large heavy iron skillet. Over medium-high heat, cook the steaks until brown on both sides. Do this in batches if necessary.

3. Remove the meat and cook the onions until limp

and golden. Lay the meat over the onions and add the remaining ingredients. Cover tightly, reduce the heat to low, and simmer the mixture gently for 30 to 40 minutes, until the meat is very tender. Do not let the mixture boil. Remove the bay leaves and adjust the seasoning. If the sauce is too thin, remove the steaks and raise the heat; boil until the liquid thickens slightly. Serve with mashed potatoes or buttered noodles.

- 2 bay leaves
- 3 sprigs fresh thyme or ½ teaspoon crumbled dried
- ¼ cup beer
- 1 cup beef stock

Serves 4 to 6.

VARIATIONS

Sour Cream Swiss Steak

It was my pleasure to serve as one of the judges at the Third Annual Portland, Oregon, James Beard Cooking contest, a few years ago, and Mrs. Ethel Richman's recipe was one of the winners. It has become a favorite around our house.

- Steak, flour, salt, and pepper as in basic recipe
- ½ teaspoon hot paprika
- ½ teaspoon dry mustard
- 2 tablespoons vegetable oil
- 3 tablespoons butter
- ½ cup chopped onion
- 1 garlic clove, finely minced
- ¾ cup water
- 3 tablespoons soy sauce
- 3 tablespoons brown sugar
- ¾ cup sour cream

≈

1. Follow steps 1 and 2 of the basic recipe, adding paprika and mustard to the flour.
2. Brown the steak pieces in a mixture of vegetable oil and butter, and set aside. Pour off all but one tablespoon of fat.
3. Mix together the onion, garlic, water, soy sauce, brown sugar, and sour cream. Add to the skillet and mix with the pan drippings. Add the browned steak, cover, and bake in a preheated 300-degree oven for 30 to 35 minutes, or until tender.

Serves 4 to 6.

Grandma Ellis' Country-Fried Steak

Steak, flour, salt, and pepper as in basic recipe
3 slices bacon, cut into 1-inch pieces
1 cup sliced mushrooms
1 cup beef broth

Mashed potatoes are a must with this!

≈

1. Follow step 1 of the basic recipe (page 30). Cut the steak into 4 pieces.

2. Fry the bacon to render some of the fat. Push the bacon to the side of the pan. Brown the steaks in the bacon fat, remove, and set aside.

3. Sauté the mushrooms in the same pan. Pour off all but 1 tablespoon of fat. Put the steaks back, add the beef broth, cover tightly, and cook over low heat for 30 to 35 minutes, or until tender.

Serves 4.

Chapell Ranch Smothered Steak

Steak, flour, salt, and pepper as in basic recipe
2 tablespoons lard or vegetable oil
2 large onions, thinly sliced
1 bell pepper, sliced into rings
2 stalks celery, thinly sliced
1 teaspoon hot red-pepper flakes
1 15-ounce can tomato sauce*

* Charlotte likes Hunt's Special Sauce, the one with bits of onions and peppers.

Charlotte Reed has been the ranch cook for the Chapell Ranch, just outside of Tucumcari, New Mexico, for many a year. She hails from Minnesota, where she was once a cook at a boarding school. "Cookin' for schoolboys and cookin' for cowboys is a lot alike," she says.

≈

1. Follow steps 1 and 2 of the basic recipe (page 30). Lay the sliced onions, pepper rings, and celery over the steaks. Sprinkle with pepper flakes and pour the tomato sauce over all.

2. Cover and bake in a preheated 350-degree oven for about 1 hour, until tender.

Serves 4 to 6.

Barbed Wire

Issac Leonard Ellwood, a storekeeper from De Kalb County, Illinois, and Joseph Farwell Glidden, a local farmer from the same area, are credited with changing the West by their invention of barbed wire. In July of 1874, the two formally joined forces under the banner of the Barb Fence Company and began peddling their product in Texas.

One of their salesmen, John Gates, built a barbed-wire corral in San Antonio and invited Texas cattlemen to "Bring your steers, gentlemen—the cattle ain't been born can get through this here fence." Twenty-five of "the worst fence busters in Texas" were brought together in San Antonio's city plaza. As expected, they charged the fence—it hurt! They gave up, and that day Gates sold six hundred miles of what the cowboys came to call "bob wire." It changed the West!

Baked Steak with Mushrooms and Onions

My grandmother made this recipe using canned mushrooms and canned onions. Fresh was hard to find in Nebraska in the 1930s, particularly in the winter, when smothered steaks somehow seemed to taste best. I use fresh mushrooms and onions now. You can use, as my grandmother would say, "whatever you have a mind to."

- 2 tablespoons butter
- 1 tablespoon olive oil
- A 2-pound top-round steak cut ½ inch thick
- 2 medium onions, sliced thin
- 1 pound fresh mushrooms
- 1¼ cups catsup
- ¾ cup strong black coffee
- one shot whiskey (optional)

≈

1. Melt the butter in a heavy skillet over medium heat and add the olive oil. Brown the steak well on both sides in the hot fat. Remove and set aside.

2. In the same skillet, sauté the onions until just limp.

Baked Steak with Mushrooms and Onions *(cont.)*

Add the mushrooms and cook for a couple of minutes. The mushrooms can be left whole, quartered, or halved, depending on their size.

3. Stir in the catsup, coffee, and whiskey. Return the steak to the skillet, spoon some of the sauce over the meat, cover, and bake in a preheated 350-degree oven for 15 to 20 minutes.

4. Cut the steak into thin slices across the grain, on the diagonal. Pour the sauce over the slices and serve.

Serves 4 to 6.

Odelia Prudhomme's Steak Etouffée

- 2 large onions, finely chopped
- 2 cloves garlic, finely chopped
- 2 teaspoons salt
- 2 teaspoons cayenne pepper
- 1 teaspoon freshly ground black pepper
- 1 tablespoon dry mustard
- 1 tablespoon Worcestershire sauce
- A 2-pound, 2-inch-thick slice of top round
- 2 tablespoons A-1 steak sauce
- 2 tablespoons vegetable oil

"Steak Etouffée" is a sort of Cajun Swiss steak with a kick. Etouffée means "smothered" in French. This recipe comes from a lady in Opelousas, Louisiana, who is the sister-in-law of the best Cajun cook I know, Paul Prudhomme, who says she's the best Cajun cook *he* knows.

≈

1. Mix half the chopped onions, half the chopped garlic, 1 teaspoon of the salt, 1 teaspoon of the cayenne pepper, ½ teaspoon of the black pepper, the dry mustard, and the Worcestershire sauce in a small bowl. Cut slits in the steak and stuff each slot with a teaspoon or so of the mixed seasonings.

2. Rub the steak well on both sides with a mixture of the A-1 sauce and the remaining salt, pepper, and cayenne. Heat the oil in a heavy skillet over medium-high heat and brown the steak on both sides. When brown, push the steak to the side and add the bell pepper, and the remaining onion and garlic. Sauté until the vegetables are limp.

3. Add the beef stock, sugar, and Tabasco sauce to

taste. Cover, reduce the heat, and simmer for 45 minutes to an hour. Slice the steak across the grain and serve the slices moistened with sauce. Serve with rice.

Serves 6 to 8.

1 medium bell pepper, finely chopped
2 cups beef stock
1 teaspoon sugar
2 or 3 dashes Tabasco sauce

Cowboys

The word "cowboy" captures the romance, the dreams, and the struggle to tame the American West. But being identified as a cowboy wasn't always something to be proud of. Revolutionary War patriots used the term, contemptuously, to describe Tory supporters of King George III who would lure colonial militiamen into dense woods with gently tinkling cowbells and then would mow them down with musket fire. It wasn't until the late 1870s that the proud cattlemen of the emerging West gradually embraced the name and made it their own. By then, the cowboy was in his heyday, a legend in the making. And to this day, the term "cowboy" is applied to a man who works cattle on a ranch or in a feedlot.

Grandma Simpkins' Chicken-Fried Steaks

FOR THE STEAK

- 2 tablespoons flour
- 1 teaspoon salt
- 1 teaspoon freshly ground black pepper
- 2 pounds top-round steak, cut ¾ to 1 inch thick
- 2 eggs
- 2 tablespoons heavy cream
- ½ cup lard or vegetable shortening
- 1 cup finely crushed saltine-cracker crumbs
- 1 large onion, sliced thin

FOR THE GRAVY

- 3 tablespoons flour
- ½ cup heavy cream
- 1 cup chicken stock
- Generous dash Worcestershire sauce
- Generous dash Tabasco sauce

A delicious variation on the smothered-steak theme is chicken-fried steak. (It gets an egg coating, as a lot of fried chicken does.) I proclaim myself the world's foremost authority on chicken-fried steak. I acquired my vast knowledge of the subject in my Grandma Simpkins' kitchen, helping her cook for fifteen to twenty hired hands at harvest time, when I was too young to work in the fields. She would cook mountains of steaks on a wood-burning stove, fueled not with wood but with corncobs, which Nebraskans used back then.

It is important to pound flour into the steak. I don't mean "dust" with flour, I mean *pound* it, hit it, beat it, whack it. Grandma used the edge of a heavy plate, and I've never found anything better. Pound in a crisscross pattern to flatten the steak to a thickness of a half-inch.

You can fry your steaks in lard or vegetable shortening. You must use a black iron skillet; nothing else will do. And you *must* use saltine crackers crushed with a rolling pin as fine as dust. Any other crumbs make a crummy chicken-fried steak!

Now, about the gravy. Cream gravy is traditional, and a good heavy cream is important, but you need more than just cream. Grandma kept a pot of chicken stock simmering on the back of the stove, and a dipperful of stock made all the difference to her cream gravy. Here's my grandma's recipe.

≈

1. Mix the flour, salt, and pepper together. With the edge of a heavy plate, pound the mixture well into the meat. Cut the meat into 4 to 6 serving pieces.

2. Beat the eggs together with the cream. Heat the lard or shortening in a large, heavy iron skillet over medium-high heat. Dip the floured steaks into the egg

mixture, let them drip a little, then dip into the cracker crumbs, turning them. When the fat in the pan sizzles, cook the steaks, turning once, until brown on both sides.

3. Reduce the heat to moderate. Cover, and cook 15 to 20 minutes, turning occasionally, until the meat is tender. Chicken-fried steak should be well done but not dry. Remove the steaks and drain on brown paper bags or paper towels. Keep the steaks warm.

4. Cook the onion slices in the fat until soft, about 7 minutes, turning occasionally. Remove the onions before making the gravy.

5. Make the gravy. Pour off all but 3 tablespoons of fat, stir in the flour, gathering up any browned bits in the pan, and cook for 2 minutes. Stir in the cream to form a thick paste, then add the chicken stock, stirring to make a smooth gravy. Return the onions to the gravy. Add the Worcestershire and Tabasco sauce, and adjust the seasoning. Serve the steak and gravy with lumpy mashed potatoes, homemade biscuits, or corn bread. Hey! That's chicken-fried steak!

Serves 4 to 6.

The Return of the Longhorn

The Texas Longhorn was nearer extinction than the buffalo or the whooping crane when, in 1927, the federal government appropriated $3,000 for the requisition and preservation of a herd of Texas Longhorns. For example, Mr. Will C. Barnes found it necessary to travel almost five thousand miles through South Texas and Mexico to discover and acquire twenty cows, four calves, and three bulls with which to develop a herd that was the remains of some forty million cattle in Texas only sixty years before.

The Return of the Longhorn (continued)

In 1960, there were about twenty-five hundred Texas Longhorns in the United States; in 1964, the Texas Longhorn Breeders Association of America was created to preserve the cattle.

A couple of universities, Texas Tech and Texas A&M, began doing research on transferring the Longhorn blood lines into other breeds. Some Texas cowboys feel that the program may be at least part of the answer to providing more beef for a hungry world. Longhorns can live on marginal rangeland, eating cactus and scrub grass—a definite advantage, given the high cost of feed and fertilizer. They have small calves, which means that few die at birth. And they have a very strong natural instinct for self-preservation, which means that fewer calves are likely to be lost to range predators.

Today there are more than forty thousand registered Longhorns in America, and millions of crossbreeds. It is hard to imagine what the beef cattle of tomorrow will look like. But if cattlemen of this country can manage to survive recurring economic crises, boycotts, and the rather bewildering "one-less-hamburger-a-day-will-save-the-world" logic of some groups, if they survive long enough to produce the ideal steer, it will probably be very large, lean, meaty, and mostly steak. It will have lived a reasonably long part of its relatively short life on little more than sagebrush and scrub grass. And it may very likely have, like its ancestors years and years ago, horns—long horns.

THE MIDDLE MEAT—STEAKS AND ROASTS

Selecting Tender Steaks

The main steak area of a beef animal makes up just 20 percent of the carcass. There are only about thirty-three one-inch-thick steaks on an average side of beef. Because of the great demand for steaks—particularly during barbecue season—and because of the limited supply, good steaks are expensive. A short lesson in basic animal anatomy may be a big help when it comes to selecting a good steak for grilling or broiling. It may also save you some money.

Tender steaks come from three sections of the carcass, which we called the "middle meat." They are the short loin, the sirloin, and the rib section.

The cuts of beef that you see labeled "steak" in any meat case can be divided into three basic categories: *tender,* steaks that are naturally tender enough to toss on the barbecue grill just as they are; *next to tender,* steaks that will work on the grill given a little loving care and perhaps a bit of tenderizer; *not so tender,* steaks that are awfully close to tough and are better braised than grilled or broiled.

The most naturally tender steaks from the beef animal come from a section right in the middle of the back called the "short loin." When the short loin is cut into steaks with the bone left in, it yields three different steaks, with which, I am sure, you are all familiar: porterhouse, T-bone, and club steaks. If, however, the bone is removed from the short loin before it is cut into steaks, the selection and terminology can be a bit confusing, and even more expensive. The boneless short loin yields, for example, New York steaks, except in New York City—they don't call these New York steaks in New York City. The proper name no matter what part of the country you're in is "top loin" or "strip loin"; it's the top muscle of the short loin, and one of the most tender muscles of the animal. This is exceeded in tenderness only by the other muscle of the short loin, the tenderloin. You can often save a good deal of money on both "strip steaks" and "tenderloin steaks" if you buy a bone-in porterhouse and bone it out yourself.

As you move away from the short loin in either direction, the meat becomes increasingly less tender, but it's a gradual change. Behind the short loin, for example, is the sirloin section. The various muscles of the sirloin are naturally tender enough to grill and broil beautifully. The same is true in the rib section, just in front of the short loin. Rib steaks and rib-eye steaks have a wonderfully rich beefy flavor.

Aging

More people, I think, are disappointed with the beef they buy primarily because it has not been properly aged. Proper aging accomplishes several things that greatly benefit the tenderness and flavor.

Confirmed beef eaters of long standing, like me, have always known that aged beef is best, but there are not many butchers aging beef these days. Aged beef is more than a little hard to find. There are those who advertise it, but they'd like you to believe that beef ages in those Cryovac plastic bags that most meat today comes to market in—it doesn't! Some tenderizing may occur in those plastic bags, but aging in the traditional sense—no way! Old-fashioned-style aging is now referred to as "dry-aging," meaning that the beef is aged, usually in carcass form or primal cuts, outside the plastic.

Aging is a simple process, but an expensive one. It requires that meat be stored for up to twenty-one days, sometimes longer, at a temperature of between thirty-four and thirty-eight degrees. This accomplishes several things: (1) The deterioration of the connective tissue holding the muscle bundles together—controlled decomposition, if you will—which helps promote tenderness. (2) The evaporation of moisture, which produces a steak with a firm yet tender texture, but which also causes shrinkage. As much as 15 to 20 percent moisture loss can result from long dry-aging, which accounts for why a good aged steak is expensive. (3) An incomparably rich beefy flavor that makes a great steak the essence of good eating.

If you can find one, go to a butcher that still handles carcass of beef and ask him for a standing rib or short loin of beef. Then ask him if he will age it for you. You will need to buy and pay for the weight of the piece as it is, but once it is yours, some butchers will be willing to "hang it back" for a couple of weeks with your name on it.

In two or three weeks, your loin or rib will have developed the incomparable flavor and tenderness that only those who have tasted really well-aged beef can truly appreciate. And you will be in for a treat that will spoil you for any other kind of beef. You also will have spent a small fortune, but it is worth it at least once in your life, if only to learn what the phrase "aged to perfection" really means.

Next to Tender

A few steaks that lie just outside the tender zone can be grilled or broiled if treated right, and they are often very good buys. These I call the "next to tender." The first cut of the blade chuck is a good example of such a steak. It comes off the carcass from the tender rib section and is only the thickness of a knife blade; it contains a large portion of the same muscles that make the rib a tender steak. Look for the first-cut blade chuck, the one with the long thin shoulder-blade bone tipped with white cartilage. That is the chuck next to the tender rib.

At the other end of the carcass, both the sirloin tip and the first cut of the top round come off right next to the tender sirloin, and with the help of a little tenderizing both work rather well for broiling or grilling. They are also good cuts to select for quick pan-frying, stir-frying, or sautéing.

Butcher Steaks

There's a group of meat cuts that over the years have come to be called "butcher steaks," so named because there are not enough of them on the carcass of beef to make a display in the meat case, and traditionally the butcher took them home. Now they have been "discovered" by the consumer. While not plentiful, they are still available. However, they are a whole lot more expensive than before, when nobody but the butcher knew about them. Flank steak and skirt steak fall into that category.

Flank steak is a lean, flat boneless muscle with a long coarse grain that comes from the flank section of the beef carcass. It is one of the most versatile cuts of beef in the meat case today. Fortunately, it is also one of the least expensive.

The classic recipe for flank steak is London broil, simply seasoned with salt and pepper and quickly broiled; sliced thin across the grain, it makes the ideal quick dinner. It can also be a real money saver when you have time to spend in the kitchen doing a little stuffing, rolling, and sauce making. (See pages 56–57.)

Skirt steak is the diaphragm muscle of the beef animal, the muscle that controls the flow of air into and out of the lungs. That's probably more than you wanted to know about skirt steak, but that's what it is. What you should know is that the skirt is one of the most flavorful cuts on a carcass of beef. It has a rich, beefy flavor not found in many cuts these days, and it is a very tender morsel. Skirt steak became popular when the rest of the world discovered the South Texas food specialty called fajitas (see page 52).

Other cuts of "butcher steaks" are much more difficult to find. Some are all but extinct unless you know a butcher.

Oyster steaks are small round-shaped ½-to-¾-pound pieces of meat. They are removed from the inside of the hip bone in the process of boning out a top round. Today these usually end up in the ground-beef trimmings.

Hanging tender anatomically is the "pillar of the diaphragm," a narrow, thick 1½-to-2-pound muscle to which the two diaphragm muscles (skirt steaks) are attached. There is but one per carcass, and it comes to market hanging just below the tenderloin on the left hindquarter. Like the oyster steaks, this one you're not apt to find in any but a market that still handles carcass beef.

Butcher steaks can be cooked any way that you would cook a more expensive steak.

Another cut of beef that is not common in many American markets but that every steak lover should be aware of is the *tri-tip*. The tri-tip is a triangle-shaped muscle weighing about 1½ to 2 pounds, from the bottom-sirloin section of the beef carcass. Every beef animal has two, just like skirts and flanks. The reason that the cut is so little known in much of the country is that until recently most butchers cut sirloins with the bone in, and a small piece of the tri-tip was a nondescript part of a sirloin steak. Since boxed beef has become the norm, the entire carcass is boned out at the packing plant and individual muscles are shipped out in vacuum packages. Now the tri-tip is available in any market, but not every butcher knows about it. If you don't see it in your market, ask for it. It has a good beefy flavor and makes a great steak.

Myths of Meat Cookery

There are almost as many theories on how best to cook a steak as there are backyards, briquettes, and barbecue buffs combined, and if you've found the "perfect" way, don't let me talk you out of anything. But if your steaks sometimes come out dry, perhaps I can help.

I disagree with most of the cooks in the modern cookbook-writing world when it comes to how to grill a steak. With very few, old-fashioned exceptions, most cookbooks recommend barbecuing or grilling a steak so many minutes on one side, then turning the steak only once and grilling for an equal amount of so many minutes on the other side. That notion is, to my mind, a myth, one of several on cooking meat.

Heat forces the juices to the uncooked surface of a steak. If you let a nice thick steak sizzle over the coals for a full half of its required cooking time, a good-sized puddle of delicious, nutritious juice will accumulate. Then, when you turn the steak only once after half the cooking time, what do you do? You dump all those good juices onto the coals in one big sizzle! What a waste!

A better way, to my way of thinking, is to sear the steak first on both sides over high heat. Then spread out the coals to lower the heat and cook the steak, turning every three to four minutes until it is done to your liking. When you turn the steak, that sort of confuses the juices; they start to rise to the top, but before they get there, you turn the steak and they have to change course. This keeps all the juices in the steak. One myth dismissed!

There are a couple of other myths of meat cookery passed along regularly by mothers and cookbook writers, having to do with the juiciness of meat or how to maintain it. Those need to be dispelled.

- "Never salt meat before you cook it; salt draws the moisture out!" Myth! Yes, if you pack six pounds of salt around a leg of pork and "put it down" for six weeks, the salt draws the moisture out and you have a ham. But when you're grilling a steak or frying a pork chop, salting it first won't dry it out. If you don't season meat before you cook it, the seasoning doesn't mix with the meat juices to make for great flavor.

- "Never turn meat with a fork; you'll let all the juices escape." Myth! Meat is not a balloon that bursts when punctured. It's a multicellular structure, like a sponge, and you can turn it with a fork without letting the juices out.

Great Grilled Steak

A 1½-to-2-inch-thick well-aged porterhouse, T-bone, club, rib-eye, or strip steak
Olive oil
Salt, preferably sea salt
Coarse-ground black pepper

If you want a really great steak for the barbecue grill, don't look for it in a supermarket. Go to a little "old-fashioned" butcher shop where they buy and sell Prime beef or the high end of the Choice grade, with a good bit of marbling, and where they age their beef. Fat and age make for a great grilled steak!

≈

1. Trim any excess fat from the edge of the steak. Drizzle on and rub into each side a bit of olive oil. Sprinkle on and rub into each side a bit of sea salt and pepper. Let stand at room temperature for about an hour.

2. Heat up the grill (gas, electric, or charcoal). If you're using charcoal briquettes, follow the directions on the package for starting, and let the briquettes burn until covered with fine gray ash.

3. Sear the steak quickly on one side (about 2 minutes), then turn and sear on the other side for 2 minutes. Remove the steak from the grill and lower the grill temperature to moderate. If you're cooking with charcoal, spread out the charcoal to reduce the heat.

4. Put the steak back on the grill, being careful to turn the steak at a slight angle (45 degrees) from its first position to achieve a pleasing grill pattern on the surface of the steak. We taste things first with our eyes. Grill the steak another 2 to 3 minutes on each side to the desired degree of doneness, as tested on an instant-read thermometer (125 to 130 degrees for medium rare).

5. Remove the steak from the grill and serve immediately. A well-marbled, well-aged steak needs nothing but a bit of salt and pepper to taste great. Most of the steaks you buy at your local supermarket, however, can't possibly compare. Whatever the grade, whatever the price, they will very likely be improved by a bit of butter.

Serves 1, 2, or 3, depending on size of steak (count on about 8 ounces per person).

Butter Works Magic with Steak

A delicious way to put some flavor back in lean beef is simply to use a bit of butter. Even a patty of plain butter on top of a sizzling steak will add to your enjoyment as it melts and mingles with the meat juices. But an herb butter made especially for the purpose can work flavor-enhancing magic. All that is required is a quarter-pound stick of butter, a few of the herbs and spices you like best, and a bit of imagination in combining them.

To make an herb butter, soften the stick in a mixing bowl, then beat with a wire whip until creamy. Stir in any desired herbs and flavorings. Around our house, we mix in fresh tarragon or basil, or add a little mustard seed to the butter. My wife, Neva, likes a couple of anchovy fillets minced and mixed in with lemon and parsley.

When you have the butter seasoned to your taste, set the bowl in the refrigerator and let the butter begin to firm up until you can mold it. Then scrape the mixture onto a piece of waxed paper and shape it into a roll like a sausage, about an inch and a half in diameter. Roll it up in the waxed paper and refrigerate it to harden. Use as needed to add a bit of flavor to your steaks.

When your steaks come off the skillet or grill, simply slice off a few patties of your herb butter and lay one on each steak before you serve it. This makes a pretty presentation, and makes a good steak even better.

MAÎTRE D'HÔTEL BUTTER

1 tablespoon lemon juice
¼ pound butter, softened
1 tablespoon minced parsley
Salt and pepper to taste

Beat the lemon juice into the softened butter slowly, a few drops at a time. Blend in the parsley and season with salt and pepper.

NEVA'S ANCHOVY BUTTER

Add 2 or 3 mashed anchovy fillets to the above recipe.

Butter Works Magic with Steak (continued)

MUSTARD BUTTER

¼ pound butter, softened
1 tablespoon hot mustard
1 teaspoon white-wine vinegar
Salt and pepper to taste

Cream the butter and mustard together. Beat in the vinegar and season with salt and pepper.

BASIL BUTTER

¼ pound butter, softened
1 or 2 cloves garlic, minced
1 teaspoon lemon juice
1 tablespoon finely chopped fresh basil
Salt and pepper to taste

Cream the butter, beat in the garlic and lemon juice. Mash in the basil and season with salt and pepper.

GARLIC BUTTER

5 or 6 cloves garlic (*I like garlic!*)
¼ pound butter, softened
Salt and pepper to taste

Crush the garlic into a paste in a mortar or with a garlic press. Cream the crushed garlic into the softened butter and season with salt and pepper.

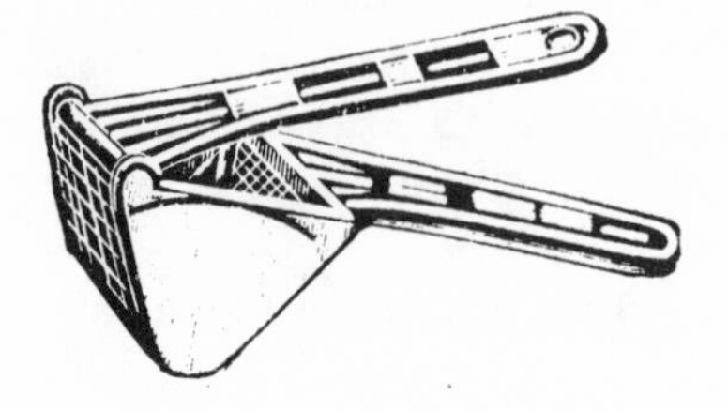

Pan-Broiled Steak

Backyard barbecues are right up there with apple pie as an American icon. Now, I sure don't want to be a spoilsport, but when it comes to cooking one of today's leaner beef steaks, barbecuing—in my opinion—is not the best way.

Steaks, I think, do best when cooked in an iron skillet. I also recommend a simple sauce made right in that skillet. Stir a bit of booze and a touch of imagination into whatever is left in the pan; the process is called "deglazing." It only takes a moment.

A 1½-to-2-inch-thick porterhouse, T-bone, club, rib-eye, or strip steak
Salt, preferably sea salt
Coarse-ground black pepper
¼ cup either red wine, brandy, beef stock, or (as a last resort) water
2 tablespoons butter

≈

1. Trim any excess fat from the edge of the steak and reserve. Sprinkle each side of the steak with salt and pepper and let stand at room temperature for 1 hour.

2. Heat a heavy black iron skillet over high heat. Grease the skillet with the reserved beef fat. Sear the steak quickly on both sides, no more than 2 minutes per side. Then reduce the heat to medium and continue cooking for an additional 2 to 3 minutes on each side to the desired degree of doneness, as tested on an instant-read meat thermometer (125 to 130 degrees for medium rare).

3. Remove the steak to a warm platter and keep warm in a warm oven while you make a sauce by deglazing the pan.

4. To make the sauce, first discard all but 1 tablespoon of fat from the skillet. Put the pan back over moderate heat and add about ¼ cup of an appropriate alcohol. It could be a bit of the wine you plan to drink with the meal, brandy (the classic), or whatever strikes your fancy. You can use stock or even plain water, but without a little alcohol the sauce, in my opinion, will lack zip.

5. As the liquid boils, scrape the pan with a wooden spoon to loosen all the good stuff stuck to the bottom. Continue cooking until the liquid has reduced in volume

Pan-Broiled Steak *(cont.)*

and is slightly thickened. Stir in 2 tablespoons of butter and you have a wonderful sauce, perfectly suited to the meat. Pour the sauce over the steak and serve.

Serves 1, 2, or 3, depending on size of steak (count on about 8 ounces per person).

VARIATIONS

- Stir in a teaspoon of chopped fresh tarragon, rosemary, or thyme, and a tablespoon of Dijon or whole-grain mustard.
- Add a teaspoon of capers and a squeeze of lemon.
- Add a few sautéed mushrooms and a teaspoon of tomato puree.
- A dollop of cream mellows the sauce; a bit of horseradish or a dash of Tabasco sauce peps it up.
- Use your imagination! Following are a few of our favorite pan-broiled steaks to stimulate your creativity.

Pan-Broiled Steak with Whiskey Sauce

A 2-inch-thick porterhouse or 4 small 1-inch-thick strip steaks
1 tablespoon black peppercorns, coarsely crushed
2 or 3 cloves garlic, finely chopped
½ teaspoon kosher or rock salt

A well-marbled porterhouse steak cooked this way and served with a simple tomato-and-onion salad is "soul food" for this country boy!

≈

1. Trim any excess fat from the steak or steaks. Press the crushed peppercorns and garlic onto both sides of the steak and let it stand at room temperature for 1 hour.
2. Heat a heavy iron skillet over high heat. Grease the skillet with a piece of the fat trimmed from the steak. Toss in about half of the salt. Sear the steaks quickly on one side, then lift out; add the remaining salt to the skillet, turn the steak, and sear the other side. Reduce the heat to

moderate and cook the steaks as desired. Remove to a warmed platter.

3. Make the sauce. Pour off the fat from the skillet. Melt the butter in the skillet over low heat; add the onion and garlic and cook slowly until soft, stirring often. Add the remaining ingredients and simmer for 1 to 2 minutes. Pour over the steak or steaks and serve.

Serves 4.

WHISKEY SAUCE

¼ pound unsalted butter
2 tablespoons chopped onion
1 clove garlic, finely chopped
2 tablespoons whiskey (I like Jack Daniel's)
1 tablespoon Worcestershire sauce
½ teaspoon dry mustard
Dash Tabasco sauce

Mustard Steak

There are all kinds of wonderful mustards on the market: Dijon and coarse-grain, honey mustards, Italian-style with sun-dried tomatoes—take your pick.

≈

2 large or 4 small steaks (about 2 pounds in all), top round, T-bone, or rib-eye, cut ¾ inch thick
Salt and freshly ground black pepper to taste
2 tablespoons of your favorite mustard
2 tablespoons butter
2 tablespoons olive oil
2 tablespoons gin (or your favorite booze)
¼ teaspoon cumin seeds
4 tablespoons sour cream
2 tablespoons chopped parsley

1. Season the steaks with salt and pepper and spread the mustard generously on both sides of the steak. Heat the butter and olive oil over high heat in a very large heavy cast-iron skillet. Brown the steak on both sides, then lower the heat to moderate and cook to desired doneness, turning the steak every 4 minutes to prevent the juices from evaporating.

2. Remove the steaks to a warmed serving platter. Splash in the gin, raise the heat, and cook until it evaporates; or flame the gin, if you wish.

3. Add the cumin seeds to the pan. Stir in the sour cream, blending thoroughly with the pan juices. Add the parsley. Cook over high heat until the sauce reduces slightly. Pour over the steaks and serve.

Serves 4.

New Yorker's Steak

- Boneless top-sirloin steak, about 2 pounds, cut 2 inches thick
- 1 clove garlic, bruised
- 1 tablespoon butter
- 1 tablespoon vegetable oil
- 1 shallot, finely chopped
- 1 tablespoon Dijon mustard
- ¼ cup dry red wine
- ½ cup beef broth
- Chopped parsley

The late Bert Greene, a New York food writer, included a marvelous recipe for steak in his book *Honest American Fare.* I had the pleasure of helping Bert prepare this dish at a cooking school in San Antonio, and I can assure you that it is very good.

≈

1. Rub the steak on both sides with the garlic clove. Heat the butter and oil over high heat in a large heavy skillet. Brown the meat well on both sides and transfer to an ovenproof platter.

2. Drain all but 1 tablespoon fat from the skillet. Add the shallot and cook, stirring, over low heat for 5 minutes. Add the mustard, wine, and beef broth, heat to a boil, and boil until the liquid reduces to a syrup. Pour the sauce over the steak.

3. Place the platter in the oven and bake in a preheated 400-degree oven for approximately 15 minutes for rare. Sprinkle with parsley, slice the steak on the diagonal, and serve.

Serves 4.

Butcher's Barbecue Sauce

- 4 tablespoons (½ stick) butter
- 2 onions, minced
- 2 or 3 cloves garlic, minced
- 1 stalk celery, finely chopped
- 1 small green pepper, seeded and finely minced

Whether you're barbecuing steaks or chicken or ribs or just plain old hamburgers 'n' hot dogs, you gotta have a good barbecue sauce. I've got a good barbecue sauce. For a great sandwich, slice leftover beef or pork roast into thin slices and heat them in the sauce, thinned, if you like, with a splash of beer. Serve on warm hamburger buns.

≈

1. Melt the butter in a good-size heavy pot over medium heat. Add the onions, garlic, celery, and green

pepper. Cook until limp and tender but not browned. Add all the remaining ingredients. Bring to a boil, reduce heat, and cover. Simmer for 1 hour, stirring occasionally.

2. Remove the bay leaves. Then either blend sauce in a blender or food processor, or force it through a sieve. Keep refrigerated. Use on anything you barbecue—steaks, ribs, hamburgers, chicken, franks, whatever.

Makes about 3 pints.

- 1 28-ounce can stewed tomatoes
- 1 12-ounce can tomato paste
- 1 tablespoon dry mustard
- 1 tablespoon salt
- 1 or 2 bay leaves
- ½ cup cider vinegar
- ½ cup dark molasses
- 1 tablespoon Tabasco sauce
- 1 tablespoon liquid smoke
- Juice of 1 lemon

Neva's Teriyaki Sauce

For the Oriental flavor, Neva has a terrific and easy teriyaki sauce that's great for meat, fish, and fowl.

≈

Mix all of the ingredients together and refrigerate. This makes a great marinade, but *do not* marinate longer than 1 hour or the flavor will be too strong.

Makes approximately 1 cup.

- 4 tablespoons brown sugar
- 1½ tablespoons ground ginger
- ¼ teaspoon red-pepper flakes
- ½ cup soy sauce
- 2 cloves garlic, minced
- 1 to 2 tablespoons sake or white wine

Fajitas

- 1 beef skirt steak, about 1 to 1½ pounds
- ½ cup lime juice
- ¼ cup tequila (optional, but good)
- 3 or 4 cloves garlic, minced
- 1 teaspoon salt
- ½ teaspoon black pepper
- 1 package (12) corn tortillas

Fajitas have become popular all across the country in the past few years; in South Texas they have been found for a long time. They originated in the area bordered by Mexico to the south and west, the Nueces River to the north, and the King Ranch to the east.

One account of the introduction of fajitas was given by a cowboy who worked on the King Ranch in the 1940s. In those days, cattle roundups could last three months. Usually, two to five cattle were slaughtered daily to feed the seventy cowboys involved. The *jefes* (bosses) always had first priority for the inside belt—the fajitas. The word "fajita" is Spanish for "little belt" or "sash," and the piece of meat involved resembles a cummerbund. Fajitas (pronounced "fah-*hee*-tuhs") come from the diaphragm muscle (the skirt steak) of the beef animal. The resemblance of the diaphragm muscle to a belt led to the use of the word "fajitas."

Fajitas were placed directly on the coals, because there is a skinlike membrane on both sides of the meat. After a few quick turns, the meat was taken off the fire and the membranes were peeled off. The meat was then cut into strips across the grain and wrapped in a tortilla. Traditional condiments added to the sizzling fajitas were: Pico de Gallo, a spicy relish made of onions, green chilies, tomatoes, and cilantro; Salsa Picante, a hot tomato relish; sour cream; grated cheese; chopped green onions; and guacamole.

≈

1. Cut the skirt steak into 3-to-4-inch pieces. Put the steak in a plastic bag and add the remaining ingredients except the tortillas. Tie the bag securely and marinate in the refrigerator for 2 or 3 hours. Drain the marinade and discard it.

2. Broil the steak over coals—mesquite if you want to be authentic—or pan-broil in a heavy skillet over moder-

ately high heat. Either way, cook only 2 or 3 minutes per side. Carve into thin slices across the grain. Serve on warm tortillas with your choice of assorted condiments suggested above. Recipes for Pico de Gallo and Salsa Picante follow.

Serves 4 to 6.

Pico de Gallo

The name is Spanish for "rooster's bill." This salsa is a must as an accompaniment to fajitas, but it is also good with any grilled meat.

- **½ cup chopped green onions**
- **1 serrano pepper, chopped**
- **½ tablespoon corn oil**
- **1 15-ounce can tomatoes with green chilies**
- **1 large fresh tomato, chopped**
- **2 medium ripe avocados, chopped**
- **Juice of a large lemon**
- **Salt and pepper to taste**
- **5 or 6 sprigs fresh cilantro, chopped**

≈

Combine all the ingredients and chill at least 1 hour before serving.

Makes approximately 2 cups.

Salsa Picante

3 "chilitos"—jalapeño, serrano, or waxed green
2 fresh tomatoes
½ onion
Lemon juice (a squeeze)
1 tablespoon olive oil
Salt and pepper to taste
1 tablespoon chopped cilantro

This spicy hot sauce is traditional with almost all Tex-Mex grilled meats or as a dip with tortilla chips. It will keep in a closed jar in the refrigerator for about a week.

≈

1. Remove the stem ends from the chilies. If using fresh jalapeño, remove most of the white seeds and veins at the stem end (this is already done for you if the chilies are canned). The more seeds and veins left in, the hotter the sauce. Be sure you wash your hands in cold water immediately after handling the chilies.

2. Chop the chilies, tomatoes, and onion. (Chop the chilies quite fine, the tomatoes and onions in small dice.) Scrape them into a bowl. Be sure to get all the oil from the chilies off the cutting board and your hands by washing carefully.

3. Add the lemon juice, oil, salt, and pepper. Chill. Before serving, top with chopped cilantro.

Makes approximately 2 cups.

Carpetbag Steak

4 tablespoons butter
10 ounces shucked oysters, or 1 10-ounce jar, drained
A 3-pound top-round steak, cut 2 inches thick

A complementary, contrasting filling inside a plump and juicy steak adds a touch of sophistication to a meal. In California's Gold Rush days, the specialty of the house in some of San Francisco's finest food establishments was Carpetbag Steak, a thick cut of beef tenderloin stuffed with sautéed oysters. When some old forty-niner struck it rich and could afford the most expensive, steaks and oysters were what he ordered.

≈

1. Melt the butter in a large skillet. Add the oysters and cook over moderate heat, turning occasionally, until the oysters are firm and plump. Lift them from the pan with a slotted spoon and set aside. Raise the heat and boil the pan juices, stirring, until only the butter and browned bits remain; take care not to burn. Set aside.

2. Cut a pocket in the steak by making a small incision with your boning knife right in the center of the side without any fat cover; that's the inside of the steak. Do not cut a large opening; rather, pivot your knife so that you enlarge the pocket inside the steak to within a half-inch from the outside. Try to keep the slit small; a few inches will do. Then spoon the oysters and as much of the cooking butter as you can into the opening. Skewer the opening closed with 4 toothpicks and lace tightly with string to hold in the stuffing.

3. Broil the steak or barbecue it over a solid bed of evenly burning coals, with the heat source 6 inches from the surface of the meat. Cook for about 12 minutes on each side for rare, brushing occasionally with the remaining oyster butter.

4. Remove the skewers and string. Slice the steak into ½-inch-wide slices across the grain and place the meat on a warm platter. Season with salt and pepper, and serve at once.

Serves 6 to 8.

Salami-and-Cheese-Stuffed Steak

3 pounds top-round steak, cut 2 inches thick
2 cloves garlic, minced
1 tablespoon olive oil
1 cup diced Italian-style salami
1 cup diced Monterey Jack cheese
Salt and pepper

One of my family's favorites for stuffing steak is salami and cheese. Cut little cubes of cotto or Italian-style salami and toss them together with similar-size cubes of jack or Cheddar cheese. Stuff the mixture snugly into the pocket of your steak and broil. It adds a delicious contrast of flavor and texture while at the same time contributing a richness that helps make a steak go a lot further.

≈

1. Cut a pocket in the steak as in step 2 of the previous recipe.

2. Sauté the garlic in the olive oil until just limp. Add the salami and cheese and mix thoroughly. Stuff the mixture into the pocket. Skewer the opening shut with three or four toothpicks and lace closed with string to hold in the stuffing.

3. Broil or barbecue the steak, approximately 12 minutes on each side. Remove the skewers and string and slice into ½-inch-wide slices. Spoon any sauce that flows out over each portion. Season with salt and pepper, and serve at once.

Serves 6 to 8.

Rolled Stuffed Flank

4 tablespoons unsalted butter
4 tablespoons olive oil
8 to 10 mushrooms, sliced
8 scallions, chopped
½ cup diced ham (can be leftover boiled

Flank steak is the cut called for in the classic recipe for London broil. Quickly broiled or pan-fried and carved very thin across the grain, a typical 2-to-2½-pound flank steak will provide London broil for three or four people. But to make a flank steak feed a small army, stuff it. You can use any kind of stuffing you like—bread, corn bread, oysters, whatever. This recipe was made up of what was in the refrigerator when friends dropped by. We had to make a flank steak and leftovers feed not four but eight. Everybody loved it, and it has become a family favorite. There are occasional variations depending on "what's in the fridge." You will have leftover dressing. Use it to stuff tomatoes, or stuff two flank steaks and freeze one for future use.

ham, Canadian bacon, or whatever)
- ½ cup diced smoked sausage, such as kielbasa
- ½ cup pine nuts and slivered almonds, combined
- 1 recipe Neva's Quick Pilaf (follows)
- A 2-to-2½-pound flank steak
- 1 cup grated cheese (Cheddar or Monterey Jack)
- 1 cup flour, combined with 2 teaspoons salt and 1 teaspoon pepper
- 1 10-ounce can beef bouillon
- 1 cup dry red wine
- 1 tablespoon cornstarch dissolved in 3 tablespoons cold water

≈

1. In a heavy skillet heat half of the butter and oil. Over moderate heat cook the mushrooms and scallions until limp. Add the ham, sausage, nuts, and pilaf. Mix well and set aside.

2. Butterfly the flank steak. Place it on a cutting surface and with a sharp knife slice almost through horizontally, leaving the meat attached at one end, like a hinge. When folded out, the meat will be twice the size it was to begin with. With a mallet or heavy frying pan, pound the butterflied steak a few good whacks to make it thinner. Liberally sprinkle with the grated cheese and cover with a layer of the mushroom dressing from step 1, using about half of it (reserving the rest for some future use).

3. Roll up the butterflied steak like a jelly roll. Secure with toothpicks and lace closed with string. Roll it in the seasoned flour and brown it in the remaining oil and butter. Add the bouillon and wine, cover, and simmer the meat until tender; approximately 2 hours. Add more stock if needed.

4. Slice the steak ½ inch thick and arrange the slices on a warm platter. Thicken the sauce in the pan with the cornstarch mixture and serve with the flank steak.

Serves 6 to 8.

Neva's Quick Pilaf

- 1 cup rice or any combination of rice, barley, and bulgur wheat
- 2 tablespoons unsalted butter
- ½ package dry onion-soup mix
- 2 cups water

My wife, Neva, is very like my grandmother in her creative use of good canned and packaged products that can speed up a recipe and shorten her time in the kitchen. We have a whole file of recipes labeled "Neva's Quick." In this recipe she uses dry onion-soup mix rather than cooking onions from scratch; not only does the mix provide the onions, it provides all of the seasonings as well.

≈

Brown the rice or grain mixture in the butter and add the onion soup mix. Add water, cover, and simmer until the water is absorbed and the grain is tender, approximately 20 to 30 minutes.

Serves 4 to 6.

Strips and Cubes for Quick Cooking

It doesn't take long to cook steaks; they are, I think, one of the original convenience foods. Yet in this fast-paced world we live in there are those for whom even a steak takes too long, or they don't want that much meat, or both.

Most any of the cuts that we call "steak" can be sliced very thin or cut into small cubes to be cooked very quickly in recipes that have come to be called collectively and respectively "stir-fries" and "kabobs."

Stir-fry is an Oriental cooking technique that is usually done in a wok, but in America today the technique of stir-fry knows no national boundaries and any skillet will do.

The word "kabob" comes from "shish kabob," which is the Turkish name for skewered mutton seasoned with salt, pepper, thyme, and powdered bay leaves and grilled over hot embers. In America we skewer all kinds of things and call them kabobs. The favorite meat on the skewer for most is beef.

Following are a few recipes for using beef strips and cubes for quick cooking. One word of caution: do not buy strips or cubes in little trays labeled "meat for stir-fry" or "beef kabobs" in your supermarket meat case. Buy a steak and cut your own. You'll likely get better quality; you'll know what you're getting, and you'll probably pay less for it!

Green-Pepper Steak, Chinese Style

Sometimes we pay a premium for what we perceive as "convenience foods." I made this recipe up reading the ingredients list on the back of a package of Stouffer's frozen Green Pepper Steak—Chinese Style and leaving out all the things I couldn't pronounce. It cooks in less time than it takes the water to boil to cook the frozen "convenience" variety, and you can feed four or more people for the price of one frozen single-serving package.

1 to 1½ pounds lean beef, cut into thin strips for stir-fry
2 tablespoons soy sauce
2 tablespoons white wine
2 tablespoons corn-starch
¼ cup peanut oil
1 medium onion, sliced thin
1 green pepper, seeded and sliced thin
1 tomato, cut into wedges
1 cup beef broth
1 teaspoon red-pepper flakes (optional)

≈

1. Put the beef strips in a small mixing bowl. Mix together 1 tablespoon each of soy sauce, white wine, cornstarch, and peanut oil. Pour the mixture over the meat and toss to coat the meat well.

2. Heat 2 tablespoons of peanut oil in a wok or sauté pan, add the meat and brown quickly, tossing to brown well on all sides. Remove the meat from the pan and set aside. Sauté the onion in the same pan, adding a bit more oil if needed.

3. Add the sliced pepper to the pan with the onion and cook until the pepper and onion are just limp (3 minutes). Add the tomato wedges to the pan along with 1 cup of beef broth.

4. Put the beef strips back in the pan. Bring everything to a boil; simmer for a minute or two. Mix together the remaining soy sauce, white wine, cornstarch, and peanut oil, and stir that into the pan. Add red-pepper flakes if desired and continue cooking until the sauce thickens slightly. Serve over cooked rice.

Serves 4 to 6.

Szechwan Beef Stir-Fry

- 1 pound beefsteak (tenderloin, top loin, sirloin, or top round) cut 1 inch thick
- 2 tablespoons soy sauce
- 4 teaspoons Oriental dark roasted sesame oil
- 1½ teaspoons sugar
- 1 teaspoon cornstarch
- 2 cloves garlic, crushed
- 1 tablespoon finely minced fresh ginger
- ¼ teaspoon red-pepper flakes
- 1 red bell pepper, cut into 1-inch pieces
- 1 8-ounce package frozen baby corn, defrosted
- ¼ pound fresh green beans, cut into julienne strips

The sesame oil and pepper flakes are what give this dish the spicy zip that makes it Szechwan. If you like a milder version, use peanut oil, skip the pepper flakes, and call it Cantonese. This makes a hearty, filling meal served over hot cooked rice or barley, but it can also be served on a bed of crisp greens for a light, refreshing summer entrée.

≈

1. Cut the beefsteak lengthwise into 2 strips so that you have the meat in strips about 2 inches wide and 1 inch thick. Slice the strips across the grain at a slight angle in ⅛-inch slices.

2. Combine the soy sauce, 2 teaspoons of the sesame oil, sugar, and cornstarch. Pour over the beef strips and toss.

3. Heat the remaining 2 teaspoons of oil in a large skillet over medium-high heat. Add the garlic, ginger, and pepper flakes; cook, stirring, for 30 seconds. Add the bell pepper and the corn and stir-fry for another minute or two. Add the beans and stir-fry for another 30 seconds. Remove the vegetables and set aside.

4. In the same pan, stir-fry the beef strips (half at a time) for 2 or 3 minutes, stirring constantly. Add the beef strips to the vegetables as they are done.

5. Return everything to the skillet and heat through before serving.

Serves 4 to 6.

Mexican Beef Stir-Fry

This is great served on crisp lettuce for a hot beef salad or rolled up in a warm tortilla (and called "almost fajitas").

- 1 pound beefsteak (tenderloin, top loin, sirloin, or top round), cut 1 inch thick
- 2 tablespoons vegetable oil
- 1 teaspoon ground cumin
- 1 teaspoon dried oregano leaves
- 2 cloves garlic, crushed
- 1 red or green bell pepper, cut into thin strips
- 1 medium onion cut in half and then into thin slices
- 1 or 2 jalapeño peppers, interior ribs and seeds removed, thinly sliced
- 3 cups thinly sliced iceberg lettuce

≈

1. Cut the beefsteak lengthwise into 2 strips so that you have the meat in strips about 2 inches wide and 1 inch thick. Slice the strips across the grain at a slight angle into ⅛-inch slices.

2. Combine the oil, cumin, oregano, and garlic; reserve half. Heat the other half of the seasoned oil in a large nonstick skillet over medium-high heat. Add the bell pepper, onion, and jalapeño pepper; stir-fry 2 to 3 minutes, or until crisp-tender. Remove and reserve.

3. In the same skillet, stir-fry the beef strips (half at a time) in the remaining oil for 1 to 2 minutes. Return the vegetables to the skillet and heat through. Serve beef mixture over lettuce.

Serves 4 to 6.

Italian Beef Stir-Fry

This recipe calls for spaghetti, though any cooked pasta will work. We often serve it over orzo, but always with toasted garlic bread.

- 1 pound beefsteak (tenderloin, top loin, sirloin, or top round), cut 1 inch thick
- 2 or 3 cloves of garlic, crushed
- 1 tablespoon olive oil
- Salt and pepper to taste

(recipe continues)

≈

1. Cut the beefsteak lengthwise into 2 strips so that you have the meat in strips about 2 inches wide and 1 inch thick. Slice the strips across the grain at a slight angle into ⅛-inch slices.

2. In a nonstick skillet cook the garlic in oil over medium-high heat for 1 minute. Add the beef strips (half

Italian Beef Stir-Fry *(cont.)*

- 2 small zucchini, thinly sliced
- 1 cup cherry-tomato halves
- ¼ cup bottled Italian salad dressing
- 2 cups hot cooked spaghetti
- 1 or 2 tablespoons fresh-grated Parmesan cheese

at a time); stir-fry for 1 to 2 minutes. Season with salt and pepper, remove with slotted spoon, and set aside.

3. Add the zucchini to the same skillet; stir-fry for 2 to 3 minutes, or until crisp-tender. Return the beef to the skillet with the tomato halves and the dressing; heat through.

4. Serve the beef mixture over hot pasta; sprinkle with Parmesan cheese.

Serves 4.

Three-Pepper Beef Kabobs

- 1 pound beefsteak (tenderloin, top loin, sirloin, or top round), cut into 1-inch-thick cubes
- 2 tablespoons vegetable oil
- 1 tablespoon fresh lemon juice
- 1 tablespoon water
- 2 teaspoons Dijon-style mustard
- 1 teaspoon honey
- ½ teaspoon dried oregano leaves
- ¼ teaspoon black pepper
- 1 medium green, 1 red, and 1 yellow bell pepper, seeded and cut into 1-inch pieces
- 8 large mushrooms

You will often find ready-made kabobs in the meat case with cubes of beef (who knows what cut) threaded on skewers with bell peppers, mushrooms, and usually cherry tomatoes. Stay away from them-there kabobs! Why pay high beef prices for vegetables? Make your own kabobs!

≈

1. Cut the beefsteak into 1-inch pieces.

2. Whisk together the oil, lemon juice, water, mustard, honey, oregano, and pepper in a large bowl. Add the beef, bell peppers, and mushrooms, stirring to coat.

3. Preheat the broiler. Alternately thread pieces of beef, bell pepper, and mushrooms on each of four 12-inch skewers, with the colored peppers arranged to achieve a pleasing presentation. Place the kabobs on a rack in the broiler pan so the surface of the meat is 3 to 4 inches from the heat.

4. Broil for 9 to 12 minutes for rare to medium, turning occasionally. Season with salt and pepper if desired. You can also grill the kabobs over medium coals for 8 to 11 minutes.

Serves 4.

VARIATIONS

Peppercorn Beef Kabobs Cut the beef into 1-inch cubes. Combine 1½ teaspoons crushed black peppercorns, ½ teaspoon each of salt and pepper, and 1 clove of crushed garlic into a shallow dish. Add the beef cubes and toss to coat. Thread the beef cubes on skewers alternately with small wedges of onion. Grill or broil as above.

Serves 4.

Beef and Pineapple Kabobs Cut the beef into 1-inch cubes. Combine 1 small diced onion with ½ cup bottled teriyaki sauce. Put the beef cubes in a small bowl, add the onion-teriyaki marinade and stir to coat. Let marinate for a few minutes, tossing occasionally. Cut fresh pineapple into 1-inch cubes or use canned chunks, and open and drain an 8-ounce can of whole water chestnuts. Alternately thread beef cubes, pineapple, and water chestnuts on skewers. Grill or barbecue as above, using the marinade to baste occasionally.

Serves 4.

Rosemary Walnut Beef Skewers

1½ pounds beef tenderloin or boneless top-sirloin steak
Salt and freshly ground pepper to taste
2 red bell peppers

SAUCE

¼ cup finely chopped walnuts
1 stick (½ cup) melted butter
¼ cup fresh lemon juice
4 cloves garlic, finely chopped
1 tablespoon fresh rosemary, finely chopped, or 1 teaspoon dried rosemary
2 teaspoons coarse-grain mustard
6 sprigs fresh rosemary (optional)
6 lemon wedges (optional)

This recipe, created by Karen Kevan of Saratoga, California, won top honors at the 1995 California Beef Cook-Off. Having a lot of rosemary in my herb garden, I decided to try the recipe using rosemary branches for the skewers. It was delicious. We do it quite often. I don't have very much rosemary left.

≈

1. Trim the fat from the beef. Cut the beef into 1-inch cubes. On 6 long metal skewers or 6 rosemary branches,* thread the beef cubes, leaving spaces between the pieces for more even cooking. Season the beef with salt and freshly ground pepper to taste.

2. Remove the stem, ribs, and seeds from each pepper. Cut each pepper into 6 strips. Season with salt and pepper to taste.

3. In a skillet over medium heat, toast the walnuts, stirring frequently, about 3 minutes, or until well browned and fragrant.

4. In a small bowl, mix the remaining ingredients, and add the toasted walnuts. Brush the sauce generously over the beef and peppers.

5. Place the skewers and peppers on a preheated grill over medium coals. Grill 10 to 14 minutes for medium-rare to medium doneness for the beef; the peppers should be tender. Baste and turn the skewers frequently, using the remaining sauce, if any. Do not overcook.

6. If desired, garnish with fresh rosemary sprigs and lemon wedges.

Serves 6.

* Use thick rosemary branches, tufts of leaves left at one end, scraped smooth and cut at an angle at other end for easy threading.

Sukiyaki

When I was courting my Polynesian bride in San Francisco in the late 1950s, one of our favorite spots was a little out-of-the-way Japanese restaurant called the Mingei Ya. A specialty of the house was Sukiyaki. It has become a specialty around our house and the requested dish for the birthday dinner of our youngest daughter for most of her thirty years. It's a great dish for small dinner parties. Once the mincing, slicing, and chopping are done, Sukiyaki is prepared at the dining-room table.

- 2 tablespoons sugar
- 1 teaspoon black pepper
- ½ cup soy sauce
- ½ cup beef broth
- 2 cups green onions cut on a diagonal into 2-inch lengths
- 1 cup celery cut on diagonal into 2-inch slices
- 1 cup thinly sliced fresh mushrooms
- 1 5-ounce can water chestnuts, drained and sliced
- 1 5-ounce can bamboo shoots, drained and sliced
- 5 cups small spinach leaves with stems removed
- 1 cup fresh bean sprouts or 1 can, drained

≈

1. Just before cooking time, mix the sugar, pepper, soy sauce, and beef stock in a small pitcher. Arrange the vegetables, meat, tofu, and bean threads attractively on large platters, keeping each item separate.

2. Preheat a large 12-inch electric skillet. When your guests are seated, add the oil or suet and cover the bottom and sides well. If using suet, remove and discard after you have rendered about 2 tablespoons of fat. When the pan has reached medium-high heat, add the beef and cook briskly, turning it over and over, until just browned, for a minute or two.

3. Pour the liquid mixture over the meat and push the meat to one side of the pan.

(recipe continues)

Sukiyaki *(cont.)*

1 pound beef tenderloin, top loin, or rib-eye, sliced paper-thin across the grain
1 pound bean curd (tofu), drained and cubed* (optional)
4 ounces dry bean threads, soaked 1 hour in hot water and drained* (optional)
2 tablespoons peanut oil or some small pieces of beef suet

* Bean curd (tofu) and dry bean threads (shirataki) may be found in Oriental food stores and in many supermarkets all over the United States.

4. Keeping them in separate groups, add the onions, celery, and mushrooms. Continue cooking and toss-stirring over high heat for 1 minute, then push to the side of the pan.

5. Again in separate groups, add the remaining vegetables in the order given, then the bean curd and bean threads. Cook and toss-stir each food until heated through. Serve over hot fluffy rice.

Serves 4.

Roasts

Put in lots of cobs to get the oven right hot. The meat should be wiped, then dredged all over with salt, pepper and flour. Place bits of butter or lard over the top and add enough boiling water to cover the roaster by 1½ inches. Place in a hot oven; baste every ten minutes. Allow twenty minutes to the pound. Don't shake the grate much. You want the cobs to burn down slow.

That's how Grandma used to roast a roast in the oven of her wood burner in 1911. Times have changed a great deal since then. So have the stoves, and as we know, so has the meat we roast in them.

If your roasting method is entirely satisfactory, don't let me talk you out of anything or into any changes. But if your roast on occasion comes out dry or lacking in flavor and tenderness, let's talk about it.

Before you blame your roasting failures on your butcher or his beef, be aware that one of the major factors affecting tenderness, juiciness, and flavor is under your control: the cooking temperature. Meat is *always* more tender when cooked at a low temperature, between 275 and 325 degrees. The lower temperatures also produce more juicy results, because the natural moisture in the meat does not evaporate away as it does when the temperature is too high.

Meat cooked at a low temperature also has more flavor, because meat flavor is contained, to a large extent, in the fat. Under high temperature, the fat is rendered to the bottom of the roasting pan, where it can, at best, flavor the gravy.

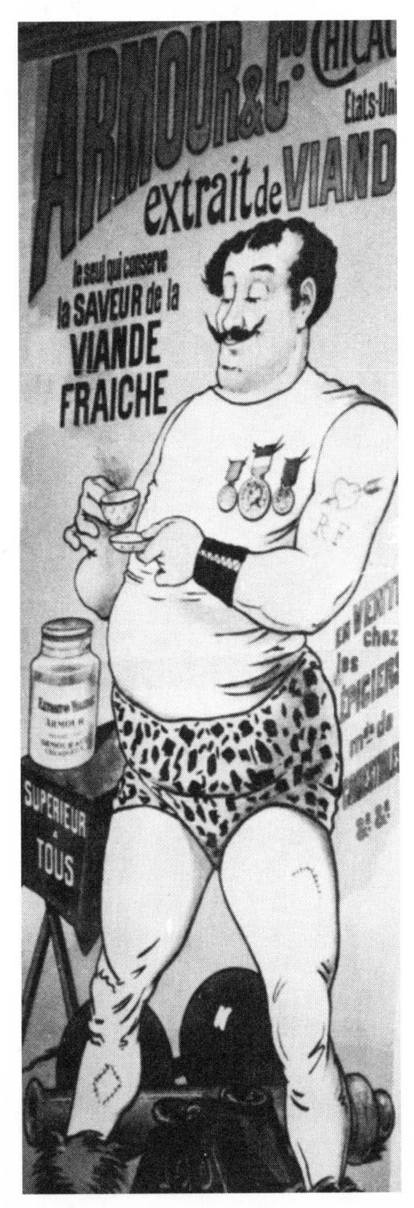

So—how low is too low and how high is too high? Unfortunately, there are no absolutes. It would be wonderfully simple if we could say, for example, twenty minutes per pound at 325 degrees and guarantee perfect results, but we can't. Roasting times and temperatures depend on a number of factors, including the kind of meat, its size, and its shape. Large roasts need lower heat for a longer time than small roasts. Roasts with the bone in cook more quickly than roasts that are boneless, since the bone helps conduct the heat into the meat. A thick, blocky roast will take longer to cook than a flat roast even though they may weigh exactly the same. Aged meat tends to cook more quickly than meat that has not been aged.

These many variables are enough to confuse all but the most experienced cooks. But help is at hand, with the aid of a good meat thermometer. A meat thermometer is the only accurate guide to the doneness of meat, especially roasts. Buy the best; I prefer an instant-read model. One person's "rare" is another's "well done." The instant-read thermometer will tell you what the internal temperature is, so you can arrive at what you like. For me, a perfect rare roast will read 120 to 130 degrees. Medium rare reads 140 to 150 degrees. With the thermometer, and careful attention to keeping oven temperature low, you'll have great roasts every time.

The Meat Heat Test

To show how much is lost in dollars and cents when meat is cooked at too high a temperature, Clifford G. Bowes, a top meat consultant from Chicago, ran a test a few years ago for a group of professional chefs. He took two standing rib roasts that were as nearly alike as any two roasts could be, taken from the left and right sides of the same carcass of beef. The roasts were cooked at different oven temperatures: the roast from the left side at 275 degrees, the one from the right at 400. Both were cooked to the same level of doneness: medium, 160 degrees internal temperature. Here are his results:

Roast Cooked at 275 Degrees

Weight before cooking: 28 pounds 12 ounces. Weight after cooking: 25 pounds 4 ounces. Weight loss: 3 pounds 8 ounces. Percentage lost: 12.1.

Roast Cooked at 400 Degrees

Weight before cooking: 28 pounds 6 ounces. Weight after cooking: 20 pounds 2 ounces. Weight loss: 8 pounds 4 ounces. Percentage lost: 29.1.

There was a 17-percent difference in weight loss. If you think about that in terms of money, it means that 17 cents out of every dollar that was spent on the roast cooked at 400 degrees was wasted. It quite literally went up in smoke. On a roast the size of those Cliff was cooking, that amounts to more than $4.75 wasted!

Prime Rib with Yorkshire Pudding

A 4-rib prime rib of beef
Salt and freshly ground black pepper

YORKSHIRE PUDDING

3 large eggs
1½ cups milk
1 teaspoon salt
1½ cups flour
½ cup hot beef drippings
1 13¾-ounce can beef broth

A marvelous slab of roast beef and a light airy Yorkshire pudding, both slathered with pan juices—delicious. Great for holidays, great anytime!

≈

1. Trim the roast of any excess fat. You may want to "French" the rib bones for an elegant presentation; to do so, remove an inch of meat from the ends of the rib bones, as you would for a rack of lamb (see page 171). Rub the roast with salt and pepper and place it on a rack or on its rib bones in an open roasting pan (the bones form a natural arch under the meat).

2. Roast in a preheated 325-degree oven for about 2 hours for rare. Test the meat with an instant-read meat thermometer; the temperature should read 120 to 130 degrees. For medium rare, roast 2½ hours, to register 140 to 150 degrees. For well done (I don't approve!), roast 3 hours, to 160 degrees. Transfer the roast to a warm platter to rest before carving. Letting the roast rest in a warm place near the stove while you make the Yorkshire pudding allows the juices to redistribute themselves evenly through the meat, so that every slice will be juicy and done to perfection.

3. As the roast cooks, make the Yorkshire-pudding batter. In a medium bowl, beat the eggs with a wire whisk until foamy. Beat in the milk and salt. Gradually add the flour, beating to make a nice smooth batter. Let the batter rest as the roast finishes cooking.

4. After removing the roast, raise the oven heat to 450 degrees. Have a 12-cup muffin pan ready. With a bulb baster, draw up ½ cup of drippings from the bottom of the roasting pan. Divide it among the muffin cups, approximately ½ teaspoon for each. Place the muffin pan in the hot oven for 5 minutes. Remove the hot pan and pour

Prime Rib with Yorkshire Pudding *(cont.)*

3 tablespoons of batter into each cup. Bake for 25 to 30 minutes.

5. Meanwhile, spoon off as much fat as you can from the roasting pan and discard. Stir the beef broth into the remaining meat juices; reduce over high heat on top of the stove, stirring up the good browned bits into the "au jus," and keep warm. Carve the roast just before the Yorkshire pudding comes from the oven. Serve the slices with the hot Yorkshire pudding and the au jus.

Serves 6 to 8.

GROUND BEEF—WHATEVER HAPPENED TO HAMBURGER?

Whatever happened to hamburger? Considering that we Americans are reported to eat more of the stuff than does any other nation on the face of the earth, I have often wondered why we never see "hamburger" in the meat cases of our local supermarkets anymore. Today we see "ground chuck" and "ground round," "ground beef" and "lean ground beef," "extra lean ground beef" and "super lean ground beef," even "ground sirloin," but not "hamburger."

What is hamburger, and how does it differ from all of those other ground meats in the meat case?

The United States Department of Agriculture makes the following distinction between "hamburger" and "ground beef" when those two products are ground and packaged in a federally inspected or state-inspected plant: "Hamburger is ground beef to which seasonings and pieces of fat *may* be added while the meat is being ground. No added water, extenders or binders are permitted." "Ground beef" (by USDA standards) is just what the name implies—ground beef—no extras, no binders or extenders, no water, not even any extra fat. "Seasonings," however, may be added as long as they are identified on the label. So, according to the USDA, the only difference between "hamburger" and "ground beef" is the addition perhaps of a bit of extra fat.

When I first began grinding the stuff, we had two different kinds and we called them *both* "ground beef." Regular ground beef was a mixture of trimmings from all parts of the carcass. In those days, beef came to market in carcass form, and all of the breaking and cutting into steaks and roasts was done in the cutting room at the market; there were a lot of trimmings. The flank portion (after the flank steak was removed), the neck (after I had boned it out—a job I hated), the plate (the belly of the beef animal), the miscellaneous trimmings from steaks and roasts, all were ground together to make "ground beef."

To make the second kind, "lean ground beef," we added a bit of bull! Not the same kind of "bull" that is under discussion with regard to ground-beef labeling these days, but real bull. Frozen lean bull meat came to the market in sixty-pound boxes; it was sliced up into strips on the electric saw and mixed with the block scraps and lean trimmings to make "lean ground beef."

In more recent times, ground beef (hamburger) has been labeled with more sophisticated terms: "ground chuck," "ground round," "ground sirloin." There is a lot of bull in those terms too, but it's not real bull, it's another kind. The only difference between one kind of ground beef and another is fat content. They don't grind only chuck meat to make "ground chuck," and they sure as hell don't use sirloin to make "ground sirloin." How can a butcher take the bone and most of the fat off the sirloin section of a beef carcass, run it through the meat grinder, and sell it for a dollar or more *less* than he's getting for a sirloin steak? It doesn't make sense! It's bull!

Supermarkets may label their packages of ground beef according to their own preferences. In some places it's "regular," "lean," and "extra lean," while in other markets it's "ground beef," "ground chuck," and "ground round." But underneath all of those lean labels and tender terms, the only difference between one ground beef and another is the same as the USDA's difference between "hamburger" and "ground beef"—*fat content.*

Most meat markets make their ground beef from the trimmings that are a natural part of the meat-cutting process. When the butcher trims the tail off a T-bone steak, or "squares up" a rolled roast, these trimmings go into the ground beef. The less tender portions of beef—the plate, shank, flank, and often brisket (the cuts that just won't sell)—are trimmed of their excess fat and ground. From these "lean trimmings" we get ground beef.

In these days of boxed beef, with most meat being cut and trimmed not at the meat market but, rather, at the packing house, retail butchers can buy coarse-ground trimmings—"70% lean," "80% lean"—direct from the packer to mix with their own "lean trimmings." It's my guess that there is a little bull in those too!

At the retail level, there is no accurate way to measure the exact percentage of fat content. It is at best guesswork. In most markets the fat content of ground beef is determined by an age-old technique called "eyeballing it." So don't pay too much attention to percentage labels when it comes to picking ground beef. Pick out a package and check the color and the price. Don't pay a lot more money for a little more lean. Selecting lean beef, whether it's in the piece or ground, is relatively easy to do if you remember the simple fact that lean meat is *red,* and fat is *white.* If the more expensive "extra lean ground beef" doesn't look a whole lot redder than "regular ground beef," then it's not so "extra lean" at all.

The Best Burger

1½ pounds lean ground chuck or round
¼ pound beef suet (kidney fat)
Salt and pepper to taste
1 tablespoon butter
1 tablespoon vegetable oil

Any of us fortunate enough to be on the scene in "The City"—San Francisco—back in the 1950s know that no one ever built a better burger than Jack Falvey at what may go down in the history books as the restaurant that created the first "gourmet hamburger"—The Hippo.

I knew Jack Falvey back then, and learned a lot about what it takes to make a great hamburger from him. "You can dress up a hamburger in many ways," he said. "You can sauce it with all kinds of sauces and you can give it eye appeal with all kinds of things from caviar to candy canes, but you must remember, the meat that makes up the hamburger makes it a success!"

"When I buy hamburger," said Falvey, "I buy round or chuck and add suet to it to bring the total fat content to about 15 percent. Ground meat, when cooked without suet, is very dry. Have the meat and suet put through the grinder twice to ensure an even distribution of the fat. A thick patty is best—thin patties dry out in cooking. One-third of a pound, about one to one and a quarter inches thick, is the perfect size. How you form the patty is very important, too. The less you touch the meat the better. One of my biggest problems here at the restaurant is with cooks who insist in overpatting the meat patties.

"Avoid buying ground meat from markets that use those machines that stamp out square, flat, bricklike loaves of ground beef. The machine already has overpatted the meat before you even get your hands on it. Grind your own or have the butcher do it."

≈

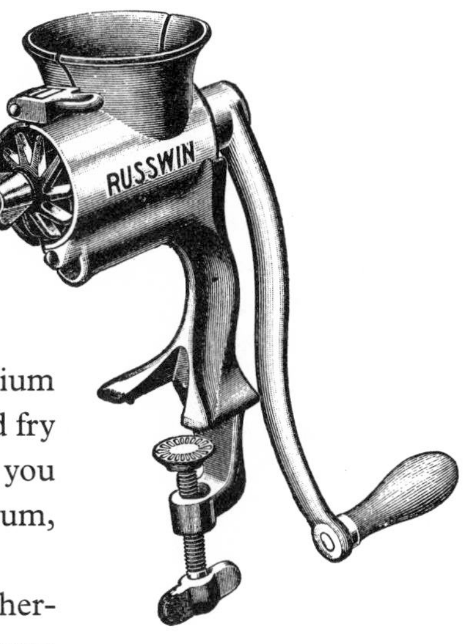

1. Grind the meat and suet twice through the fine plate of your meat grinder, or ask your butcher to do it for you. If you have a food processor you can use that, but do it gently, with a pulsing action—don't overgrind the meat!

2. Season the mixture with salt and pepper and mix gently. Shape into four patties about 1 inch thick; don't overpat the patties.

3. Melt the butter and oil in a skillet over medium heat until bubbling. Lay in the hamburger patties and fry 2 to 3 minutes on each side for rare (rare is OK when you grind your own), 4 to 5 minutes on each side for medium, and 6 minutes per side for well done (if you must).

4. Test for doneness with an instant-read meat thermometer, 125 to 130 degrees for rare, 140 to 145 degrees for medium, and 155 to 160 for well done. Don't squish the patty with a spatula to see what color the juices are or there won't be any juices left!

5. Finally, Falvey advises, "Never put anything *in* your hamburger except salt and pepper, but be as wild as you want with the sauces that go on it." Jack's wild Hippo hamburger sauces can be made ahead of time and stored in the refrigerator to use not only on burgers, but on steaks, chops, and cutlets of all kinds.

Serves 4.

Hippo Hamburger Sauces

Stroganoff Sauce

≈

½ cup chopped onions
1 teaspoon butter
½ cup thinly sliced mushrooms
½ teaspoon beef-bouillon base or 1 bouillon cube dissolved in 1 tablespoon warm water
1 teaspoon Worcestershire sauce
Salt and pepper to taste
1 pint sour cream

1. Cook the onions in the butter over a low flame until they are translucent. Add the mushrooms and cook for about 5 minutes more, stirring constantly. Stir in the remaining ingredients and heat thoroughly.

2. *Do not* allow the mixture to boil, or the sour cream will separate. Serve with your hamburger. Refrigerate any unused sauce to be heated again for another meal.

Makes 3 cups.

Game Sauce

≈

2 strips bacon, diced
1 cup currant jelly
4 tablespoons water
1 garlic clove, finely minced
½ teaspoon lemon juice
5 teaspoons Worcestershire sauce
¼ cup sherry
¼ cup bourbon
1 tablespoon catsup
½ teaspoon paprika
¼ teaspoon salt

1. Fry the bacon bits to render the fat. Add the rest of the ingredients and simmer for 10 minutes.

2. Ladle the sauce over your cooked hamburger, and refrigerate any leftover sauce for later use.

Makes approximately 2 cups.

Mexican Sauce

≈

1. Heat the ½ cup of water in a small saucepan and dissolve the bouillon cubes in it. Add all the remaining ingredients except the flour mixed with water, and bring to a boil.

2. Reduce the heat and simmer for 30 minutes.

3. Add the flour-water mixture and cook gently to thicken the sauce to the consistency of cream.

4. Serve over hamburgers.

Makes approximately 2 cups.

½ cup water
2 small beef-bouillon cubes
½ cup tomato puree
1½ tablespoons chili powder
2 tablespoons dry white wine
1 tablespoon Maggi seasoning
1 small pinch cayenne pepper
1 pinch salt
1 pinch black pepper
½ teaspoon Worcestershire sauce
1 tablespoon flour mixed with ¼ cup water

The French Connection

≈

1. In a large skillet melt the butter and cook the onion until the onion rings are translucent. Add the other ingredients and keep stirring until the sauce simmers and ingredients are thoroughly mixed.

2. Put cooked hamburger patties in individual casseroles and cover with sauce, scooping up generous amounts of onion. Serve with hunks of French bread to help mop up this glorious sauce.

Makes approximately 2 cups.

1½ tablespoons unsalted butter
1 large yellow onion, sliced thin
1 tablespoon Bovril (concentrated liquid beef bouillon)
Salt and pepper to taste
½ teaspoon Worcestershire sauce
1 cup dry vermouth

Burger with the Blues

½ pound blue cheese
2 pounds ground beef
¼ cup minced scallions, including the tops
¼ teaspoon Tabasco sauce
½ teaspoon Worcestershire sauce
1 teaspoon salt
½ teaspoon black pepper
¼ teaspoon ground red pepper (a little less if you don't like red-hot "blues")
8 hamburger buns

Even though some authorities recommend never putting anything *in* your burger, James Beard, the Dean of American Cooking, liked burgers with a bit of blue cheese. It was my good fortune to study with Mr. Beard, and though he agreed with Jack Falvey on every other count of what it takes to make a great burger, Jim still liked a bit of blue cheese with the following seasonings in his.

≈

1. Crumble the blue cheese into the ground beef and add the minced scallions, Tabasco, Worcestershire, salt, and peppers. Mix lightly to combine. Let stand in the refrigerator for an hour or two so the flavors can blend.

2. Gently press the meat into patties. Broil, pan-fry, or grill over moderate coals to the desired degree of doneness. Serve on toasted hamburger buns.

Serves 8.

Taverns

1 cup water
2 pounds ground beef
¾ cup catsup
3 tablespoons French's mustard
1 teaspoon chili powder, or to taste
1 small onion, finely chopped
Salt and pepper to taste
Hamburger buns

The controversy continues, in the part of the country where I grew up, over the origin of the "Tavern." Those of you from the other parts of the country know them now as "Loose-Meats," "Yum-Yums," "Maid (or Made) Rights," or, most commonly, as "Sloppy Joes." The truth, I am confident, is that the Tavern was originally created at the 14th Street Tavern in Sioux City, Iowa, on or just prior to my first date with Diane in 1944. I didn't have the foresight to ask for the recipe then (I had other things on my mind), but I have since developed my own recipe, and it comes very close to the original. My kids don't call them Taverns. Around our house they're "Sloppy Butchers."

≈

1. Bring the water to a boil in a large saucepan. Crumble up the ground beef and add it to the water. Add the

rest of the ingredients, except the buns. Bring the mixture back to a boil for a minute or two. Reduce the heat, cover, and simmer for 20 minutes.

2. To serve, spoon the hamburger on warm hamburger buns and serve with carrot and celery sticks. Delicious! The kids will eat 2 or 3 of these.

Makes 6 to 8 sandwiches.

Chicago

Chicago's first recorded slaughterhouse, located on the north bank of the Chicago River, was operated in 1827 by Archibald Clybourne, who had a government contract to supply Fort Dearborn with meat. The first livestock markets in Chicago were taverns that provided stock pens for dealers who brought cattle to the city to trade. Records differ on the opening dates and locations of Chicago's earliest markets, but an article in a 1929 *Provisioner* says the Bull's Head Live Stock Market was established in 1848 at Madison Street and Ashland Avenue, and the Lake Shore Stock Market (Myrick's Place) in 1856 at 31st Street and the lakefront.

Meat Loaf

A well-made meat loaf can make a marvelous meal not only for a family pot luck but for guests who are epicures as well. Meat loaves are easy to make and easy to serve, offer an almost endless variety, and don't cost much. What more could anyone ask? No wonder they're making a comeback!

Basic Meat Loaf

- 1 pound ground beef
- ½ pound ground veal
- ½ pound ground pork
- ¼ cup chopped onion
- ⅛ teaspoon black pepper
- ¼ teaspoon salt (or more if not using bacon)
- 1 medium carrot, grated
- 1 medium potato, grated
- 2 eggs, beaten until lemon yellow
- ¾ cup milk or cream
- 2 cups bread crumbs
- 2 to 3 slices of bacon (optional)

The best meat loaves are made with more than one kind of meat. Beef, pork, and veal are the meats most often called for. The meat loaf that follows is one of our favorites. A good meat loaf should be firm, not dry—much like the texture of a country pâté. Like a pâté, it's as good, if not better, served cold. Make two while you're at it.

≈

1. Mix well all the ingredients except the bacon, in the order in which they are listed. Press into a greased 9-by-5-by-3-inch loaf pan or shape into an oblong free-form loaf.
2. Should you choose to use the bacon, lay the slices over the top. Bake the loaf in a preheated 350-degree oven for one hour.

NOTE: There are a couple of variations that we use on occasion just for fun. One is to "ice" the loaf with mashed potatoes after it has baked and then return it to the oven for 10 to 15 minutes to brown the potatoes. Another is to lay a row of peeled hard-boiled eggs in the center of the mixture before baking.

Serves 4 to 6 (hopefully with leftovers).

Pizza Burger Loaf

This is a surefire recipe for teenagers and for the rest of us too. It's great for a Super Bowl or any other TV party.

- ½ pound hot or sweet Italian sausage
- 2 pounds ground beef
- 1 cup crushed saltine crackers
- 1 onion, chopped
- 2 cloves garlic, minced
- ¼ cup chopped parsley
- 1 egg, beaten
- 1 teaspoon salt
- ¾ teaspoon dried oregano
- ½ teaspoon black pepper
- 1 15-ounce can tomato sauce
- 3 ounces mozzarella cheese, grated
- 6 stuffed green olives, sliced

≈

1. Take the sausage out of its casing and crumble it. Combine it with the ground beef, cracker crumbs, onion, garlic, parsley, and egg. Stir the salt, ½ teaspoon of the oregano, and the pepper into the tomato sauce. Set aside ½ cup seasoned sauce, add the remainder to the meat mixture, and mix thoroughly.

2. Place the mixture in a 9-by-5-by-3-inch loaf pan. Spread the reserved seasoned sauce over the loaf. Bake in a preheated 350-degree oven for 1 hour and 30 minutes. Sprinkle the top with grated cheese and the remaining ¼ teaspoon oregano and arrange the olive slices in a nice pattern. Continue baking for 5 to 8 minutes. Let the loaf stand for 10 minutes before serving.

Serves 6 to 8.

Ham-Hamburger Meat Loaf

- 1½ pounds ground beef
- 1 pound ground ham (any leftover ham or boiled ham will work, but the meat from a country ham is the best)
- 2 eggs, beaten until lemon yellow
- ½ cup bread crumbs
- ¼ teaspoon dry mustard
- ¼ teaspoon black pepper
- ¼ to ½ teaspoon salt, depending on the saltiness of the ham
- ⅛ teaspoon ground cloves

This is another meat-loaf favorite that uses up the last of the country ham we usually have around the holidays. It makes wonderful sandwiches. If you like, you can garnish this loaf with pineapple rings on top, sprinkled with brown sugar before baking.

≈

1. Mix together all of the ingredients, press into a greased loaf pan, or shape into an oblong loaf.
2. Bake in a preheated 350-degree oven for 1 hour.

Serves 6 to 8 (hopefully with leftovers).

Meatballs

Meatballs offer another way to take advantage of a good buy on ground beef. They can be made ahead and frozen IQF (that's industry jargon for Individually Quick Frozen). Mix up a good big batch of meatballs using any of the following recipes, any of the meat mixtures listed in the meat-loaf section (pages 78–80), or your favorite meat mixture. Shape the meat into balls about ¾ inch to 1 inch in diameter, lay them out on a cookie sheet, and freeze them. Package up the frozen meatballs in freezer bags. Because they were frozen before they went into the bag, they will not stick together. When you want a meal of meatballs, simply take out as many as you need and finish your recipe.

A good and easy way to form meatballs is to use a small 1-inch-diameter ice-cream scoop. Scoop up one, place it on a cookie sheet, then scoop up another.

Dilled Meatballs

Dill adds a wonderful zest to these meatballs. They are great served with noodles or rice.

≈

1½ pounds ground beef
¾ cup quick-cooking oats
1 teaspoon salt
½ teaspoon freshly ground black pepper
1 egg, beaten
2½ teaspoons dry dill weed
1 cup cooking oil
1 cup beef bouillon
1 tablespoon Kitchen Bouquet or Bovril (concentrated liquid beef bouillon)
1 cup sour cream

1. Mix the beef, oats, salt, pepper, egg, and ½ teaspoon of the dill weed. Mix gently, trying not to compress the meat. Shape the mixture into 1-inch meatballs.

2. Heat 1 inch of oil in a large heavy skillet until the surface ripples. Cook the meatballs in batches, turning until browned. Drain on paper towels. Add more oil as needed. When all the meatballs are cooked, discard the oil.

3. Return the meatballs to the skillet, and stir in the bouillon and Kitchen Bouquet. Heat until boiling. Cover, lower the heat, and simmer for 15 minutes. Stir in the remaining dill weed and the sour cream. Heat thoroughly and serve at once.

Serves 6.

Crunchy Meatballs

These make great appetizers on the buffet table at a cocktail party. Everything can be made ahead.

≈

1½ pounds ground beef
½ cup dry bread crumbs
2½ tablespoons finely chopped onion
1 cup beer
1 egg
1 teaspoon salt
½ teaspoon freshly ground black pepper
Vegetable oil for frying

1. Mix together, gently but thoroughly, the ground beef, bread crumbs, onion, 1 cup of beer, 1 egg, 1 teaspoon salt, and ½ teaspoon pepper. Shape the mixture into 1-inch meatballs and set aside. (For appetizers you may want to make them smaller—½- or ¾-inch balls.)

2. Make the Batter: Blend together the ⅔ cup of beer, 2 eggs, and 4 teaspoons oil. Mix in the flour, baking powder, 1½ teaspoons salt, and ¼ teaspoon pepper. Blend well.

(recipe continues)

Crunchy Meatballs *(cont.)*

BATTER

⅔ cup beer
2 eggs
4 teaspoons vegetable oil
1⅓ cups flour
1 teaspoon baking powder
1½ teaspoons salt
¼ teaspoon freshly ground black pepper

MUSTARD SAUCE

1 cup mayonnaise
½ tablespoon French's mustard
½ teaspoon sugar
1 teaspoon salt
¼ teaspoon cayenne pepper
½ teaspoon paprika

3. Make the Mustard Sauce: Blend all the ingredients together and refrigerate until needed.

4. In a large deep heavy skillet, heat 3 inches of the oil to register 325 degrees on a deep-fry thermometer, or until a cube of bread dropped into the hot oil browns quickly without burning. Coat the meatballs with the batter and fry in batches until golden brown. Cook only a few at a time to keep the temperature of the oil constant. Drain on paper towels and keep warm in a preheated 200-degree oven. Serve with the Mustard Sauce.

Serves 6 (more if served as appetizers).

Bar-B-Sauced Meatballs

3 pounds ground beef
2 cups quick oats (uncooked)
1 13-ounce can evaporated milk
1½ cups chopped onion
2 eggs, beaten
2 teaspoons chili powder
2 teaspoons salt
½ teaspoon black pepper

This recipe doesn't qualify as true barbecue, so I call it "bar-b-sauced," but even the barbecue purists in my acquaintance seem to like it.

≈

1. Thoroughly mix the ground beef, oats, evaporated milk, 1 cup of the chopped onion, eggs, chili powder, salt, pepper, and ½ teaspoon of the garlic powder. Shape into 1-inch balls. Place meatballs in a single layer in two 13-by-9-inch baking dishes.

2. Combine the catsup, brown sugar, liquid smoke,

and the remaining garlic powder. Stir in the remaining ½ cup chopped onion; pour over the meatballs. Bake in a preheated 350-degree oven for 1 hour. Place the meatballs on a serving platter and garnish with parsley.

Serves 12.

1 teaspoon garlic powder
2 cups catsup
1½ cups brown sugar
2 tablespoons liquid smoke
Parsley

Italian Meatballs

Spaghetti and meatballs is a regular meal in many households. This is a basic recipe that can be altered to your own personal preference.

1 pound ground beef
¼ pound Parmesan cheese, grated
1 cup bread crumbs
2 tablespoons chopped parsley
¼ cup chopped onion
2 eggs
2 teaspoons salt
½ teaspoon black pepper
2 teaspoons dried savory
5 tablespoons olive oil
2 large cloves garlic, crushed
2 cups chopped onions
½ pound mushrooms, sliced
2 No. 2½ cans Italian-style tomatoes
2 6-ounce cans tomato paste
1 teaspoon dried rosemary
½ teaspoon dried thyme
1 bay leaf
1 teaspoon dried oregano

≈

1. Mix the ground beef, cheese, bread crumbs, parsley, onion, eggs, 1 teaspoon salt, ¼ teaspoon pepper, and 1 teaspoon savory, and shape into 1-inch balls. Brown the meatballs in 1 tablespoon of the oil. Remove the meat from the pan and set aside.

2. Add the rest of the oil and sauté the garlic, onions, and mushrooms for 2 or 3 minutes, until just soft but not brown. Drain the excess oil and discard.

3. Add the remaining salt, pepper, and savory and the remaining ingredients and mix well. Add the meatballs and simmer for 45 minutes. Serve over cooked spaghetti and top with additional Parmesan cheese.

Serves 6.

Mariachi Beef Balls and Rice

- 2 pounds ground beef
- 1 cup crushed corn chips
- ½ cup milk
- 1 egg, slightly beaten
- 2 teaspoons salt
- 2½ tablespoons flour
- 2 tablespoons butter
- 2 cups sliced onion
- 1 clove garlic, crushed
- 1 teaspoon chili powder
- ¼ teaspoon powdered cumin
- 1 19-ounce can whole tomatoes, undrained
- 1 4-ounce can green chilies, drained
- ½ cup sliced ripe olives
- Mexican Rice (recipe follows)

These meatballs would be good served over most any kind of pasta, but around our house the preference is over Mexican Rice.

≈

1. In a large bowl, lightly combine the ground beef with the corn chips, milk, egg, and 1 teaspoon salt. Cover and refrigerate for 1 hour.
2. Shape into meatballs. Lightly roll the meatballs in 2 tablespoons flour, coating completely. In a large frying pan, cook the meatballs in hot butter, half at a time, stirring until evenly browned. Remove the meatballs and set aside.
3. In the same frying pan, cook the onion and garlic for 5 minutes, stirring occasionally.
4. In a small bowl, combine the remaining ½ tablespoon flour and 1 teaspoon salt, chili powder, and cumin. Stir into the onions. Add the tomatoes, green chilies, and olives. Bring to a boil, stirring constantly; reduce the heat and cover tightly and cook slowly for 30 minutes.
5. Add the meatballs to the tomato mixture, cover tightly, and cook slowly for 20 minutes. Uncover and continue cooking for 10 more minutes. Serve meatballs and sauce over hot Mexican Rice.

Serves 6.

Mexican Rice

≈

1 pint sour cream
1 4-ounce can chopped green chilies
¼ teaspoon salt
3 cups cooked rice
½ pound Monterey Jack cheese, cut into strips
¼ cup grated Parmesan cheese

1. Combine the sour cream, chilies, and salt. In a 13-by-9-inch baking pan, layer 1 cup cooked rice, half of the sour-cream–chili mixture, and half of the cheese strips. Repeat the layers and top with remaining rice.

2. Bake in a preheated 350-degree oven for 25 minutes. Sprinkle with Parmesan cheese and top with meatballs and sauce. Continue baking for 5 minutes or until the cheese melts.

Serves 6.

Pork

≈

A LITTLE HOG HISTORY

The first pigs to set hoof in the New World were the eight that came with Columbus on his second voyage, in 1493. Their descendants soon provided a large pig population in the Spanish West Indies. Cortés brought the next load—not on his first expedition, in 1519, but in 1521, after things had calmed down a bit in Honduras and Mexico. As the exploration of Mexico progressed northward, hogs went along. It was practical in those days of conquest for invaders to come equipped with their own meat supply on the hoof. Hogs travel well.

The first hogs to land on the East Coast of what would become the United States were the dozen or so that Hernando de Soto picked up in the West Indies and brought to Florida in May of 1539. Over the following three years, their number increased to over three hundred swine. De Soto's band tramped across the territory that is now Georgia, North and South Carolina, Tennessee, Alabama, Mississippi, and Louisiana. Hogs went with them, thereby exposing the Indians of the area to hog meat. They liked it, and that led to more than a few instances of hog rustling and Indian raids.

Pigs in the Colonies

The British colonists who settled in Jamestown in 1607 brought a few hogs with them, but most of the offspring were eaten, the Indians getting more than their fair share. The main swine reinforcement came in 1611, when Thomas Dale, the new governor of Virginia, brought some to the colony. Because of the Indians, he confined them to an island in the James River, halfway between Jamestown and what is now the town of Smithfield. The hogs not only survived, they thrived. By 1627, a local livestock census was able to determine the exact number of cattle, horses, sheep, and so on, but "the swine population was innumerable." The island became known as Hog Island, and Smithfield became famous—and remains so today—for the quality of the hams that were produced there.

Farther north, in the Massachusetts Bay Colony, the Puritans were having their problems with pigs and Indians, too. Their solution was a law requiring all Englishmen to mark the ears of their hogs, whereas the Indians were forbidden to do so. When the Indians brought their pigs to town to sell, they had to display unblemished ears to prove that the pigs were indeed of Indian ownership, not English.

Wall Street Is Born

It wasn't the bulls and the bears but the hogs that gave Wall Street its name.

Pigs reached the middle-Atlantic colonies about the same time as they did New England. Peter Evertson Hulft, a director of the Dutch West Indies Company, brought 103 animals, including pigs, to New Amsterdam in the early 1600s. Since New Amsterdam was intended to be primarily a trading post and not an agricultural colony, a stout wall was built on the north side of the settlement to keep the animals in their place. The road that developed alongside that wall became, in time, Wall Street. Outside the wall were the farms, or "bouweries," antecedents of the Bowery of today.

The First Great Hog Colony

Thanks to the early Swedish settlements on the Delaware, the English in the "Jerseys," William Penn's colony of Quakers, and the Germans called Pennsylvania Dutch, the first great hog colony was in Pennsylvania. William Penn, determined to make Pennsylvania self-supporting, encouraged his Quakers to buy livestock but not to sell it, and to provide feed and shelter for their animals. Within a decade, the colony had enough surplus to be able to export pigs and pork products. In 1640, when England was entangled in its Civil War, New England farmer-packers were able to take over a profitable meat trade that England had been developing with the West Indies.

As the seventeenth century drew to a close, a typical American farm family owned four or five hogs, which not only supplied the family with pork for the table and the smokehouse, but helped initiate the salt-pork barrel trade of the next century, upon which our first commerce—other than fisheries and lumber—was based.

Westward Ho the Hogs

A real advance for hogs in America came with the opening of the trails to the West during the first half of the nineteenth century. As Western territory was made safe for settlement and the wagons began the long trek, hogs went along. They were perfectly suited to the challenge. Pigs are far more prolific and far better foragers than any other domestic animal. They could root for themselves in the lush prairies and thick timberlands on the way west and, like the pioneers they accompanied, they were hearty critters perfectly able to defend themselves against wolves, coyotes, wildcats, and snakes. For pig and pioneer both, it was "root, hog, or die."

Pigs meant food on the table. Pork could be smoked and cured or cooked and packed in lard to provide meat through the long winter months and far into the summer, when it was unsafe to keep other meats without refrigeration.

When the frontiers were pushed beyond the Alleghenies, and the prairies of the Midwest were opened to farming in the early 1800s, hogs began to be produced in large numbers; by 1840, the Midwestern hog population reached an estimated ten million. The meat could be brought to the markets in the East only by driving large herds (droves) of hogs over the mountains on trails which later became the route of the New York Central, Pennsylvania, and Baltimore and Ohio railroads.

Driving hogs through the streets of Cincinnati, 1860.

The Louisiana Purchase in 1803 brought New Orleans into the Union and opened a large area of the country to agricultural development. As river towns sprang up, small packing plants and slaughterhouses were built where farmers could get cash for their hogs. The cured meats were shipped down the Ohio and Mississippi rivers to New Orleans and then up the Atlantic coast.

By the early 1800s, Cincinnati was processing so many hogs the city became known as "Porkopolis," having "perfected the system that packs fifteen bushels of corn into a pig, packs the pig into a barrel, and sends him over the mountains and over the ocean to feed mankind," noted a writer of the day.

The opening of the Erie Canal in 1825 allowed livestock and processed pork products to be shipped east by barge. Chicago, because of its central geographic location on the Great Lakes and its proximity to the large hog-raising areas of the country, was in the perfect position to take over from Cincinnati as "hog butcher of the world" when the Civil War of 1861–65 interfered with shipping pork down the river.

After the homestead days, when free land was exhausted, pigs rightfully earned the titles of "mortgage lifters" and "the gent that pays the rent." Because of their short gestation period, large litter size, and rapid growth rate, pigs could be counted on to help provide funds for a hardworking farm family. Any hogs that were not needed to feed the family became "cash crop."

Hog-butchering season was an exciting time in every farming community. For the kids it was an excuse to miss a day of school. For wives, a get-together to exchange neighborhood gossip and share a meal. "Hog-killin' time"—ah, yes, I remember it well.

Hog-Killin' Time

When I was a boy, late-fall mornings were so cold you took your clothes to the kitchen to get dressed behind the woodstove, and you didn't have to wear any overshoes 'cause the mud in the road was frozen solid. That time of year was "comin' up hog-killin'." In those days every farm family put down some meat for the winter, and that usually meant butchering a pig, smoking the hams and hocks, canning, salting, and pickling; and, with whatever was left, making sausage, scrapple, headcheese, and souse. It was a lot of work, but even though I was too young to help, I knew it was worth the effort.

In my family, hog-killin' was always done at "the Girls'," the home of my granddad's two unmarried sisters. They lived on the "Homeplace" with a hired man named Daryl. (You can imagine there was more than a little lip waggin' and a few raised eyebrows.) Daryl, Dad, and Gramps slaughtered, scaled, and scraped the hogs. Then Dad dressed them out,

Hog-Killin' Time (continued)

sending every last bit of the beasts to the kitchen to be turned into all manner of marvelous meats.

Each pig provided *two loins* to be cut into chops for frying, or to make roasts for special occasions like the crown roast of pork the Girls often had at Christmas. Then there were the *picnic shoulders,* the front legs of the pig, which were sometimes smoked to make some extra hams but were most often cut up and boned out for pork pot roasts, stews, cutlets, and kabobs. The hocks were cooked up with beans or greens. The *belly* of the pigs went for makin' bacon, after the spareribs were trimmed off to be saved for the barbecue.

The *Boston shoulder* or *Boston butt* (they can't seem to get their anatomy straight in Boston) came off the pig just in front of the loin and above the picnic, and offered the same quality pork for smoking and pickling, and for sausage, as the front leg of the pig, with the added advantage of having only one little bone to take out. I could do that when I was just a kid.

My brother and I would take turns rotating the handle of the meat grinder to grind up all the trimmings for sausage. Aunt Gert simmered the head of the hog—all except the ears—till the meat fell from the bone and the cooking broth turned into a rich gelatin, all of which was made into headcheese.

"Everything but the squeal is used for food," Daryl used to tell my brother, Gary, and me, "and that's what they use to make whistles." But far and away the best part was the hind leg of the pig, cured and smoked to make ham! The watered-down, mild-flavored, chipped, flaked, and formed, plastic-packaged stuff that passes for "ham" in most markets today couldn't hold a candle to the rich, flavorful, tangy, dry-cured oak-and-corn-cob-smoked hams Dad and Daryl used to make on the Homeplace.

One hind leg of one pig always went to the kitchen, where Aunt Helen would roast it to a crispy golden brown, to serve for dinner on hog-killin' day, but the rest were cured to make hams. Daryl would also buy a few extra legs of pork from other farmers, who didn't have as big a smokehouse as the Girls. He usually cured a dozen or so.

The hams were first put down in salt on the floor of the curing shed. Daryl would add cure and I think a little sugar to the layer of salt. The hams got rubbed well all over with the same mixture, then laid down on the salt and covered with more salt. They'd stay in the salt for a month or more before they went to the smokehouse, where they'd hang to age for several months before they got any smoke. Sometimes he didn't even smoke them at all, but I always liked best the ones that had just a hint of the smell of smoke. I don't think there was really much difference in the flavor of the meat, but I sure did love that smell.

TODAY'S PORK

Until recently, we bred pigs in this country to be fat. We wanted them fat. We needed them fat. Pork fat—lard—was what we cooked with. We fried chicken in it, and potatoes. We used it to make pie crusts (I still do). Our pioneer forefathers packed bacon and sausage in lard to preserve them for the long trek westward. Things are different now. Today's hogs are scientifically bred and fed specifically for the meat they provide—and that meat contains 22 percent more protein and 57 percent less fat than the pork of twenty years ago. This could change again. It was recently confirmed in "scientific studies" that pure lard is every bit as healthy as olive oil. It could make a comeback.

In Granddad's day a good percentage of the pigs raised in this country were "kept on the place" by small farmers to help them clean up. After every meal, table scraps were used to "slop the hogs." When the corn or peanuts or potatoes had been harvested, the pigs were turned into the fields to clean up there. Then, when they had done all their work, along about October or November, the pigs were sent off to market, fat from the summer of stuffing themselves with whatever was left of everything. It was a pretty slipshod system of producing pork but it worked, and nothing went to waste around the place. The quality of pork that resulted, however, was nowhere near as uniform or as uniformly good as it is today. Nobody paid too much attention to breeding for quality meat. As a result, hogs came to market ranging from magnificent well-marbled meat types to ones so fat that they were good for little but lard.

Because of the widespread practice of feeding raw garbage to hogs, there was the constant danger of trichinae. So it was recommended that all pork be cooked to death, to an internal temperature of 185 degrees. Times have changed. The pork available in today's supermarket is a different product entirely from the pork of even two decades ago, the result of a very carefully controlled scientific process. Ninety-eight percent of the nation's pigs are now raised on grain and other vegetable feed. Since 1952, in most states, if garbage is fed at all, it must be cooked.

COOKING TODAY'S PORK

Cooking today's pork is also a far cry from cooking yesterday's. The pork you buy now comes to market younger and therefore far more tender than it did back then. It does not require—indeed, cannot tolerate—the kind of treatment we gave the fat pigs we used to have. To cook today's pork to the 185 degrees of doneness that was recommended in most cookbooks of a generation ago would be akin to cremation.

I would venture to guess that if any of you are having trouble with the quality of the pork you are putting on the table, the fault lies not with the pig but with the way you're cooking it. The most oft-committed crime in the kitchen is that of overcooking. It is committed with equal brutality against all kinds of foods, vegetables as well as meat. But pork, it seems, is the most viciously victimized. Much of the problem stems from old cookbooks. When Grandma was a girl, cookbooks recommended emphatically, to the point of preaching, that pork must be cooked well done. Good advice in those days, when trichinosis was a very real problem. These days, trichinosis is a clinical rarity in the United States. Years ago, scientists discovered that the trichina parasite is destroyed at 137 degrees, and that cooking pork to an internal temperature of 155 to 160 degrees develops the best flavor and juiciness.

Pork roasts will be much juicier and more flavorful if cooked at a moderately low temperature for a longer period of time. A 300- or 325-degree oven setting produces better results than 350 or 375, but the meat will, of course, take a bit longer to cook through. Boneless roasts will take slightly longer to cook than those with the bone left in, since the bones act as conductors to carry heat to the meat.

The shape and dimensions of a roast are far more important in determining cooking time than is the total weight. Many good roasts are ruined by following the old-fashioned "so many minutes per pound of meat" formula. It just doesn't work, particularly with pork.

A six-pound pork loin that is four inches wide and twelve inches long and is roasted for thirty minutes per pound would take—according to the formula—three hours to cook. Half of that same pork loin would be four inches wide and six inches long, and would weigh three pounds. It should, therefore, cook in half the time. But the "so many minutes per pound" formula does not take into account the fact that heat penetrates meat uniformly; thus heat takes no longer to reach the center of the four-by-six roast than it does the larger one. Heat must penetrate two inches to reach the center of the meat in either case; weight has absolutely nothing to do with it.

An absolute essential for success in roasting any meat, particularly pork, is a good meat thermometer. My preference is one that is not left in the meat as it cooks but, rather, inserted periodically to give you an instant reading. Taylor's Bi-Therm is a good one that is available wherever cooking equipment is sold. I would have a hard time cooking any meat without mine.

Pork chops and steaks will also be more tender, juicy, and flavorful if cooked at a lower temperature. High grill or broiler temperatures overcook the outside before the center reaches the proper degree of doneness.

Turn down the heat; you'll eat better pork if you do!

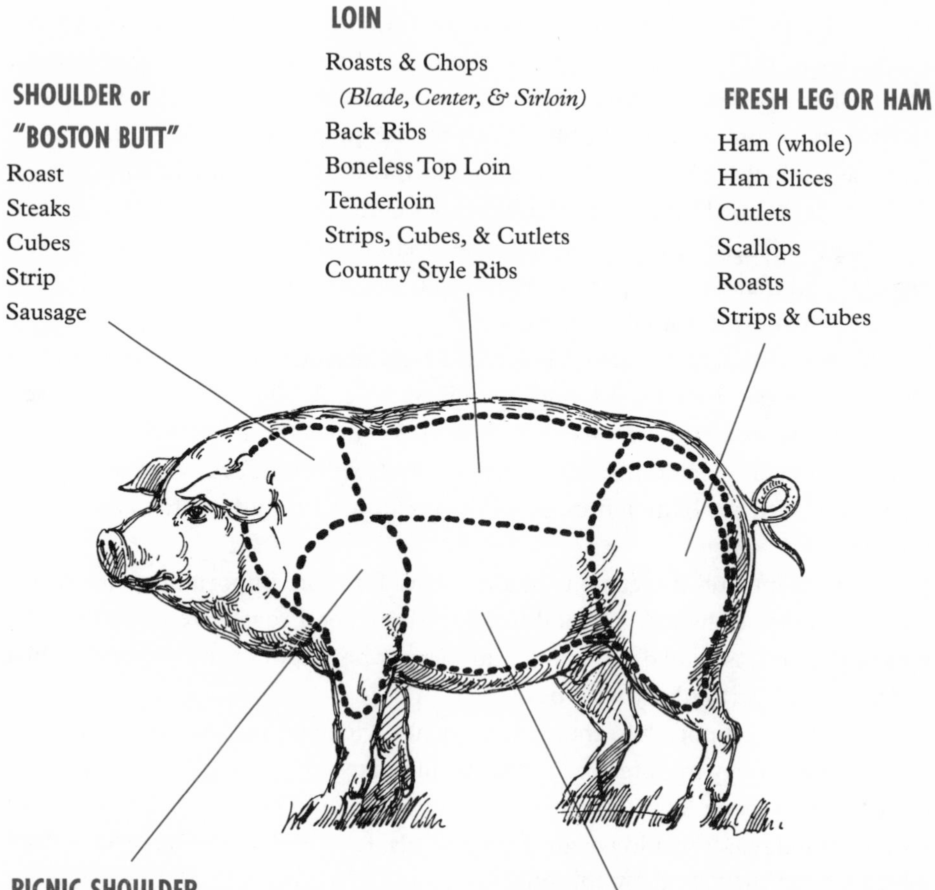

PICNIC SHOULDER

"Smoked Picnic Ham"
Hock *(Smoked or Fresh)*
Roast

SPARE RIBS & SIDE PORK

Spare Ribs
St. Louis Ribs
Bacon
Fresh Side Pork

BASIC FORMS OF PORK

Pork comes to market today, as it has for centuries, in two basic forms: fresh and smoked. Most hind legs of the pig are cured and smoked as hams. The same is true of the belly, which after curing and smoking becomes bacon.

Most fresh pork in the marketplace today comes from the pork loin and the shoulder or "Boston butt." These are cut into all manner of chops, steaks, roasts, cubes, and strips.

Pork Loin

The most tender part of the pig is the loin, right in the middle of the back. Extending from the shoulder (Boston butt) on the front to the hind leg (ham) on the back side, it contains two of the choicest, most tender muscles the pig has to offer, the top loin and the tenderloin.

The loin is usually marketed in three separate parts, the rib end and sirloin end for roasts and less expensive chops, and the center portion for the more expensive center-cut loin, and rib chops and roasts.

There is a new method of marketing fresh pork loin that could offer big savings to any consumer with a sharp knife and a willingness to do some cutting up in the kitchen. Several pork processors now furnish *boneless pork*; all of the bone and most of the fat are removed at the packing plant, then the boneless cuts are vacuum-packed in plastic for shipment to the supermarket. The most popular and most available of these boneless cuts are the top loin and the tenderloin. Dividing up one of these cuts is as easy as slicing a loaf of bread—you don't need a highly paid butcher to do it for you.

A whole vacuum-packaged top loin will weigh between ten and twelve pounds, more meat than you might want for a single meal. You can easily turn one into a gold mine of goodies to stock your freezer for many meals to come.

Simply remove the loin from its plastic wrap, pat it dry with paper towels, lay it out on your cutting board, and make of it what you will. Cut off a six- or eight-inch piece for a roast; cut some for chops as thick as you like; cut some thin slices for cutlets; cut a portion into cubes for kabobs or strips for stir-fry. Use your imagination. Remember, you are saving money!

Package everything in freezer bags in serving-sized portions for your family and put them, clearly labeled, in the freezer to be taken out and cooked as needed. Pork keeps well for six to eight months in the freezer, so take advantage of a good buy on top loin when the price is right.

Tenderloins are another cut readily available in supermarkets today. They usually come two to a package, for a total weight of only one and a half to two pounds. They are a boon to the hurried cook, because they cook quickly. They are very lean, and there are so many things to do with them that I have devoted a special section on ways to cook tenderloins (see pages 116–121).

Boston Butt

Pork shoulder is called "Boston shoulder," "Boston butt," "Western butt" in the East, "city butt" in the country, and "fresh Cala butt" in parts of California. But whatever it's called, a pork butt is apt to be the best pork buy in the meat case, no buts about it.

Butts are generally merchandised whole, cut in half, sliced, cubed, or ground. By far the best buy is the whole butt. It is one of the simplest cuts of meat to cut up yourself. If you can't find a whole pork butt in your butcher's meat case, ring the bell and ask. Most butchers will be happy to sell you a whole one, and usually at a considerable saving over the price of the various component parts. It keeps them from having to cut it up.

Butts are usually packed and shipped in cartons with weight ranges from four to six pounds, six to eight pounds, and eight to twelve pounds. The lighter butts, under eight pounds, are likely to be much leaner and, therefore, the best buy.

The simplest way to cut up a butt is to divide it approximately in half by cutting along the edge of the blade bone, part of the shoulder blade of the pig. It is partially visible on two sides of the roast. Simply put the blade of your knife against the edge of the bone on one side and, following the bone with your knife, cut through to the edge of the bone on the other side. You will remove a small (about one-third of the whole) triangular-shaped piece that contains the blade bone. The remainder of the roast is boneless.

The boneless piece may be sliced into strips for stir-fry dishes or cut into cubes for stews. It may be ground for pork patties or made into sausages. You can slice all or part of it into pork steaks to be fried, broiled, or braised. The list is almost endless.

Boston Butt and Picnic Ham

Boston butt: In pre-Revolutionary New England and into the Revolutionary War, some pork cuts (not those highly valued, or "high on the hog," like the loin and ham) were packed into casks or barrels also known as "butts," for storage and shipment of pork supplies. The choicer cuts of loin were consumed fresh, and ham, the pork hind leg, was given the popular cure-and-smoke treatment we are fond of today. The particular way the hog shoulder was cut in the Boston area became known *in other regions* as "Boston butt." This moniker stuck, and today Boston butt is called just that almost everywhere in the United States—even in Boston!

Picnic ham: The lower part of the front leg, below the butt, became known as the "picnic shoulder" when, in the late nineteenth century, its scrappy meat was boned and cured for a less expensive ham-type product. It was suitable for casual occasions like picnics; the highly prized cured and smoked hind-leg ham was reserved for Sunday dinner.

PORK CHOPS

Chops are one of the most familiar pork cuts. There are many kinds: center loin, rib chops, sirloin chops, boneless, or bone-in. They can be prepared by panbroiling, grilling or broiling, roasting, braising, or sautéing. Thin chops (¼ to ⅜ inch) are best quickly sautéed. Thicker chops (¾ to 1½ inches) can be panbroiled, grilled, roasted, or braised. Boneless chops cook more quickly than bone-in chops.

Picking Pork Chops

Pork in a pile can be a pig in a poke. Picking a good package of pork chops out of a pile causes more problems than it should. To a large extent, when it comes to selecting pork from your butcher's meat case, you are very much on your own. With beef you can look to the USDA grade (or lack of it) as some indication of the quality you can expect from a steak or roast. Not so when it comes to pork. So what do you look for as an indication of quality when you're picking through pork chops?

The first thing you look for is fat. I'm not talking about the outside layer of fat that covers a pork chop, which is waste and should be avoided. What I mean is "marbling," those little flecks of fat inside the lean. Marbling has proved to be an important factor in quality pork. Look for it! Without at least a slight amount of marbling, pork tends to be dry. Too much, on the other hand, will result in an equally undesirable pork chop. Learn to recognize the happy medium.

Color is another important indicator. A pinkish gray is most desirable, and the fat should be creamy white. Avoid chops that are pale and watery-looking; they will almost certainly dry out and shrink up in the cooking process. Don't worry about a bit of "two-toning." It is natural for certain muscles of the pig to be darker than others. In a pork chop the tenderloin, that tiny muscle on the other side of the T-bone, is almost always darker in color than the loin muscle, on the top of the T-bone. The larger top-loin muscle is the one that should be a nice pink-gray color.

One of the things often misused as a quality indicator is size. It does not always follow that because a pork chop is small it came from a young pig and thus is more tender than a larger pork chop. These days all pigs come to market at a young and tender age. A smaller chop is apt to be the result of an overly fat pork loin that has been trimmed down, not necessarily coming from a younger pig.

Poor-quality pork often has a small loin muscle covered by an excess of fat. By the time the fat is trimmed away, the chop is small, but not younger and no better than a big chop without all of the excess outside fat. The ratio of meat to bone is better in a bigger loin. This means you get more for your money, and that's important.

Pork Chops, German Style

In Great-Grandmother's day, meat markets were the source of supply for sauerkraut. Every market had a big barrel of the stuff in the cooler and a crock-full on top of the counter that was put back in the barrel every night and refilled every morning. Many butchers, I'm sure, made their own, but my dad bought his by the barrel from a woman in town who made "the best sauerkraut around." I've forgotten her name, but her pork-chop recipe has been in our family for years.

- 4 to 5 slices bacon
- 1 32-ounce jar sauerkraut
- 4 to 6 pork chops, bone-in or boneless
- Salt and pepper to taste
- 1 or 2 onions, sliced
- 2 or 3 potatoes, peeled and sliced very thin
- 1 22-ounce can solid-pack tomatoes, squished
- 1½ teaspoons caraway seeds

≈

1. Cover the bottom of a large casserole dish (approximately 9-by-13-by-2 inches) with the bacon. Layer the sauerkraut and its juice on the bacon. Lay the pork chops close together on the kraut. Season with salt and pepper.
2. Cover the chops with onions, then place a layer of sliced potatoes over the onions. Cover with the tomatoes and shake the casserole sideways a little to let their juice mingle with the other ingredients. Sprinkle the top with caraway seeds.
3. Cover the casserole and bake in a preheated 350-degree oven until done, approximately 1½ hours.

Serves 4 to 6.

Tex-Mex Chops

- 1 tablespoon cooking oil
- 4 bone-in or boneless loin pork chops, 1¾ inches thick (about 1 pound)
- 1½ cups bottled salsa, chunky style, hot or medium
- 1 4-ounce can diced green chilies, drained
- ½ teaspoon ground cumin
- ¼ cup grated Cheddar cheese

An easy recipe, and you'll think you're in Santa Fe! I've cooked this dish on many a television program. In TV, getting off on time is of paramount importance; with this recipe you will get it on the table in time.

≈

1. Heat the oil in a heavy skillet over medium-high heat. Brown the chops on both sides for about 2 minutes each.

2. Add the salsa, chilies, and cumin to the skillet. Lower the heat, cover, and barely simmer for 8 minutes. Uncover and top each chop with 1 tablespoon of cheese. Cover and simmer an additional minute, until the cheese melts. Serve immediately.

Serves 4.

Lemon Pork in Cream

- 4 boneless pork chops, approximately ⅓ pound each
- Juice of 1 large lemon
- 6 tablespoons butter
- 6 to 8 pippin (or any other tart) apples, cored and sliced into rings
- 1 teaspoon flour
- 1 pint half-and-half
- Salt and pepper

Here is my more contemporary and quick version of pork cooked in milk, which I think Grandma would have liked.

≈

1. Trim off any excess fat. Marinate the chops in half the lemon juice for 15 to 20 minutes. Drain.

2. Brown the chops in 3 tablespoons of the butter on both sides, turning once. Be careful not to scorch the butter. Do not overcook the pork.

3. In another pan melt 2 tablespoons of the butter and cook the apple slices until tender. Put the pork and apples on a warm platter in a warm oven while the sauce cooks.

4. Put the remaining tablespoon of butter into the pan that held the pork. Over medium heat sprinkle in the flour and cook a few seconds; do not let it brown. Slowly add the half-and-half, stirring constantly. Add salt and pepper to taste.

5. Gradually add the remaining lemon juice, blending well. If the sauce is too thick add more half-and-half (or a bit of milk). Pour over the warm pork and apples and serve immediately.

Serves 3 to 4.

Grandma's One-Dish Meal

Pork cooked in milk was standard fare in many a Nebraska farm when I was growing up. Here's a recipe that my grandmother used. I present it just as it was printed in the *Allen, Nebraska, Cook Book,* published in 1918.

> *Take about two pounds of pork chops and dredge them in flour with the necessary salt and pepper. Brown well on all sides in shortening. Place in a baking dish that has been greased with butter. Peel and core four apples; fill the centers with raisins, mixed with sugar and cinnamon, and place them around the meat.*
>
> *Add a layer of diced or halved carrots and tuck enough peeled and sliced potatoes around to complete the meal. Pour over 2 to 3 cups of rich sweet milk and bake until the meat is tender. Use sufficient milk to have plenty of gravy.*

Pork Chop–Sweet Potato Casserole

6 pork chops, approximately ⅓ pound each
Salt and pepper to taste
1 tablespoon solid shortening
4 sweet potatoes, peeled
½ cup brown sugar
1½ cups milk

Here's another old-time dish the Ellis family enjoys.

≈

1. Season the pork chops with salt and pepper. Heat the shortening in a heavy skillet and brown the chops well on both sides.

2. Place a layer of sweet potatoes, sliced crosswise into ¼-inch slices, in a well-buttered casserole. Top with a layer of chops. Dust with salt and pepper and the brown sugar. Continue the layers until the casserole is about two-thirds full (or until the potatoes are gone—whichever comes first).

3. Heat the milk and pour it over the top layer, cover, and bake in a preheated 350-degree oven for 1 hour. Remove the cover and continue cooking another 10 minutes until the chops are tender and the casserole is nicely browned on top.

Serves 4 to 6.

Pocketing Pork Chops

"Would you put a pocket in these, please," she said, handing a package of nice thick pork chops to the young chap who answered the bell. I was observing the transaction from my favorite spy spot: pawing through the pot roasts looking for steak. What the "meat cutter" did to those pork chops in the name of putting in a pocket was appalling. He virtually sliced them in half, cutting through the back fat and clear to the bone from one end to the other. He handed back what was, for all intents and purposes, two thin pork chops held together by a bone. When you stuff a chop that's cut that way, the stuffing falls out and the pork chop dries out.

There are much better methods for putting a pocket in a pork chop.

(1) To pocket a loin chop, lay the chop on your cutting board so that the chine bone (that's the flat bone that runs along one side of the chop) is away from you and the outside back fat covering is to your right. Use a stiff-bladed, five- or six-inch boning knife; one with a flexible blade is difficult to control. At the narrow, tip end of the chop, insert the point of your knife (sharp edge to the left if you are right-handed) and push it along the underside of the back fat all the way up, until you make contact with the chine bone. Be careful not to cut through the membrane that separates the back fat from the meat; that's what holds the dressing in. When you have made contact with the chine bone, cut along it through the meaty part of the chop from right to left to form a pocket. Try to keep the opening not much larger than the width of the knife blade. To stuff, spoon stuffing in a teaspoonful at a time or, if you have one, use a sausage-stuffing tube.

(2) Easier to stuff is a rib chop, with the pocket cut along the rib. Have your butcher hand-cut, with a knife, an inch or inch-and-a-quarter pork rib chop "between the ribs," leaving one rib in each chop. *Do not* let him "buzz" them off on the saw or he'll louse up your whole pork-stuffing project! You'll want one rib to each chop. To make a pocket, put a chop on the cutting board with the chine bone away from you as before, but with the back fat covering to your left and the rib bone on the right. Slide the point of your knife in on top of the rib bone and along the chine bone. Then cut down along the rib to form the pocket. Be careful not to cut through the back fat on the opposite side. When you put a pocket in this way, you can make the opening much larger, which makes the chop easier to stuff. Simply spoon in the stuffing and bake. As the chop cooks, the membrane along the inside of the rib will contract, closing the opening and trapping in the stuffing—no toothpicks or sewing necessary.

(3) To put a pocket in a boneless pork chop, first butterfly it. Cut through the back fat of each chop and down through the meat to within about a quarter of an inch of the cutting board. Be careful not to cut all the way through. You want to have two sides to be hinged together like the wings of a butterfly. Next turn the chop over and cut a pocket in the center of each wing. Now, when you fill these pockets with your favorite stuffing and open the wings up again, the stuffing is locked inside and you have a lovely meaty stuffed pork chop nicely outlined with a border of back fat. Beautiful!

Maytag Blue-Stuffed Iowa Chops

- 3 tablespoons butter
- ¼ cup finely chopped onion
- ½ cup very thinly sliced mushrooms
- 4 to 6 ounces crumbled blue cheese (Maytag, if you want to be authentic)
- 1 cup fine dry bread crumbs
- 6 pork chops (about 3 pounds), 1½ inches thick
- Salt and pepper to taste

Growing up in Iowa, where Maytag Blue cheese is a state treasure, may have something to do with this being one of my favorite recipes for stuffed pork chops.

≈

1. Melt the butter in a heavy skillet over medium heat. Add the onion and mushrooms and cook for 5 minutes. Remove them from the heat and stir in the blue cheese and bread crumbs.

2. Cut a pocket in each pork chop (see page 103). Season the pockets of the chops with salt and pepper. Divide the stuffing evenly and stuff the chops. Bake in a preheated 375-degree oven for 45 minutes or grill over moderate coals for 20 to 30 minutes.

Serves 6.

Fruit-and-Cheese-Stuffed Pork Chops

- 6 pork chops (approximately 3½ pounds), 1¼ to 1½ inches thick
- Salt and pepper to taste
- 1½ cups toasted bread cubes
- ½ cup chopped unpared apple

Fruit is often a nice accompaniment to a pork dish, so why not stuff your chops with some fruit and cheese?

≈

1. Cut a pocket in each chop (see page 103). Sprinkle the pockets with a little salt and pepper.

2. Combine the bread cubes, apple, cheese, and raisins; toss to mix well. Stir together the melted butter, orange juice, salt, and cinnamon. Pour over the bread-cube mixture; toss gently.

3. Stuff the chops. Place them in a shallow baking pan and bake in a preheated 325-degree oven for 45 minutes. Cover lightly with foil; bake 15 minutes more.

Serves 6.

½ cup shredded sharp natural Cheddar cheese
2 tablespoons golden raisins
2 tablespoons butter, melted
2 tablespoons orange juice
¼ teaspoon salt
⅛ teaspoon ground cinnamon

Stuffings

Here are two stuffing recipes. Each makes enough to stuff six chops.

Mediterranean Stuffing

≈

In a small pan gently sauté the nuts, garlic, and red pepper in the butter until the nuts are just golden. Remove the mixture from the heat and add the lemon peel, scallions, parsley, and seasonings. When cool, divide the stuffing among 6 chops.

½ cup pine nuts
1 clove garlic, minced
1 large red bell pepper, seeded and finely minced
1 tablespoon butter
1 teaspoon grated lemon peel
1½ tablespoons minced scallions
1½ tablespoons minced parsley
⅛ teaspoon oregano
⅛ teaspoon salt
⅛ teaspoon black pepper

Apple Raisin Pecan Stuffing

≈

- 1 medium tart apple, cored and diced
- 1 tablespoon butter
- ¼ cup raisins
- ¼ cup coarsely chopped pecans
- ⅛ teaspoon cinnamon
- Pinch nutmeg
- Pinch allspice
- Salt to taste

In a small pan, sauté the apple in the butter for about 2 to 3 minutes, until it begins to brown. Remove from the heat and add the remaining ingredients; mix thoroughly.

ROASTS

A roast is a large, whole cut of pork, taken from the loin, leg, or shoulder. Pork can be roasted in the oven, or over indirect heat on the barbecue grill. It can also be stewed or braised on the stovetop. Both methods yield a flavorful finished product.

Rio Grande Pork Roast

- 3-to-4-pound pork loin or shoulder roast
- ½ teaspoon salt
- 2 cloves garlic, minced
- 1 teaspoon chili powder
- ½ cup apple jelly
- ½ cup barbecue sauce

Pork cooked long and slow in a barbecue pit is as good as it gets. This recipe comes about as close as you can get in your oven.

≈

1. Rub the surface of the roast well with the salt, garlic, and ½ teaspoon of the chili powder. Place the roast in

a shallow baking pan, and roast in a preheated 350-degree oven for 30 minutes.

2. Combine the remaining chili powder, apple jelly, and barbecue sauce in a small saucepan and simmer for 2 minutes. Pour this sauce over the roast. Continue roasting, basting occasionally, until an instant-read thermometer registers 155 degrees, about 45 to 50 minutes. Remove the roast from the pan. Let it rest for 5 to 10 minutes as the internal temperature rises to 160 degrees.

3. Remove the pan drippings to a saucepan, and add enough water to make 1 cup. Bring to a boil. Carve the roast and serve with the sauce.

Serves 6.

Rhubarb Pork Roast

This was a standard recipe back on the farm when rhubarb was in season.

- 3-to-4-pound pork loin or shoulder roast
- 2 cloves garlic, peeled and sliced thin
- 1 teaspoon crushed dried rosemary
- 4 ribs rhubarb, sliced (about 2 cups)
- ¼ cup cider vinegar
- 6 tablespoons honey
- 6 whole cloves
- ½ teaspoon salt
- ½ teaspoon dry mustard
- 2 to 3 drops red food color, if desired

≈

1. Preheat the oven to 350 degrees. Place the pork roast in a roasting pan. Cut 8 to 10 slits in the surface of the pork and insert slivers of garlic. Rub the surface of the roast with the rosemary. Roast for approximately 50 minutes.

2. Meanwhile, combine the remaining ingredients in a heavy saucepan; bring to a boil, then reduce the heat and simmer about 10 minutes. Pour the rhubarb sauce over the pork and continue to roast, basting often, until the pork reaches an internal temperature of 155 degrees on an instant-read thermometer, about 45 to 50 minutes. Let the pork roast rest for 10 minutes, as the internal temperature rises to 160 degrees. Slice thin and serve with the rhubarb sauce.

Serves 6.

Fritz's Pork and Sauerkraut

- 1 large onion, finely chopped
- 8 strips bacon, minced
- A 2½-to-3-pound pork shoulder
- 2 tart apples, peeled, cut into matchsticks
- 3 pounds (1 32-ounce and 1 16-ounce jar) sauerkraut, drained
- 1 to 2 teaspoons sugar, or to taste
- 3 whole cloves
- 2 bay leaves
- Salt and pepper to taste
- ¼ cup or more water
- Dash cider vinegar
- 1 medium raw potato, peeled

This recipe for pork and sauerkraut is for people who think they don't like sauerkraut. It is fabulous! Fritz, who was a friend of our daughters' fifth-grade teacher, introduced it to our family.

≈

1. Cook the onion and bacon in a heavy Dutch oven over low heat until the onions are translucent and the bacon is cooked but not crisp. Remove and drain on paper towels. Brown the pork in the pan drippings. Return the onion and bacon to the pan and add the apples, sauerkraut, sugar, cloves, and bay leaves, and season with salt and pepper.

2. Add the water, cover, and cook over medium-low heat for about 1 to 1½ hours, adding a little more water if necessary. Remove the pork and keep warm. Season the sauerkraut mixture with the vinegar and, if desired, more sugar, adding salt and pepper as needed.

3. Grate the potato into the sauerkraut, mix well, and continue cooking until the potato is done, about 10 minutes. Serve the pork and sauerkraut with boiled red new potatoes, using the bacon as garnish.

Serves 6 to 8.

Pork Pot Roast

Say "pot roast" and most people think beef. But in the wintertime in Nebraska, pot-roasted pig was mighty welcome. This recipe can be made with a boneless or bone-in roast. Obviously a boneless roast will be easier to carve.

≈

- A 4-to-5-pound pork shoulder roast
- 2 medium onions, chopped
- 2 cloves garlic, minced
- 2 teaspoons mustard seeds
- ½ teaspoon ground cinnamon
- ½ teaspoon ground nutmeg
- 1 teaspoon salt
- ½ teaspoon black pepper
- 2 cups chicken broth
- 3 tablespoons grated orange peel
- 12 small red new potatoes
- 12 small boiling onions
- 5 stalks celery, diagonally sliced into 2-inch pieces
- 2 teaspoons cornstarch dissolved in ¼ cup cold water
- 2 oranges, peeled and sliced
- 1 tablespoon chopped parsley

1. Brown the roast in a large Dutch oven, using a bit of rendered pork fat. When nicely browned on all sides, remove the meat and set it aside. Pour off all but about 2 tablespoons of the fat and discard. Put the chopped onions, garlic, mustard seeds, cinnamon, and nutmeg in the same pan. Cook over low heat until the onions are soft. Push the onions to the side of the pot and return the roast.

2. Sprinkle on the salt and pepper and pour in the chicken broth. Top with the grated orange peel, cover, and simmer on top of the stove over low heat for approximately 2 hours, or until the meat is tender. Baste occasionally with pan juices. About 30 minutes before the roast is done, add the potatoes, boiling onions, and celery.

3. Remove the roast and vegetables to a warm serving platter. Reduce the pan juices over high heat to about 1 cup. Skim off the fat. Stir the cornstarch mixture into the pan juices and heat to thicken. Garnish with orange slices and chopped parsley.

Serves 6 to 8.

VARIATIONS

Apple Cider Pork Roast

Grandma Ellis often cooked a pork pot roast in apple cider and served it up with sautéed apple slices instead of oranges.

≈

- A 4-to-5-pound pork shoulder roast
- 2 tablespoons vegetable oil
- 2 cloves garlic, minced
- 3 onions, sliced
- 1 teaspoon tarragon
- ½ teaspoon salt
- ½ teaspoon black pepper
- 2 cups apple cider
- 2 bay leaves
- 3 potatoes, peeled and cubed
- 4 carrots, sliced diagonally
- A small cabbage head, cut in wedges
- 2 cups small fresh mushrooms
- 2 teaspoons cornstarch dissolved in ¼ cup water
- 1 tablespoon chopped parsley

Proceed as in Pork Pot Roast (page 109).

Serves 4 to 6.

Oriental Pork Roast

My "Polynesian Princess" wife has altered Grandma's recipe for Pork Pot Roast to give it an Oriental flair.

≈

- A 4-to-5-pound pork shoulder roast
- 2 tablespoons vegetable oil
- 2 medium onions, chopped
- 2 tablespoons grated fresh ginger root
- 2 cloves garlic, minced
- 1 teaspoon salt
- ½ teaspoon black pepper
- 2 cups chicken broth
- ⅓ cup soy sauce
- ¼ cup cider vinegar
- 2 tablespoons brown sugar
- 4 cups fresh sugar peas
- 2 tomatoes, cut into wedges
- 1 8-ounce can sliced water chestnuts
- ½ pound fresh mushrooms, sliced
- 2 teaspoons cornstarch mixed with ¼ cup cold water

Proceed as in Pork Pot Roast (page 109).

Serves 4 to 6.

CUBES AND STRIPS

Pork cubes can be cut from the boneless loin, shoulder, leg, or tenderloin. They can be used for all kinds of dishes, from grilled kabobs to stews. Small ½-to-¾-inch cubes work best for quick braised dishes like Braised Pork with Peppers (page 113); they can also be used instead of pork strips in the stir-fry recipes contained in the section beginning on page 114. Larger, 1-to-1½-inch cubes from the loin or tenderloin work well for kabobs; for moist-heat cooking, like stews, use large cubes cut from the shoulder (butt).

Pork with Red Cabbage

This makes a hearty dish for a chilly winter evening. Served up with a mug of hot cider, it will make you think you're in the country.

- 1 large tart green apple, peeled and sliced
- 1 medium onion, sliced
- 2 tablespoons bacon fat or butter
- 2½ cups water
- ¼ cup sugar
- 1 teaspoon salt
- ½ teaspoon black pepper
- 2 whole cloves
- 1 small bay leaf
- 1 small head red cabbage, cut as for slaw
- ½ cup red-wine vinegar
- 2 tablespoons vegetable oil
- 1½ pounds pork butt, cut into 1-inch cubes
- 1 clove garlic, minced
- ½ cup dry vermouth or water
- 2 teaspoons cornstarch mixed with ¼ cup cold water

≈

1. Sauté the apple and onion in the bacon fat just until the onion slices are translucent. Add the water, sugar, salt, pepper, cloves, and bay leaf and bring to a rolling boil, stirring all the while. Add the cabbage, reduce the heat, and simmer gently, turning over with a spoon from time to time, for 10 to 15 minutes. Add the red-wine vinegar and continue simmering, uncovered, until the cabbage is tender, another 15 minutes.
2. In the meantime, in a heavy skillet, heat the vegetable oil and brown the cubes of meat. Add the garlic and stir. Add the vermouth, cover tightly, and simmer gently, stirring from time to time, for 10 minutes.
3. Stir the cornstarch mixture into the cabbage mixture. Cook and stir a minute or two, until the liquid is slightly thickened, then pour the cabbage mixture over the pork cubes. Gently mix the meat and vegetables, cover, and simmer for an additional 5 minutes.

Serves 4 to 6.

Ginger Melon Pork

- 1 tablespoon vegetable oil
- 1 pound lean pork, cut into 1-inch cubes
- ½ onion, thinly sliced
- 1 clove garlic, minced
- 1 tablespoon grated fresh ginger
- 2 tablespoons soy sauce
- ¼ cup dry sherry
- 2 tablespoons white-wine vinegar
- 1 tablespoon cornstarch
- 3 cups cubed melon (cantaloupe or honeydew)
- ½ cup diced pickled watermelon rind

This is a simple, fast, and flavorful dish, perfect for a summer lunch. It is best with very lean pork cubes cut from the loin or leg.

≈

1. Heat the oil in a large skillet over medium heat. Brown the pork cubes, stirring until lightly browned, about 4 to 5 minutes. Stir in the onion, garlic, and ginger; cook, stirring, for 2 to 3 minutes.

2. Mix together the soy sauce, sherry, vinegar, and cornstarch, then add to the skillet. Cook, stirring, until the sauce thickens. Gently stir in the melon and the watermelon rind. Heat through.

Serves 4.

Pork Kabobs

- 1 cup plain low-fat yogurt
- 2 tablespoons orange juice
- 1 tablespoon ground coriander
- ½ teaspoon turmeric
- ½ teaspoon ground cumin
- ½ teaspoon salt

If you are counting calories, this recipe is for you. Choose lean pork and low-fat yogurt and enjoy. Even if you're not counting calories, enjoy—I do!

≈

1. In a medium bowl, stir together the yogurt, orange juice, and seasonings. Add the pork cubes to the bowl. Stir to coat with the marinade. Cover and refrigerate for 4 to 24 hours.

2. Preheat broiler, or prepare and preheat barbecue

grill. Remove the pork from the marinade and lightly pat dry with paper towels. Skewer the pork evenly on the skewers. Broil or grill over medium-hot coals, turning frequently, for about 8 to 10 minutes, until nicely browned.

Serves 4.

¼ teaspoon ground ginger
2 pounds boneless pork, cut into 1-inch cubes
4 barbecue skewers (if using bamboo skewers, first soak in cold water for an hour)

Braised Pork with Peppers

This is a braised-pork recipe the way Grandma would have done it in Nebraska in the winter after hog-killin' time, using canned tomatoes and dried herbs. If they are available to you, use 2 or 3 fresh tomatoes, chopped, and fresh herbs; the result will be even better than Grandma's. When using fresh herbs, use two or three times the amount of dry herbs.

2 tablespoons olive oil
2 pounds boneless pork, cut into 1-inch cubes
4 cloves garlic, minced
2 cups (29-ounce can) tomatoes, undrained
½ teaspoon dried basil
1 teaspoon dried oregano
¼ teaspoon dried thyme
½ cup dry white wine
1 large onion, peeled and sliced
1 sweet red bell pepper, seeded and sliced
1 green bell pepper, seeded and sliced
Salt and pepper to taste

≈

1. Heat 1 tablespoon of oil in a large heavy skillet or Dutch oven over medium-high heat. Add the pork and garlic; cook, stirring to brown the pork, for about 4 to 5 minutes. Add the tomatoes, seasonings, and wine. Reduce the heat, cover tightly, and simmer until the pork is tender, about 12 to 15 minutes.

2. Meanwhile, sauté the onion and peppers in the remaining oil in a large skillet for about 3 minutes. Add to the pork mixture, and blend gently. Adjust the seasonings and simmer for 2 to 3 minutes.

Serves 8.

Strips for Stir-Fry and Saté

Stir-frying is a favorite quick method for cooking fresh pork. Pork stir-fry strips can be cut from virtually any fresh cut. Most retailers now offer stir-fry strips ready-cut in the store, but it's easy to do at home, too. Trim any visible fat and cut ⅛-inch-wide strips, ½ inch by 2 inches long. Wider strips can be threaded on skewers for a quick-grilled saté. Partially freezing the pork makes slicing thin strips easier.

Southwestern Stir-Fry

- 1 pound lean pork
- 2 tablespoons dry sherry
- 2 teaspoons cornstarch
- 1 teaspoon ground cumin
- 1 clove garlic, minced
- ½ teaspoon salt
- 1 tablespoon vegetable oil
- 1 green pepper, seeded and cut into strips
- 1 medium onion, thinly sliced
- 12 cherry tomatoes, halved

This is delicious served hot, with a green-chili salsa.

≈

1. Cut the pork into ⅛-inch-thick strips about 2 inches long. Combine the sherry, cornstarch, cumin, garlic, and salt in a medium bowl; add the pork slices and stir to coat the meat.

2. Heat the oil over medium-high heat in a large heavy skillet or sauté pan. Add the pork mixture and stir-fry for 3 to 4 minutes.

3. Add the remaining ingredients, cover the pan, and simmer for 3 to 4 minutes.

Serves 4.

Cashew Pork Stir-Fry

This tasty dish is reminiscent of the flavors of Hawaii.

- 1 pound lean pork
- 1 tablespoon grated orange rind
- ¾ cup orange juice
- 1 tablespoon cornstarch
- 3 tablespoons soy sauce
- ⅓ cup light corn syrup
- ¼ teaspoon ground ginger
- 2 tablespoons vegetable oil
- 2 large carrots, peeled and sliced diagonally
- 2 ribs celery, sliced diagonally
- ½ cup cashew nuts

≈

1. Cut the pork into thin strips. Set aside. Combine the orange rind and juice, cornstarch, soy sauce, corn syrup, and ginger, stirring well.
2. Heat 1 tablespoon of the oil in a large skillet over medium heat. Add the carrots and celery, and stir-fry for about 3 minutes. Remove the vegetables and set aside.
3. Pour the remaining tablespoon of oil into the skillet. Add the pork and stir-fry for about 3 minutes. Return the vegetables to the pan, and add the orange-juice mixture and cashews. Cook, stirring constantly, over medium-high heat until thickened. Serve over hot rice, if desired.

Serves 4.

Indonesian Saté with Peanut Sauce

Thanks to our rich cultural heritage, saté (saa-tay) has become a part of our culinary language in many parts of the country. An Indonesian specialty, it consists of small cubes or strips of meat, fish, or poultry threaded on skewers and grilled. Saté is usually served with a spicy peanut sauce. This is a recipe my wife calls her "soul food" from Hawaii. All of the preparation for saté can be done well in advance, even the day before you plan to serve, making this a great and easy dish for summer entertaining.

SATÉ

- 2 pounds thinly sliced strips of pork (or beef)
- 3 tablespoons curry powder
- ½ teaspoon ground chili peppers
- 2 cloves garlic, minced
- 2 large onions, minced
- 1 tablespoon salt

(recipe continues)

≈

1. Slice the meat into thin strips, no more than ¼ inch thick and about 1 inch wide. Mix all the remaining saté

Indonesian Saté with Peanut Sauce *(cont.)*

- 4 tablespoons lemon juice
- 1 tablespoon honey

PEANUT SAUCE

- 1 cup smooth peanut butter
- 1 cup Coconut Cream (see below)
- 1 tablespoon lemon juice
- ¼ cup soy sauce
- 1 tablespoon Worcestershire sauce
- 2 or 3 dashes Tabasco sauce
- ¼ teaspoon salt

ingredients together in a large bowl. Add the strips of meat and toss well to cover with the marinade.

2. Meanwhile, prepare the Peanut Sauce. Blend all ingredients together well to make a smooth sauce. Refrigerate.

3. Thread the meat strips on bamboo skewers that have been soaked in water for 1 hour, 3 or 4 pieces per skewer. Make sure that plenty of onion and garlic bits cling to the meat. Arrange the skewers of meat on a dish, and cover with any remaining marinade.

4. Simply broil or grill the skewers of meat and serve them with the Peanut Sauce for dipping.

Serves 4 to 6.

Coconut Cream

Heat to boiling 1 cup milk and pour it over a 7-ounce package of grated unsweetened coconut. Let steep for 20 to 30 minutes. Strain the milk through cheesecloth and use it in the above sauce.

TENDERLOIN

Some consider this tender and extremely lean muscle the choicest pork cut. This ¾-to-1½-pound muscle can be roasted whole, cut into cubes for kabobs, strips for stir-fry or saté, or sliced for scaloppine or medallions.

Pork tenderloin used to be a regional specialty in this country, available only in Middle America, near packing houses that processed "Canadian bacon." Fortunately, I grew up in such a place—Sioux City, Iowa—and very early on I developed a true appreciation for this most tender and versatile cut of pork. The tenderloin of pork is by far the tenderest morsel the pig has to offer. Lying, as it does, along the underside of the pork loin, it does absolutely nothing in the process of moving the pig from one side of the pen to the other. It doesn't even have to wiggle in a waller. It's a lazy muscle, and that's why it stays so tender. As a result, tenderloins are very lean, well trimmed, and absolutely marvelous for all kinds of quick-to-fix pork dishes.

Until recently, most pork loins came to market whole, with the bone left in. The further processing of the loin into pork chops and pork roasts, etc., was done at the retail level by your friendly butcher. Seldom was the loin boned out at retail to make the tenderloin available. More and more these days, however, pork loin is being marketed boneless. The top loin and the tenderloin are separated at the packing plant, individually vacuum-packaged (in the case of the tenderloin, it's usually two to a package), and distributed for sale to customers just as they come from the packer. You don't have to live in Sioux City to get pork tenderloins these days. It's available in markets everywhere and is a marvelous cut of meat—lean, waste-free, tender, and versatile. There are dozens of things to be done with it, and since it cooks so quickly, it's a boon to the hurried cook.

Because of the somewhat conical shape, tapering from 1½ to 2 inches in diameter at the large end down to a point at the other, it is necessary to cut a tenderloin into uniform slices for frying or sautéing.

Butterflying and pounding is the technique for turning the small slices of the tenderloin into larger-diameter "cutlets" perfect for frying. To cut butterflied slices, start at the large end. (For more about butterflying, see page 103.) Cut a slice about ¾ inch thick, but *do not* cut all the way through. Stop your cut about ¼ inch short of going all the way through the meat. Move your knife over an equal distance (¾ inch) and make a second cut, this time all the way through the meat. Fold the meat open and pound lightly to expand the surface and reduce the thickness. Repeat the process, increasing the thickness of the cuts as the diameter of the tenderloin becomes smaller. After pounding, all slices should be approximately the same size. The last 2 or 3 inches of the tapered end can be split open horizontally and flattened to yield a slice the same size as the rest.

Slicing the tenderloin diagonally is the second method. Starting at the large end, cut diagonal slices about ½ inch thick, changing the angle of the knife both horizontally and vertically after each slice to keep the slices approximately equal in size. The thin tail of the tenderloin can be butterflied so that this slice will be the same size as the others.

Try wrapping two or three thick slices of tenderloin with bacon to make pork tournedos for broiling. Thread pieces of tenderloin on skewers for the most tender pork kabobs you've ever tasted.

No matter how you cut it, pork tenderloin is a wonderfully tender part of the pig.

Sautéed Pork Tenderloin

2 pork tenderloins (about 2 pounds)
1 cup flour
½ teaspoon salt
¼ teaspoon black pepper
2 tablespoons butter
1 tablespoon olive oil
½ cup chicken stock or white wine or a combination

One of the easiest, fastest, and most versatile ways to serve pork tenderloin is sautéed, or cooked quickly. It is important to have all the slices cut the same thickness and approximately the same size, so they will all cook to the desired degree of doneness in the same time.

≈

1. Slice the tenderloins into uniform slices as described above. Toss the flour, salt, and pepper together in a small brown paper bag. Add the tenderloin slices and shake to coat them with the seasoned flour.

2. Heat the butter and oil together in a sauté pan and quickly brown the tenderloin pieces a few at a time, 2 to 3 minutes on each side. Remove them to a warm serving platter; keep warm.

3. Pour the stock, wine, or stock-and-wine mixture into the pan, scraping the little bits of meat and browned flour from the bottom of the pan with a wooden spoon. Bring the liquid to a boil and keep boiling until it reduces by about half and thickens slightly. Pour over the sautéed tenderloin slices and serve.

Serves 6 to 8.

VARIATIONS

The variations on this basic sautéed pork-tenderloin recipe are almost endless. Use your imagination:

With Mushrooms Sauté ½ cup sliced mushrooms in the pan after cooking the pork, then add the wine and stock.

With Capers Use a bit of lemon juice in place of the wine and add a tablespoon of capers to the finished dish.

With Herbs Stir a teaspoon or two of your favorite herbs, chopped shallots, or scallions into the drippings before adding the stock and perhaps an extra dollop of butter.

With Nuts Nuts are often overlooked as an ingredient. They go particularly well with pork. Try adding ½ cup of peanuts, sliced almonds, pecans, or pine nuts to this recipe.

Honey Sesame Tenderloin

Another recipe for pork tenderloin that has become a family favorite is this one with an Asian influence.

- 1 cup soy sauce
- 2 cloves garlic, minced
- 1 tablespoon grated fresh ginger or 1 teaspoon dry ground ginger
- 1 tablespoon dark sesame oil
- 1 pound whole pork tenderloin
- ¼ cup honey
- 2 tablespoons brown sugar
- 4 tablespoons sesame

≈

1. Combine the soy sauce, garlic, ginger, and sesame oil. Place the tenderloin in a heavy plastic bag, pour on the soy mixture, and turn the bag to coat. Let marinate 2 hours at room temperature, or overnight in the refrigerator.
2. Remove the pork from the marinade and pat it dry. Mix the honey and brown sugar in a shallow bowl. Place the sesame seeds in a separate shallow bowl. Roll the pork in the honey mixture, coating it well, then roll it in the sesame seeds.
3. In a preheated 375-degree oven, roast the meat in a shallow pan for 30 to 40 minutes, until an instant-read thermometer inserted in the center of the tenderloin registers 155 to 160 degrees. Remove to a serving platter and slice thin.

Serves 3 to 4.

Pork Tenderloin Diane

- 1 pork tenderloin, cut crosswise into 8 pieces
- 2 teaspoons lemon pepper
- 2 tablespoons butter
- 2 tablespoons lemon juice
- 1 tablespoon Worcestershire sauce
- 1 teaspoon Dijon mustard
- 1 tablespoon minced parsley or chives

This is a spin on steak Diane, a well-known San Francisco dish, prepared in very little time.

≈

1. With the heel of your hand, press each tenderloin slice into a medallion 1½ to 2 inches in diameter and ¼ inch thick. Sprinkle with lemon pepper.

2. Heat the butter in a heavy skillet, and cook the medallions 3 to 4 minutes on each side over medium heat. Remove the medallions to a serving platter and keep warm.

3. Add the lemon juice, Worcestershire sauce, and mustard to the skillet. Cook, stirring with pan juices, until heated through. Pour sauce over the medallions, sprinkle with parsley or chives, and serve.

Serves 4.

VARIATIONS

Apricot Pork Medallions Prepare the medallions, sauté in 1 tablespoon butter, then remove and keep warm. To the skillet add ½ cup chopped dried apricots, two sliced scallions, ¼ teaspoon dry ginger powder, 1 teaspoon wine vinegar, 2 teaspoons brown sugar, and a dash of hot-pepper sauce. Cover and simmer for 3 to 4 minutes. Return the medallions to the pan and heat through. Serves 4.

West Indian Pork Medallions Prepare the medallions, sauté in 1 tablespoon butter, then remove and keep warm. Add 3 tablespoons butter to the skillet. When bubbling, cook 2 sliced bananas for 3 minutes; add ¼ cup brown sugar and ¼ cup brandy. Cook, stirring, until thick and bubbling. Return the medallions to the pan and heat through. Serves 4.

Tenderloin Tonnato

Here the tenderloins are simmered whole, then sliced before serving in a variation on the classic dish veal tonnato. This is a recipe I love to use for casual entertaining on a warm spring day.

TENDERLOIN

- 2 whole pork tenderloins (about 2 pounds)
- ½ onion, sliced
- 1½ cups water
- 1 tablespoon fresh lemon juice
- ½ teaspoon hot-pepper sauce
- 1 teaspoon pickling spice
- ½ teaspoon salt

TONNATO SAUCE

- 1 6½-ounce can white tuna, drained
- 1 cup mayonnaise
- 1 tablespoon Dijon mustard
- 2 tablespoons fresh lemon juice

- 2 tablespoons drained capers
- 4 tablespoons chopped parsley

≈

1. Place all the tenderloin ingredients in a large heavy skillet; bring to a boil, reduce the heat, cover, and simmer for 25 to 30 minutes. Remove the tenderloins to a platter, cover, and refrigerate until serving. Reserve the cooking liquid.

2. Prepare the sauce. Whirl the tuna, mayonnaise, mustard, and lemon juice in a food processor until smooth. Stir in some of the reserved cooking liquid until the sauce is the consistency of a thick syrup. Cover and refrigerate until ready to serve.

3. To serve, slice the pork ¼ inch thick, and arrange the slices slightly overlapping on a serving platter. Pour the Tonnato Sauce over the pork. Sprinkle on the capers and parsley.

Serves 8 to 10.

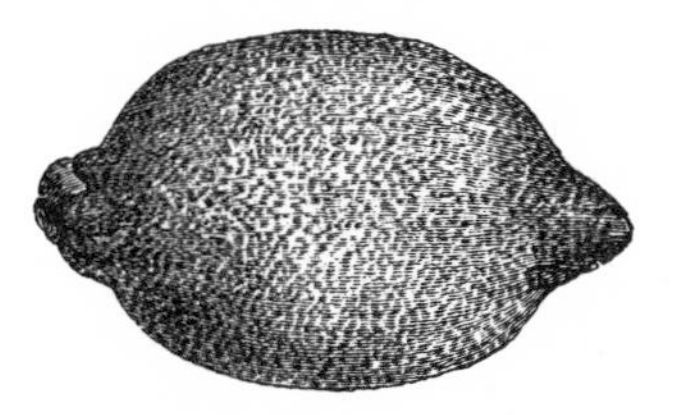

CUTLETS

Cutlets are thin slices taken from almost any boneless cut of pork—the loin, leg, shoulder, or tenderloin. The key to cutlets is their thinness (⅛ to ¼ inch). They are great for a quick sauté or braised dish.

Like veal cutlets, pork cutlets are often called by various names in meat markets and recipe books, depending upon the native language of the butcher or cook: "medallions," "scallops," or "scaloppine," for example. Pork cutlets can very successfully be substituted for veal cutlets in recipes found in the veal chapter.

Curried Pork with Peaches

- 1 tablespoon cooking oil
- 1 pound boneless pork cutlets, ¼ inch thick
- ½ onion, coarsely chopped
- ½ teaspoon ground ginger
- 2 teaspoons curry powder
- 1 cup chicken broth
- 4 teaspoons cornstarch
- ¼ teaspoon salt
- ½ cup coarsely chopped fresh peaches
- 2 teaspoons peach preserves

Pork goes wonderfully well with fruit. This recipe calls for fresh peaches and peach preserves. An equally delicious variation can be made using instead apples and applesauce, and substituting cinnamon for the curry powder.

≈

1. In a large skillet, heat the oil over medium heat. Add the cutlets and onion to the skillet and sauté the pork quickly about 2 minutes per side, until golden brown.
2. In a medium bowl, stir together the remaining ingredients. Pour the mixture over the cutlets. Cook, stirring gently from time to time, over low heat until the sauce thickens, about 8 to 10 minutes.

Serves 4.

VARIATIONS

Here are a couple of other quick and easy variations combining pork and fruit.

Mandarin Medallions

≈

- 1 teaspoon vegetable oil
- 1 pound boneless pork cutlets, ¼ inch thick
- ½ cup orange juice
- ¼ cup orange marmalade
- 1 teaspoon prepared horseradish
- ½ teaspoon cinnamon
- 2 tablespoons lemon juice
- 1 tablespoon cornstarch
- 1 10-ounce can mandarin-orange segments, drained

1. Heat the oil in a nonstick pan over medium-high heat. Brown the pork quickly, about 1 minute per side.
2. Mix the remaining ingredients except the mandarin oranges. Add to the skillet and cook, stirring, until the sauce thickens. Simmer for 3 to 4 minutes.
3. Remove the cutlets to a serving platter and garnish with the mandarin oranges.

Serves 4.

Plum-Glazed Pork Cutlets

≈

- 1 teaspoon vegetable oil
- 1 pound boneless pork cutlets, ¼ inch thick
- 1 8-ounce jar plum jelly or preserves
- ½ onion, chopped
- ¼ cup wine vinegar
- 2 teaspoons soy sauce
- 1 teaspoon ground ginger

Heat the oil in a nonstick skillet over medium-high heat. Brown the pork on both sides. Add the remaining ingredients, cover, and simmer 10 to 12 minutes.

Serves 4.

Pork Scallops in Sour Cream

- 1 pound lean, boneless pork, sliced ¼ inch thick
- 2 tablespoons flour
- Salt and white pepper
- 4 tablespoons butter
- 1 onion, cut in half and thinly sliced
- 1 pound fresh mushrooms, thinly sliced
- ¼ cup brandy
- 1 cup sour cream

Small slices from the loin or leg work best for this dish. We like it with Neva's Quick Pilaf (page 58) or Barley Pilaf (page 193). Remember, when you flame a dish, stand back! You can also just add the brandy and simmer for 3 minutes to cook out some of the alcohol.

≈

1. Pound the pork slices until they are approximately ⅛ inch thick. Dust with the flour, which has been seasoned with the salt and pepper. Heat 2 tablespoons of the butter in a large skillet over medium-high heat and brown the pork for 3 minutes on each side. Remove and set aside.

2. Add the onion to the pan and cook for 3 minutes. Add the remaining butter and the mushrooms, and cook for 5 to 6 minutes. Add the brandy and flame. When the flames have subsided, add the sour cream. Heat just to boiling. Return the pork to the pan and heat through.

Serves 4.

RIBS—AFTER MAKIN' BACON THERE'S BARBECUE

Depending on what part of the country you're from, the word "barbecue" is a noun meaning "pig, slow-cooked over hickory coals," or "beef brisket, slow-cooked over mesquite." To most of the nation, however, the word "barbecue" is a verb pertaining to the noun "rib." Swathed in any one of dozens of marvelous sauces, ribs are the epitome of what barbecue is all about.

Spareribs are the most common, the most readily available, and usually the least expensive of the various forms of pork ribs. They are the bones that are left over (spare) when the pork belly is trimmed for making bacon. They consist of the lower portion of the rib bones along with the cartilage that joins the ribs to the breastbone.

Spareribs vary in size depending on the size of the pig from which they came. The most desirable are called "three and under," meaning that each slab weighs no more than three pounds.

St. Louis–style ribs are spareribs from which the breastbone and cartilage have been removed, leaving only the rib bones.

Back ribs are cut from above the spareribs. They are the result of the butcher's boning out the pork loin to make boneless club roasts or Canadian bacon (cured and smoked top loin of pork). Most back ribs go to the hotel-and-restaurant trade. Restaurants like them because they're smaller and more uniform in size (they sometimes are called "baby back ribs"), so they make a nicer presentation and it's easier to control the size of the portions. As far as quality is concerned, they are no better than spareribs.

Country-style ribs can and do take a variety of forms in different meat cases, but they are all prepared from the same cut of pork, the blade loin end. Butchers traditionally have had a hard time selling blade-end pork loins during the summer months. This cut is usually thought of as a pork roast, and nobody wants to heat up the kitchen roasting pork in the summer. In the early 1970s, an ingenious meat man, Scott Detrie, president of Scotty's, a chain of markets in the Louisville area of Kentucky, came up with a new way of merchandising the cut. He cut the blade-end roast so that it could be divided up into thinner pieces that could be cooked on the barbecue. Not all cuts of country ribs have the rib bone; some have a portion of the blade bone, and some a portion of the backbone; but they all have a good meaty portion of the pork loin.

Boneless ribs are boneless strips of pork, usually from the loin or shoulder, cut with the barbecue grill in mind. They can be cooked as you would other kinds of rib. The only disadvantage for the true rib lover is that they're hard to eat without a knife and fork, and for many of us, ribs are finger food.

When it comes to cooking ribs, wherever *they* come from, a good deal depends on where *you* come from. In parts of the South, where "barbecue" is almost a religion, ribs are cooked long and slow with hickory smoke and served up with any one of hundreds of sauces, from sweet to hot, depending upon "where you come from."

The recipes that follow reflect some of the regional differences in rib cookery around the country. Some, to meet the demands of a true barbecue buff, must be cooked out of doors with the flavorful addition of smoke from the local wood of choice—hickory or apple in North Carolina, mesquite in Texas—but all can be cooked to finger-lickin' goodness in your oven.

Piedmont-Style North Carolina Ribs

4 pounds pork ribs
1½ cups catsup
1 cup cider vinegar
½ teaspoon cayenne pepper
Pinch crushed red-pepper flakes
1 teaspoon ground black pepper
3 tablespoons brown sugar
½ cup water
1 teaspoon liquid-smoke seasoning

In North Carolina, barbecue sauces vary from one end of the state to the other. In the east, ribs are served with a sauce made mostly of vinegar and pepper. In the mountains of western North Carolina, it is a sweet tomato-based sauce. In the Piedmont region, around Lexington, North Carolina, which bills itself as the "barbecue capital of the world," the sauce is a tasty blend of both.

≈

1. Place the whole slabs of ribs in a shallow roasting pan and roast in a preheated 325-degree oven for 2 hours.
2. Mix the remaining ingredients together in a small saucepan and simmer, stirring, until the sugar dissolves. Remove from the heat and use to baste the ribs occasionally as they roast, about every 15 minutes.
3. Cut the ribs into serving-size pieces. Heat the remaining sauce and serve with the ribs.

Serves 4 to 6.

Cowboy Barbecued Ribs

These are ribs not unlike those you might have tasted were you sitting around the campfire on a cattle drive from San Antonio to Kansas City in the late 1800s.

- 4 pounds pork ribs
- 1 cup water
- ⅓ cup butter or margarine
- 2 tablespoons fresh lemon juice
- ¼ cup dry mustard
- ¼ cup chili powder
- 1 tablespoon sugar
- 1 tablespoon hot paprika
- 2 teaspoons salt
- 1 teaspoon onion powder
- 1 teaspoon garlic powder
- ¼ teaspoon cayenne pepper

≈

1. Place the spareribs in a shallow roasting pan. Cover with foil and roast in a preheated 400-degree oven for 1½ hours.
2. Meanwhile, combine the remaining ingredients in a medium saucepan; mix well. Bring to a boil. Reduce the heat and simmer for 30 minutes.
3. Brush the sauce on the ribs. Broil 5 inches from the heat for 7 to 10 minutes on each side. Cut the ribs into serving-size pieces. Serve the ribs with additional sauce.

Serves 4 to 6.

Cajun-Rubbed Ribs

In the bayou of Louisiana, ribs may be served with no sauce at all but, rather, seasoned with a spicy dry rub that will definitely wake up your taste buds!

- 2 tablespoons paprika
- 2 teaspoons onion powder
- 2 teaspoons garlic powder
- 2 teaspoons cayenne pepper
- 1½ teaspoons ground white pepper
- ½ teaspoon ground black pepper
- 1 teaspoon salt
- 1 teaspoon crushed dried thyme
- 1 teaspoon crushed dried oregano leaves
- 4 pounds pork ribs

≈

Combine all the dry ingredients and rub on all the surfaces of the ribs. Place the rib slabs in a shallow roasting pan and roast in a preheated 325-degree oven for 2 hours. Cut the ribs into serving pieces.

Serves 4 to 6.

Sweet and Sour Ribs

2 pounds meaty ribs, cut into 2-inch pieces
Hawaiian salt or coarse sea salt

MARINADE

1 tablespoon white wine
½ cup soy sauce
1-inch piece fresh ginger, crushed, or 1 teaspoon dry, ground ginger
1 large clove garlic, crushed
¼ cup peanut oil

SAUCE

1 cup cider vinegar
½ cup water
¼ cup pineapple juice
½ cup brown sugar
½ cup white sugar
1½ tablespoons cornstarch
½ green pepper, cut into chunks
1 can pineapple chunks, drained

This was my mother-in-law's way with ribs. She fixed it for us every time we went to Hawaii. Now Neva has the recipe and, after almost thirty-four years, I haven't tired of it. Any ribs work well.

≈

1. Cook the rib pieces in boiling water to cover for 15 minutes; drain and set aside. When the ribs are cool, rub them with coarse salt. Mix the marinade, reserving 2 tablespoons of the peanut oil. Add the marinade to the ribs and let them stand for 1 hour, stirring occasionally.

2. Mix together the sauce ingredients in a large pan and cook until slightly thick.

3. Remove the ribs from the marinade and drain. Brown the marinated ribs in the remaining peanut oil. Drain the ribs and add to the sauce. Simmer for 30 minutes. Add the green pepper in the last 10 minutes. Check the seasoning and add salt and pepper if needed. Garnish with pineapple chunks and serve with rice.

Serves 4 to 6.

HAM

The hams we find in most city supermarkets these days are the well-dressed, water-added, mild-mannered, debonair, but distant city cousin of the old-fashioned "country ham," common a generation ago. "City hams," as I call them, have much to commend them, but little to distinguish them one from another with the exception of the package they come in.

The unqualified term "ham" is limited to the cured and smoked and/or cooked hind leg of a pig. By USDA regulation, the finished product may weigh no more after the curing, smoking, and/or cooking process than the fresh uncured leg of pork weighed to begin with—"the green weight." If the finished product exceeds the "green weight," it must be labeled "ham—water added."

Most city hams are water-added. The curing ingredients—salt, sugar, sodium nitrate, etc.—are dissolved in water and pumped into the leg of pork. Some water remains in the meat after the processing.

City hams come in a variety of forms and are usually boneless. They are labeled with a lot of qualifying terms: "canned ham," "gourmet ham," "buffet ham," "pressed ham." Most are fully cooked, "ready to eat," and require only heating through before serving. They are mild in flavor and preferred by many of today's consumers, but to my taste they cannot compare to an old-fashioned country ham.

Country hams are "dry-cured." The hams are "put down," in curing rooms, packed in salt mixed with the other curing ingredients. They are left for up to thirty-five or forty days. The salt draws much of the moisture out of the meat, yielding a firmer, somewhat salty, but very flavorful finished product.

The best ham buy on the market these days is not really a ham at all, it's a "picnic." A ham by definition is the "cured and smoked hind leg of a pig." A picnic ham is the cured and smoked front leg and shoulder. The only other major difference between the two is price. Picnic hams have been selling in my neighborhood with some regularity for under a dollar a pound. The other end of the pig goes for considerably more.

Selecting a good lean picnic ham is difficult to do by sight. Most of them these days come wrapped in red plastic, which makes them all look marvelous! Pick out a picnic the way you pick out a pineapple—pinch it. If it's nice and solid, chances are that it will not be excessively fatty.

Where Is Smithfield Anyway?

Say "country ham" in most parts of this country and the first name that comes to most folks' minds is "Smithfield." The country-ham tradition had its beginnings in Smithfield, Virginia, a little town located on Pagan Creek, a tributary of the James River, settled in 1619. Legend says the recipe for curing a country ham was borrowed from the Indians of the area, who preserved venison for the winter by rubbing it with "magic white sand" (*salt* to us today) and smoking it over a fire. Their recipe was applied to the hind legs of pigs that ran wild in the forests surrounding the town.

Malory Todd began curing hams in Smithfield in the mid-1700s. He became the first to produce "Smithfield Hams" in any quantity. By 1779, Mr. Todd was curing twelve thousand hams annually. Hams cured by the Todd family were among the first exports from the New World to the Old. They were a featured item on the royal dining table at Windsor Castle during the reign of Queen Victoria.

By the twentieth century, the Smithfield Ham had become so famous that in 1926 the Virginia General Assembly passed a law to protect it from imitations. The statute read: "Genuine Smithfield Hams are those cut from the carcass of peanut fed hogs raised in the peanut belt of the State of Virginia or the State of North Carolina, and which are cured treated, smoked and processed in the town of Smithfield, in the State of Virginia." The law has been changed only once, in 1966, when the legislature dropped the provision requiring that the hogs be peanut-fed.

Currently there are only four companies whose products qualify to bear the prestigious title "Genuine Smithfield Ham." They're the only companies processing ham in the "town of Smithfield, in the State of Virginia."

Unfortunately for Mr. Todd, he had moved his growing ham-processing business away from the little town on Pagan Creek to the big city of Richmond before the lawyers and legislation had their day. So today, even though the E. M. Todd Company—the oldest meat-packing company in the country and the producer of the first Smithfield Hams—is still producing hams, they cannot be called Smithfield Hams. Ironic, isn't it? There's more . . .

The best Smithfield Ham that I have ever tasted comes from Smithfield—not in Virginia but in North Carolina, so it doesn't qualify as "genuine." But country hams don't get any better than Johnston County Country Hams from Smithfield, North Carolina. Jesse Brown, the cure master at Johnston County Country Hams, has been dubbed by the national press "the King of Country Hams." He has won most every award there is in ham-curing competitions, and you would be amazed at how many that is. Last time I was in attendance at a ham competition, Jesse won top honors in every category—so many, in fact, that he got embarrassed, left, and made his son Rufus go to the stage time and time again to pick up blue ribbons for Johnston County Country Hams from Smithfield, not Virginia but North Carolina.

So . . . where is Smithfield anyway? You decide! The following is a listing of Smithfield Ham products: the first, served to queens, from Richmond, Virginia; the four "Genuine" from Smithfield, Virginia; and the "King" from Smithfield, North Carolina. Call for one of their catalogues. If you decide to call Jesse, just ask for Rufus.

Smithfield Ham Companies

1. *First Smithfield Ham Company*

E. M. Todd Company
Richmond, VA 23220
(800) 359-5026

2. *"Genuine" Smithfield Ham Companies*

Luther Smithfield Packing Company
(800) 444-9180

Gwaltney of Smithfield
(800) 678-0770

V. W. Joyner & Co.
(800) 628-2242

Amber Brand Smithfield Ham
(800) 628-2242

3. *The "King" from Smithfield, North Carolina*

Johnston County Country Hams
(919) 934-8054 (ask for Rufus!)
(800) 543-4267

There are lots of good country hams besides Smithfields. See the list in the appendix (page 320).

Cooking Hams

Cooking a "city ham," whatever the type—bone-in, boneless, buffet, canned, or picnic—is the epitome of simplicity. First read the label; if it says "cook before eating," bake on a rack, uncovered, in a 325-degree oven to an internal temperature of 160 degrees. A meat thermometer is helpful in achieving the best results. Insert the thermometer at an angle, so the tip is in the center of the meat and not resting on the fat or bone. If you don't have a meat thermometer, bake the ham approximately twenty minutes per pound.

If the label reads "fully cooked" or "ready-to-eat," bake it anyway. It will be much improved by spending some time in the oven. Fully cooked hams need only to be brought to a 140-degree internal temperature, about 15 minutes per pound.

About a half-hour before the baking time is over, remove the ham from the oven and remove the rind, if there is one. Score the fat in a diamond pattern and brush on a glaze (see page 134), and return the ham to the oven at the same temperature. Baste frequently with more glaze as the ham finishes cooking.

Cooking a "country ham" is considerably more complicated and a lot more time-consuming. It can take days, but it's worth the trouble. One set of instructions from back in Grandma's day calls for soaking "a-old-ham in 13 changes of water for 36 hours in someplace cool like by the separator." Then, "scrub thoroughly with warm water usin' a stiff pig-bristle brush."

Next, "place the ham in a lard can with a tight lid and boil one minute per each pound of ham. Take the can off-en the stove and set it by the cob box. Wrap it tight with quilts, old coats or horse blankets and leave set for 24 hours." That procedure is perhaps a bit outdated—few folks have a cob box these days—but a country ham does need soaking; how long it needs to soak can vary.

All hams are cured a little differently, and some are aged a lot longer than others. A young ham with a considerable amount of sugar or molasses in the cure won't need soaking nearly as long as a Smithfield Ham that's been hanging for a year or two.

You can tell about the cure and the age just by looking at the ham. A young ham will be a little soft and have a light-reddish color, whereas an old ham will be hard as a rock and a deep-purple color. The young ham will need only twelve hours of soaking, a really well-aged ham perhaps as much as forty-eight hours. Soaking is important! A country ham should have a nice salty tang, but if you don't soak one long enough, it can be awfully salty!

After you've soaked it, scrub it thoroughly to get any mold off. Then put it skin side up in a deep roasting pan and cover it about half over with water. Some folks like to use wine or cider or champagne—in Georgia a lot of folks use Coca-

Cola—but I just use water. Some folks tell you to put the skin down, but I like to keep the skin up and let the ham rest on the aitch (hip) bone.

Don't let the ham boil—it will toughen. You want it just to simmer, slowly, with a tight-fitting lid in about a 300-degree oven, or over low heat on top of the stove. Cooking time will vary depending on the character and age of the ham, but it's done when a thermometer registers the internal temperature at 160 degrees. If you don't have a thermometer, you can tell it's done when the aitch bone comes loose.

Don't overcook it. A lot of folks overcook ham. They'll let it set for hours in the pan after it's cooked, the way Grandma used to do, and it just keeps on cooking. When it's done, let it cool just enough so you can handle it, then skin it, and glaze it just as you would a "city ham."

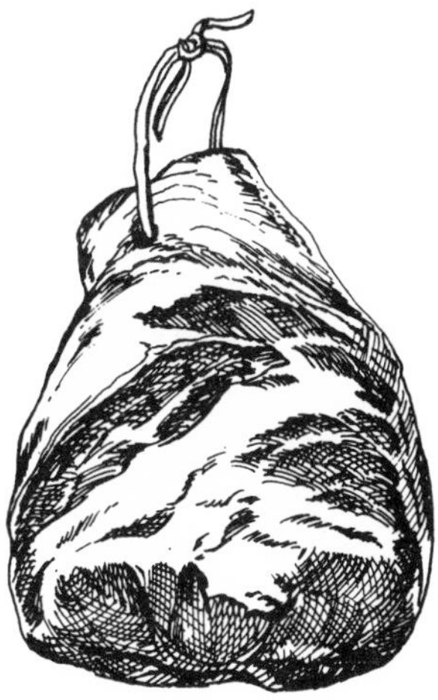

Serve "country ham" hot, cold, or at room temperature, sliced in paper-thin slices. It's a rich and flavorful treat that is well worth the time it takes to prepare.

Oh, by the way, there is an easier way to serve country ham: buy one already cooked from most any of the sources listed on page 131 or in the appendix.

Country Ham with Red-Eye Gravy

This is a traditional way of serving country ham in many parts of the South. It's usually served for breakfast with grits and hot biscuits. Water may be used in place of the coffee, but it won't have that unique flavor.

¼-inch-thick center cut of country ham
4 tablespoons black coffee
½ teaspoon sugar

≈

1. Trim off the skin from the slice of ham. Fry the ham quickly in an ungreased hot skillet for a couple of minutes on each side. Remove the ham from the pan and set aside.
2. To the hot fat remaining, add the black coffee and sugar. Stir to dissolve the sugar, cover, and simmer for a couple of minutes.
3. Pour the gravy over the ham slices and serve.

Serves 1 or 2.

Baked Ham Slice

- 1½ teaspoons dry mustard
- 2 tablespoons brown sugar
- Ham slice, 1 to 2 inches thick, preferably cut from the center of the ham
- 1 cup milk

If you use a country-ham slice for this recipe, you should simmer the slice for twenty minutes and allow it to cool in the water before you bake. A slice this thick needs precooking.

≈

Make a paste of the mustard, brown sugar, and just enough water to blend. Spread the paste over the ham slice, place in a lightly oiled baking pan, pour over it 1 cup milk, and bake in a preheated 350-degree oven until just tender. The time depends on what kind of ham you are using. It should take about an hour for country ham, and half that time for city ham.

Serves 2 to 4.

Ham Glazes

City ham, country ham, or picnic ham—the taste and appearance of all are enhanced by the application of a glaze. Here are a few of the favorite ham glazes from our family's ham files. Mix together, and baste the ham during the last thirty minutes of cooking time only.

Mustard Honey Glaze ½ cup honey, 1 tablespoon mustard, ¼ cup soy sauce.

Peanut Honey Glaze Mix ½ cup honey with ½ cup smooth peanut butter. A favorite with my kids.

Pineapple Glaze To 1 cup crushed pineapple add ½ cup brown sugar and 2 tablespoons lemon juice.

My favorite Booze Glaze Mix ¼ cup red wine with ¼ cup bourbon. Add 1 cup brown sugar and 2 tablespoons of grated orange peel.

Think Big!

Think big when buying a ham! No matter what kind of ham you buy—country, city, canned, water-added, whatever—buy a *big one*! It's a great investment! There are so many quick, easy, and delicious things to be done with ham. "A ham in the fridge is like money in the bank," my grandma used to say.

My process for dealing with cooked ham begins with boning out the remains of the leg (I always buy a bone-in ham), because it provides an extra blessing. The bone, the hock, the skin (if there is skin) go immediately into a big pot, along with some of the small scraps of meat, to make Red Beans and Rice, the traditional Cajun use for the ham bone.

The meaty parts of the ham get wrapped individually in units, and these are used for all manner of meals—sliced thin for ham sandwiches, fried with eggs, cut into strips or cubed to be tossed in salads, or added to a sauce for pasta. There are so many things to do with ham. Here are but a few, starting with Red Beans and Rice.

Red Beans and Rice

This traditional Cajun main dish gets better and better the longer it stays in the refrigerator, up to three days. However, we hardly enjoy the leftovers for very long—we've quickly eaten them up. If you don't have any leftover ham, two to three smoked ham hocks can be used.

- 6 cups water
- 1 pound (2 cups) dried small red beans
- ⅓ pound bacon, chopped
- 1 cup finely chopped scallions, including 3 inches of the tops
- ½ cup finely chopped onion
- 2 teaspoons finely chopped garlic
- ¼ pound salt pork, cubed
- 1 leftover meaty ham bone with skin if possible, or 3 smoked ham hocks
- 1 teaspoon salt

≈

1. In a heavy 3-to-4-quart saucepan, bring the water to a boil over high heat. Drop in the beans and bring to a brisk boil. Cover, then turn off the heat and let the beans soak in the hot water for 1 hour. Drain the beans in a sieve set over a large bowl; save the soaking liquid and add enough water to make 4 cups. Set the beans and liquid aside.

2. In a heavy 4-to-5-quart casserole, cook the bacon until cooked but not crisp. Remove the bacon from the pan, drain, and set aside. To the bacon drippings add ½ cup of the scallions and the onion and garlic. Over medium heat cook for about 5 minutes, stirring fre-

(recipe continues)

Red Beans and Rice *(cont.)*

½ teaspoon freshly ground black pepper
½ teaspoon crushed red-pepper flakes
½ teaspoon cayenne pepper
1 cup chicken stock (optional)
6 to 8 cups freshly cooked long-grain rice

quently, until the onions are soft and translucent but not brown.

3. Add the salt pork and cook for 5 minutes. Drain off the excess fat. Stir in the beans and their liquid, and add the ham bone, bacon, salt, and the peppers. Bring the mixture to a boil, then reduce the heat and simmer partially covered for about 3 hours, or until the beans are very soft. Check the pot from time to time, and if the beans seem dry, add up to 1 cup of chicken stock.

4. Remove the ham bone or ham hocks. When cool enough to handle, cut off any remaining meat (skin too), chop, and return to the pot. During the last 30 minutes or so of cooking, stir frequently and mash the softest beans against the sides of the pan to thicken the sauce. Taste for seasonings, add what is needed, and serve at once. Place the hot rice in individual bowls, top with the remaining ½ cup of scallions, and serve with the beans.

Serves 4 to 6.

Country Ham and Potato Casserole

3 or 4 medium potatoes, peeled and sliced very thin
1 onion, sliced very thin
1 pound ham, sliced thin or diced
1 recipe White Sauce (see below)
½ cup grated Cheddar cheese
1 tablespoon chopped parsley

This dish can be made with a milder-flavored "city ham," but that's pretty bland, to my taste. It's much better made with "country ham."

≈

1. Butter an ovenproof casserole dish and line the bottom with a layer of potatoes. Top them with a layer of onions, then slices of ham. Repeat the layers until you run out of potatoes, onions, and ham. Place the last layer of ham neatly around the edge of the casserole, leaving a space in the middle.

2. Make the White Sauce. Melt the butter in a saucepan, and blend in the flour, stirring. Stir constantly as you pour milk slowly into the mixture. Cook until

thickened. Add as much salt and pepper as you like. Pour the White Sauce over the dish, shaking the casserole gently so that the sauce mixes thoroughly through the layers. Put the grated cheese in the center of the casserole and sprinkle the surface of the dish with parsley.

3. Cover the dish with a tent of aluminum foil and bake in a preheated 350-degree oven for 30 minutes. Remove the foil and bake for another 30 minutes. Serve with beans or greens and corn bread.

Serves 4.

WHITE SAUCE

3 tablespoons butter
3 tablespoons flour
1½ cups milk
Salt and pepper to taste

Pork and Bean Casserole

Served up with a simple salad and perhaps corn bread or Scrapple Sticks (page 147), this makes a hearty family meal.

≈

1. In a heavy 3-to-4-quart saucepan, bring about 4 cups of water to a boil over high heat. Drop in the beans and bring to a brisk boil. Cover, turn off the heat, and let the beans soak for 1 hour. Drain, and cover with fresh water. Boil for 15 minutes, then drain.

2. Preheat the oven to 325 degrees. Put the beans, ham bone, pork skin, carrots, onion, and seasonings into a casserole dish. Pour on the stock. Cover and bake for 2 hours, adding more stock if the dish becomes too dry. Cut the meat off the bone, dice it and the pork skin, and add to the casserole. Stir the meat into the beans and heat through. Taste for seasoning and add more if necessary.

Serves 4.

½ pound (1 cup) beans (Great Northern, haricot, or pinto)
A meaty leftover ham bone
Pork skin, if desired
2 carrots, diced
1 large onion, chopped
1 teaspoon chili powder
½ teaspoon Tabasco sauce
½ teaspoon curry powder
Salt and pepper to taste (easy on the salt if the ham is very salty)
1 cup chicken stock

The Oldest Meat Company

The oldest company now in the meat business is believed to be Wm. Underwood Co., Westwood, Massachusetts. This meat-canning firm was started in 1822 on Boston's Russia Wharf as a mustard-and-pickle canner by William Underwood, a recent immigrant from England. Meat and fish sauces were among the early products. In 1846, Underwood erected a factory in Charlestown, Massachusetts, and also acquired a cannery in Eastport, Maine.

During the 1849 California Gold Rush, advertisements in Western newspapers proclaimed the merits of Underwood meats hermetically sealed in cans and guaranteed to keep for five years in any climate. The 1861–65 Civil War stimulated the entire canning industry as both sides sought canned products to keep their soldiers fed. In 1867, the Underwood firm began canning highly seasoned "deviled entrements," including the deviled ham that became the mainstay of the business. The company's Red Devil trademark was introduced in 1868.

Ham and Vermicelli Carbonara

This recipe was inspired by a trip to the Emilia-Romagna area in Italy, where I studied with Marcella Hazan. In Bologna they would use prosciutto, but leftover country ham works great, and it's cheaper!

- ¼ pound diced bacon
- 2 teaspoons olive oil
- 2 teaspoons butter
- 2 cloves minced garlic
- ¼ cup chopped onion
- 2 cups thin julienne strips of ham
- 1 8-ounce package vermicelli, cooked
- ½ cup grated Parmesan or Romano cheese
- ¼ cup chopped parsley
- ½ teaspoon salt
- ¼ teaspoon black pepper
- 6 eggs
- ¼ cup sliced ripe black olives

≈

1. Brown the bacon in a heavy skillet over medium-high heat until it is cooked but not crisp. Pour off the fat and set the bacon aside.

2. To the same pan add the oil, butter, garlic, onion, and ham. Sauté lightly over medium heat. Cook the pasta in boiling water, and drain. Add the cooked vermicelli, bacon, cheese, half of the parsley (save the other half for garnish), salt, and pepper; stir to mix well. Turn the heat to low.

3. Beat the eggs and pour over the pasta mixture. Toss quickly to coat the pasta evenly. Add the olives and toss again to mix them in. Transfer to a warm serving platter and sprinkle with the remaining chopped parsley. Serve immediately.

Serves 4 to 6.

Ham and Chili Quiche

1 cup chopped cooked ham
1 3-ounce can chopped green chilies, drained
1 cup grated Monterey Jack cheese with jalapeño
2 tablespoons finely chopped onion
½ teaspoon dried cumin
¼ teaspoon ground coriander
An unbaked 9-inch pie shell
1 cup milk
3 eggs

"Gaar-rahn-tee" (Cajun for "guarantee")—real men do eat quiche, when it is as hearty and delicious as this one.

≈

1. In a bowl toss together the ham, chilies, cheese, onion, cumin, and coriander. Arrange the mixture evenly in the pie shell.

2. Whisk together the milk and eggs and pour over the mixture. Bake in a preheated 375-degree oven for 40 minutes, or until a knife inserted midway between center and outer edge comes out clean.

Serves 6.

Curried Ham Salad

¾ pound boneless ham, cut into thin strips (about 2 cups)
1 cup diced celery
½ cup golden raisins
1 11-ounce can mandarin-orange segments, drained
¼ cup dry-roasted peanuts
½ cup mayonnaise
2 teaspoons lime juice
½ to 1 teaspoon curry powder

Here is a great dish for a summer luncheon that can also be a meal in itself. The curry may seem an unusual addition, but it adds a nice zip and makes the dish very big in flavor.

≈

1. In a large mixing bowl combine the ham, celery, raisins, mandarin orange, and peanuts. Arrange the mixture on individual salad plates.

2. Mix together the mayonnaise, lime juice, and curry powder and spoon the dressing over the salad.

Serves 4.

Ham Slices with Vinaigrette

This is another ham salad that is a meal in itself. The hot crisp ham on a bed of greens with onions makes an interesting and different dish.

- 8 small thin cooked ham slices (about 1 pound)
- ½ cup flour, seasoned with salt and pepper to taste
- ¼ cup milk
- 1 egg, beaten
- 2 cups fine fresh bread crumbs
- 2 tablespoons vegetable oil
- 4 teaspoons red-wine vinegar
- 1 tablespoon Dijon mustard
- 2 tablespoons olive oil
- 1 large head romaine lettuce, chopped
- ½ small red onion, peeled and sliced

≈

1. Dredge the ham slices in the flour. In a bowl beat together the milk and egg. Dip the floured ham in the egg wash, then coat with bread crumbs.
2. Heat the vegetable oil over high heat in a large skillet. Brown the slices for 2 to 3 minutes, turning once. Remove and keep warm.
3. Whisk together the vinegar, mustard, and olive oil. Toss half of the dressing with the lettuce and onion slices and arrange on a platter. Top with the ham. Serve the remaining dressing on the side.

Serves 4.

Jellied Ham with Parsley

This is a nice addition to a buffet table, and a slice served on a lettuce leaf dressed with an herb vinaigrette makes a great first course for a dinner party.

- 2 envelopes unflavored gelatin
- ¼ cup chilled white wine
- 2¾ cups defatted chicken broth
- 1 bay leaf
- ½ teaspoon black pepper
- 2 tablespoons minced onion
- ½ teaspoon dried thyme

≈

1. In a medium bowl mix the gelatin with the chilled wine. In a medium saucepan put the broth, bay leaf, pepper, onion, and thyme. Bring to a boil, lower the heat, and simmer for 10 minutes.
2. Strain the broth into the gelatin mixture and stir until the gelatin is completely dissolved. Stir in the lemon juice. Chill, stirring occasionally, until the mixture is the consistency of unbeaten egg whites.

(recipe continues)

Jellied Ham with Parsley
(cont.)

2 tablespoons lemon juice
5 cups cubed cooked ham
1 cup finely chopped parsley, plus sprigs for garnish

3. Mix together the ham and parsley, then fold into the gelatin mixture. Place in a rinsed 2-quart mold or loaf pan; chill until firm. Garnish with additional parsley sprigs.

Serves 8 to 10.

Ham Croquettes

Croquettes can be formed into small cylinders, ovals, rounds, or simply patties. I find that an ice-cream scoop is a good tool for the job.

- 2 cups chopped cooked ham
- 1 small onion, finely chopped
- 2 sprigs parsley, finely chopped
- ¾ cup cream
- 1½ cups cracker meal
- 2 eggs
- Salt and pepper to taste
- Oil for deep-frying

≈

1. In a mixing bowl, mix together the ham, onion, and parsley. Add the cream slowly, mixing well. Add 1 cup cracker meal and 1 beaten egg. Season with salt and pepper and mix thoroughly. Shape the mixture into croquettes. Heat oil in a large saucepan to 375 degrees.
2. Beat the second egg. Dip the croquettes in the egg and then roll them in the remaining cracker meal. Deep-fry until golden brown.

Serves 4 to 6.

VARIATION

Ham and Cheese Croquettes Use corn flakes in place of the cracker meal and add ½ cup shredded Cheddar cheese to the mixture.

The Best Bacon

If our pioneering forefathers had to rely on the supermarket bacon of today as the staple of the long trek westward, they wouldn't have made it much past Pittsburgh. No meat in America has suffered more from modern technology than bacon. The insipid watered-down stuff that is labeled "bacon" today is as far removed from real bacon as a horsefly is from the horse it rode in on.

The Best Bacon (continued)

Most of the bacon that you find in today's meat cases is "pumped" bacon. What that means is that the curing solution—made up of water, salt, sugar, sodium phosphate (to hold the water in), and sodium nitrite—is pumped into the pork belly with a machine made up of an arsenal of hollow needles that quickly distribute the cure through the meat and accelerate the curing process.

If you have never tasted good old-fashioned "dry-cured" bacon, you have never tasted real bacon. It takes a lot longer to make, but the end result was worth the wait. Dry-cured bacon is not pumped full of water in the curing process. Just the opposite, in fact. To make dry-cured bacon the old-fashioned way, the curing ingredients—salt, sugar, and sodium nitrate (in the old days they called it saltpeter)—were rubbed into the meat. It was left to cure for a couple of weeks before being smoked with hickory or oak, applewood or corn cobs, depending on the packer and what wood was available. An old pamphlet from the University of Kentucky Cooperative Extension Service describes the process:

> *Dry-curing bacon—an excellent sweet bacon can be made by using a mixture of 3 pounds of salt, 1¾ pounds sugar and 3 ounces of salt peter per 100 pounds of trimmed sides. Rub each piece thoroughly and stack in a cure-box skin side down (place last piece skin side up). Leave in cure two weeks. Remove, wash in lukewarm water, allow to dry, smoke and store in a cool dry place.*

The bacon that results from such a process doesn't shrivel up to nothing in the frying pan as the water evaporates from it. Most of the water has been drawn out of the meat rather than pumped in. When you've finished cooking dry-cured bacon and the room is filled with that wonderful mouth-watering aroma, you still have meat in the pan.

Dry-cured bacon is not the easiest stuff to find these days, but it *is* still available. There are several producers of good old-fashioned country hams and bacon in various parts of the country that make dry-cured bacon available by mail order. If you'd like to try some of the best bacon in America, you might want to write or call for some catalogues (see page 131 and the appendix).

SCRAPPLE

One of my favorite breakfast dishes on a cold winter morning was scrapple. Scrapple was made at "hog-killin' time" from the pig's head. It was simmered in a big pot until the meat fell from the bone. The meat was then chopped fine and put back into the broth in which it was boiled, and the whole works was thickened with cornmeal or buckwheat and seasoned with spices and herbs. When the "mash" was the consistency of thick mush, it was put into loaf pans and cooled, to be sliced later and fried crisp for breakfast. It was served with hot maple syrup.

Not many of us have a hog's head to work with these days, but good scrapple can be made from other cuts of pork more readily available at your local supermarket. If you're one of the growing number of Americans up early and out, not milking cows but jogging, you may enjoy coming home to a good country breakfast.

Basic Scrapple Recipe

Scrapple (the name comes from "scraps") is a combination of cornmeal and pork, cooked together with seasonings. The Pennsylvania Dutch are famous for it.

- 3 pounds pork with the bone (a rib-end piece of loin works best)
- 3 quarts water
- 2 cups yellow cornmeal
- 2 teaspoons salt
- 1½ teaspoons dried marjoram
- 1 teaspoon dried sage
- ½ teaspoon dried thyme
- Dash ground cloves
- 1 medium onion, finely chopped (optional)

≈

1. Simmer the pork in the water in a good-sized covered pot until the meat easily falls off the bone. Do not let boil. (With today's tender pork the cooking should take no more than 1 to 1½ hours.) Strain off and reserve the broth. Remove all the meat from the bones and chop fine, or use your food processor or meat grinder.

2. Measure out 2 quarts of the broth. If necessary, add chicken stock to make up that amount. Bring the broth to the boil and slowly add 2 cups of cornmeal, whisking. Cook the mixture until it is a thick mush, about 4 to 5 minutes, stirring constantly.

3. Add the chopped meat and seasonings and stir well. Stir in the finely chopped onion if you like. Pour the hot mixture into a 9-inch loaf pan that has been rinsed in cold water. Let stand in the refrigerator until cold and

Uncle Sam Was a Butcher

The most famous meat packer in the history of America—at least the packer with the most famous nickname—has to be Samuel Wilson of Troy, New York. Troy is on the Hudson River, north of Albany. During the War of 1812, Wilson's company, E & S Wilson Co., supplied meat to the soldiers at a nearby training camp. To his friends and neighbors in Troy, Mr. Wilson was known affectionately as "Uncle Sam." Because "U.S." was stamped on each barrel that was delivered to the army camp, the meat was referred to—in fond jest—as "Uncle Sam's beef" or "Uncle Sam's pork." The term spread, and soon any government property stamped "U.S." was said to belong to "Uncle Sam."

Cartoonists picked up on the idea, and by the time of Wilson's death, in 1854, they were drawing their conceptions of Uncle Sam as the personification of the United States government. Cartoonist Thomas Nast added the pointed beard, starry vest, striped pants, and top hat to his caricature to create a representation that enjoyed wide popularity in the 1860s and beyond. A century later, on September 15, 1961, the 87th Congress adopted a resolution officially recognizing Samuel Wilson—a butcher—as progenitor of the nation's symbol, Uncle Sam.

Basic Scrapple Recipe *(cont.)*

firm, then remove the loaf from the pan and cover with plastic wrap. This recipe makes about 3 pounds of scrapple, which won't go to waste. It keeps nicely for a week or two, but I bet it will be gone by then.

4. To serve, slice the scrapple into ¼-inch-thick slices and fry in butter until crisp and brown. Serve with hot maple syrup.

Serves 6 to 8.

City Slicker Scrapple Sticks

This recipe doesn't qualify as a "true" scrapple—it's really just a meaty corn bread—but my family loves it and it is a lot easier to make than the kind with the pig's head. Serve warm with apple butter for a breakfast reminiscent of "back on the farm."

- 1 pound bulk pork sausage
- 1 cup peeled and diced tart apple
- 2 tablespoons butter
- 1 cup cornmeal
- 1 cup flour
- ¼ cup sugar
- 4 teaspoons baking powder
- ½ teaspoon salt
- 1 egg, beaten
- ¾ cup milk
- ¼ cup butter, melted

≈

1. Fry the sausage until brown and crumbly; drain well. Set aside. Sauté the diced apple in the 2 tablespoons of butter until slightly soft. Sift together the cornmeal, flour, sugar, baking powder, and salt into a large mixing bowl. Stir in the browned pork sausage and the diced cooked apple. Add the egg, milk, and melted butter; mix well.

2. Spoon the mixture into buttered corn-stick pans or muffin tins. Bake in a preheated 400-degree oven for 20 to 25 minutes. Take the pan from the oven and let rest on a rack for 10 minutes before removing the sticks or muffins.

Makes 14.

Lamb

≈

THE HISTORY OF LAMB IN AMERICA

Spanish padres and English pioneers brought the first sheep to America. Spaniards first came to the New World on a wave of gold fever. Ships bearing conquistadors and their followers also carried the first herds of domestic sheep, important sources of food and clothing for life in the New World.

Gold hunting did not prove profitable to everyone, but animal husbandry did. By the middle of the sixteenth century, Spanish aristocrats ruled over flourishing sheep ranches throughout Central America. Despite the profits found in livestock, however, the Spaniards' gold fever grew as Indians tantalized them with tales of fantastic wealth lying in the North.

Such a tale—that of Cíbola, the legendary Seven Golden Cities—lured one of the first major Spanish expeditions into the heart of North America. In 1540, Francisco Vásquez de Coronado gathered a hunting party of soldiers and servants, a reported five thousand sheep, and hundreds of other livestock to join him in his northward quest for the legendary cities. But by 1542, Coronado, luckless in his search for gold, had retreated back to Mexico, leaving behind some sheep in the care of two Franciscan friars who remained.

Long after the Spanish aristocrats lost their faith in tales of gold, Spanish padres were still seeking to convert the Indians. Using sheep as a major source of meat and clothing, the padres built and expanded their missions for the next three centuries. By the 1800s, wealthy missions dotted the landscapes from New Mexico to California.

While the padres built missions and baptized Indians in the West, the first Pilgrims introduced domestic sheep to the East Coast of North America, where sheep raising soon grew into a vital industry. Colonial authorities, seeking to stimulate the industry, often exempted sheep from taxes and gave shepherds exclusive rights on part of the common pasturelands. By the middle of the seventeenth century, sheep had become an important, and growing, business for colonists. However, these sheep were mainly raised for their wool. As the settlers moved west during the 1800s, they took with them flocks of sheep from the Eastern Seaboard. Most of the sheep were of English breeding, more suited to producing meat than wool.

By the mid-nineteenth century, pioneer shepherds were bringing their sheep onto the vast grasslands of New Mexico, Texas, and California. Here, the flocks of the pioneers met up with those established by the padres. One of the legendary sheepherders was "Uncle Dick" Wooten, a trapper, fighter of Indians, buffalo hunter, and sheep trader. In 1852, he performed an incredible feat. He left Taos, New Mexico, with nine thousand sheep and crossed the deserts and Indian lands in what is now New Mexico, Arizona, and southern California. A year later, he arrived in Sacramento, having lost only one hundred animals along the way. At the time, his eighty-nine hundred sheep were worth $50,000—a price gratefully paid by men who were feeding the miners in California's gold fields.

The last half of the nineteenth century ushered in a new era for the sheep industry. First, the westward tide of sheep reversed itself. Ranches in and beyond the Rocky Mountains were seeking good breeding stock, so the shepherds of the Pacific coast began to trail their sheep eastward across the deserts and mountains to reach the high ranges.

About the same time that sheep numbers grew in the mountain region, the sheep-raising industry's character began to change. Industrial development on the East Coast brought in masses of immigrants accustomed to eating mutton and lamb. Soon farm-flock producers found meat more profitable than wool, and they started to raise sheep more for meat value than for wool. This changing emphasis did not take long to reach the West. By the end of the nineteenth century, the flocks moving from west to east were mostly headed for fattening and slaughter beyond the Continental Divide.

At that time, the nation's shepherds outnumbered the cowboys. (It wasn't until 1885 that the United States' cattle herds grew larger than the sheep-and-lamb population.) But as the shepherds moved their flocks into the Western rangelands in the last half of the 1800s, they found themselves the center of attention in one of the bloodiest battles of the Old West. The prized rangeland was mostly in unfenced public domain, and cattlemen, who had come first to the area, believed they had prior rights to the grass. Furthermore, the cowboys claimed: "Everything in front of a sheep is eaten and everything behind is killed."

Unfortunately, overgrazing and overcrowding gave some truth to this statement. Sheep can thrive where cattle cannot, and often shepherds would graze their flocks where the grass for cattle had given out. In these areas the sheep were allowed to eat vegetation to the roots, leaving behind a wasteland.

The old Western practice earned the epithet "hoofed locusts" for the sheep. And cattlemen tried every method possible to drive the hated shepherds out. Gangs of cowboys would hold shooting sprees on flocks of sheep. Whole herds were driven off cliffs. Dynamite charges were thrown into the closely held or corralled flocks.

A measure of peace came to the cattle wars in 1906, when the federal government set aside the National Forests, thus establishing definite government control over the summer ranges. But the conflict still simmered until 1934, when the Taylor Grazing Act corrected some remaining abuses and set up a firm system of control over all grazing lands.

Soon after entering World War I, Washington mounted an "Eat No Lamb" campaign, designed both to up wool production and to increase sheep numbers. Unfortunately, sheep men claim, the propaganda against eating lamb had an adverse effect—creating a history of prejudice against lamb that survives in many parts of America to this day.

It's interesting to note that, throughout the rest of the world, lamb is one of the very few meats against which there are almost no prejudices. Beef is not consumed in India because of religious taboos. Pork is not eaten by followers of the traditional Jewish faith, nor are the hindquarters of beef. Moslems do not eat pork. But fewer prejudices exist against lamb than against any other meat. Lamb is, to some, a symbol of purity—a reputation based at least partially in fact: fewer lambs are condemned by government inspection than any other class of meat animal.

Yet here in America, particularly in Middle America, there are, it seems, certain prejudices. They stem, I think, from the range wars of the Old West, perpetuated in the minds of our youth for generations by silver-screen cowboys dating back to Tom Mix and Hopalong Cassidy. "Why, those critters ate the grass too short, fouled the water holes . . . !"

We do not find much, if any, mutton (meat from an older animal) in the meat cases of America. What we have available to us is lamb. Mutton has a strong odor, but the only thing that can cause odor in lamb is cooking it at too high a temperature. Lamb fat is classed as "hard" fat and burns at a lower temperature than other animal fat. Anything that's burned smells bad!

If you fall into that category of folks who don't like lamb for some reason, chances are the real reason is, you've never tried it! A very large percentage of the people who don't like lamb have *never* tried it. Try it! There is no better meat.

For recipes that call for grilling, broiling, or frying lamb at a high temperature, be sure to trim the excess fat from the lamb. When roasting lamb, after the initial searing called for in some recipes, turn the oven temperature down to 325 to 350 degrees. It probably won't make the meat taste any better, but it will minimize the odor that some find objectionable.

WHAT IS LAMB?

To qualify as lamb in the American marketplace, the animal can be no more than twelve months of age. The average is usually half of that: most lamb reaches market at six months, or even younger. At that age, it's all tender. It hasn't lived long enough to get tough.

Lambs are, however, getting larger. The average dressed weight of all the lambs that came into the market when I was a kid in the 1930s was thirty-eight pounds. In 1969, the average dressed weight was fifty-one pounds—that's over 25 percent more lamb for your money, since most of the added weight is meat,

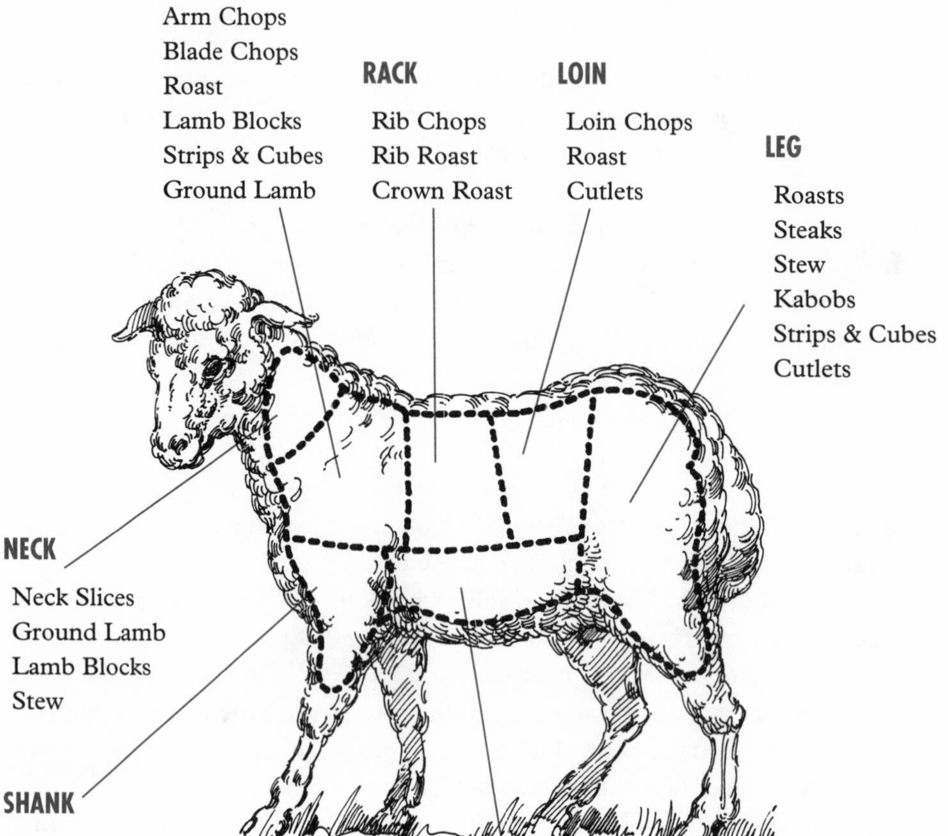
SHOULDER
Arm Chops
Blade Chops
Roast
Lamb Blocks
Strips & Cubes
Ground Lamb
RACK
Rib Chops
Rib Roast
Crown Roast
LOIN
Loin Chops
Roast
Cutlets
LEG
Roasts
Steaks
Stew
Kabobs
Strips & Cubes
Cutlets
NECK
Neck Slices
Ground Lamb
Lamb Blocks
Stew
SHANK
Roast
Grill
Braise
Ground Lamb
BREAST
Lamb Spare Ribs
Scotch Chops
Riblets
Ground Lamb
Stuffed Rolled Breast

not bone or fat. And they are still growing; it's not at all unusual to get lambs these days that weigh in around sixty pounds dressed weight.

The increase in the size of lambs over the years is no accident. In all areas of the meat industry great effort is being made to improve the genetics of meat-producing animals so that they will reach market weight sooner, consume less feed in the process, and, it is hoped, provide us with more meat for less money. The heavier, meatier, more tender lamb that comes to market these days is a good example of what better breeding stock, or efficient use of feed and selective crossbreeding, can do. A seven-pound-plus leg may have been mutton back in the days when Grandma was a girl, but today it's simply a bigger, better leg of lamb. There is very little difference in the amount of bone and waste from a five-pound leg of lamb and from a seven-pound leg of lamb. The major difference is two pounds more meat.

LAMB CHOPS, STEAKS, AND CUTLETS

Lamb chops are small cuts of lamb, generally one inch thick, taken from the loin, rib, or shoulder.

Lamb steaks are somewhat larger cuts, also usually one inch thick, cut from the leg and sirloin section.

Lamb chops and steaks with the bone removed, cut about the same thickness, are often called "medallions" or "noisettes."

Lamb cutlets are thin (¼-to-½-inch) cuts of lamb, usually boneless, cut from the leg, loin, or rib section of the carcass. Often, because it makes an attractive presentation, the long thin rib bone is left on the cutlets taken from the rib section.

In several of the following recipes, any cut of chop, steak, or cutlet can be used interchangeably.

Lamb Seasons

For years, the first Monday in March marked the beginning of spring in this country as far as lamb was concerned. Traditionally, only those lambs slaughtered between March 1 and October 1 could be stamped "Genuine Spring Lamb," according to regulations of the USDA.

The term "spring lamb" is outdated. It may have had some meaning fifty years ago, when most lambs were born in the fall and marketed in the spring, but the lamb industry has changed, and the term "spring lamb" is about as archaic and misleading as "spring chicken." We have delicious top-quality lamb available to us all year long.

The marketing season for lamb varies in different areas of the country, depending largely upon climate. For example, in California, Arizona, and certain sections of the South, and to some extent in the Northwest, where the climate is fairly mild, lambs are born in the fall and early winter. These become what is referred to in the industry as the "early lamb crop" and are ready for market in the early spring.

Most lambs, however, are born in the winter and in the spring. These lambs are raised in the high country of Colorado, Idaho, and Montana. They stay in the high country during the spring and summer to take advantage of the lush vegetation available for a period of five or six months.

In numbers, Eastern flocks do not compare to the large Western flocks, but they still provide an economic livelihood for hundreds of Eastern farmers. Eastern pastures from Maine to Florida are dotted with prize-winning flocks that produce some of America's finest lamb—winter, summer, spring, and fall.

Pan-Broiled Lamb Chops

Lamb chops at their best are simply pan-broiled and served with a slice of broiled tomato or a vegetable sauté. They can be broiled in the oven, but a heavy-duty cast-iron skillet works best, I think. Garnish—use tomatoes, if you like, with a little finely chopped parsley and garlic.

8 loin or rib chops, cut approximately ¾ inch thick, well trimmed of fat
Olive oil
Salt and freshly ground pepper to taste

≈

1. Rub the chops on both sides with a bit of olive oil and sprinkle with salt and pepper.
2. Heat a heavy skillet until a drop of water flicked into it sizzles; brown the chops quickly on both sides; reduce the heat and finish cooking, allowing about 2 to 3 minutes on each side. Serve 2 chops for each person.

Serves 4.

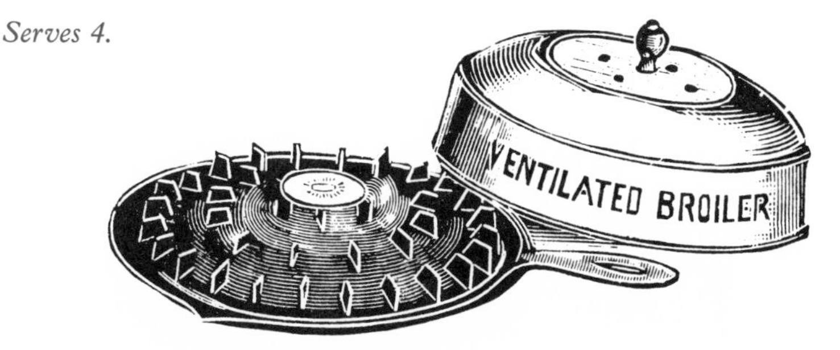

VARIATION

Pan-Broiled Kidney Chops Loin lamb chops used to be available with the kidney still attached. They were wonderful pan-broiled. They are not available now. The USDA requires removal of the kidney as part of the inspection process. But you can still enjoy kidney chops in spite of the rules. Ask the butcher to bone the loin chops and wrap a slice of kidney in the center of each. Wrap a slice of bacon around each chop and secure with a toothpick to hold it all together. Proceed as in Pan-Broiled Lamb Chops (above) for a special treat.

Lamb Chops with Peppercorn Crust

- 8 rib chops, well trimmed
- 1 cup flour combined with 1 tablespoon salt
- 2 eggs, beaten with ½ cup water (egg wash)
- 1 cup bread crumbs
- 1 tablespoon freshly ground black peppercorns
- 1 tablespoon freshly ground white peppercorns
- 1 tablespoon freshly ground green peppercorns (optional, but good)
- ½ cup oil for frying

"Fat," I know, has become a forbidden word in our contemporary gastronomic society, but lamb chops, fried crisp as they are here, are well worth the guilt feelings they may cause. So skip dessert. I first had these cooked in a black iron skillet over a campfire by a sheep man in Mendocino County, California, named Rod Shippy. Rod fried his in rendered lamb fat. I use peanut oil only because lamb fat is hard to find.

Rib chops make by far the most appealing presentation in this recipe. It is important that all the fat be trimmed, leaving just the lean rib-eye with the attached rib bone—you don't want to eat the fat, just cook with it. Specialty and gourmet shops carry green peppercorns, immature pepper berries that are less pungent than dried ones.

≈

1. Dredge the chops in the flour-and-salt mixture. Shake off the excess. Dip them in the egg wash. Mix the bread crumbs with the crushed peppercorns and press the mixture firmly on the chops.

2. Fry in the oil (heated to 350 degrees) until golden brown to achieve rare to medium-rare doneness, about 2 to 3 minutes on each side.

Serves 4.

Lamb Shoulder Chops with Sour Cream

Lamb steaks from the leg or sirloin can be substituted for the shoulder chops in this dish.

≈

- 6 lamb shoulder chops, 1 to 1½ inches thick
- ¾ cup tarragon wine vinegar
- ¼ cup olive oil
- 1 teaspoon dried dill weed
- 1 teaspoon salt
- ¼ teaspoon black pepper

SOUR CREAM SAUCE

- 1 pint sour cream
- ½ teaspoon dried dill weed
- 1 teaspoon chopped fresh tarragon leaves or ½ teaspoon crumbled dried tarragon leaves
- ¼ teaspoon salt
- ⅛ teaspoon freshly ground black pepper

1. Place the lamb chops in a glass baking dish. Mix together the vinegar, oil, dill, salt, and pepper and pour over the lamb. Cover and marinate overnight, turning the chops at least once.

2. Make the Sour Cream Sauce. In the top of a double boiler mix the sauce ingredients together. Heat gently over simmering water. Do not let boil, or the sauce will separate. (Makes about 2 cups.)

3. Heat the broiler to its highest point. Broil 6 to 7 inches from source of heat for 6 to 8 minutes on each side, or until the chops are done as you like them. Brush frequently with marinade during cooking. Serve with the Sour Cream Sauce.

Serves 6.

Greek Lamb Steaks

- 4 lamb steaks, sirloin or round, about ¼ to ½ pound each
- Grated peel and juice of 2 lemons
- 4 tablespoons butter, softened
- 3 teaspoons minced parsley
- 3 small garlic cloves, minced
- Salt and pepper to taste

Serve these with a rice pilaf and a Greek salad of tomatoes, cucumbers, and feta cheese.

≈

1. Make incisions in the lamb steaks and stuff them with bits of lemon peel. Pour the juice of 1 lemon over the steaks. Let them stand for an hour or so at room temperature.

2. Meanwhile, make an herb butter by beating together the butter, parsley, a bit of the lemon peel, and just a drop of lemon juice.

3. In a large skillet over medium heat, melt half of the butter mixture. Add the minced garlic and the lamb steaks. Cook for 5 to 6 minutes on each side for medium rare. Season with salt and pepper and place a spoonful of the remaining herb butter on each steak.

Serves 4.

Italian Lamb and Vegetable Dinner

- 12 loin or rib lamb chops
- 2 tablespoons chopped fresh oregano or 2 teaspoons dried oregano
- 1 teaspoon salt
- ½ teaspoon black pepper
- 4 tablespoons olive oil
- 3 small zucchini, sliced

This simple, hearty lamb dinner has been a favorite of ours since my wife and I visited Italy for the first time, twenty years ago. I've been trying to learn to be Italian ever since. My kids say this is about as close as I've come.

≈

1. Sprinkle the lamb chops with the oregano, salt, and pepper. Brown the chops in 3 tablespoons of the olive oil for about 4 to 5 minutes on each side. Remove and keep warm.

2. Heat the remaining tablespoon of olive oil. Sauté the zucchini, onions, and garlic until they are tender, about 10 minutes. Add the tomatoes and basil; cook 2 minutes more. Toss together with the pasta.

3. Arrange the pasta on a warm plate with the lamb chops.

Serves 6.

- 2 medium red onions, sliced
- 1 clove garlic, minced
- 3 medium tomatoes, cut in wedges
- 1 tablespoon chopped fresh basil or ¾ teaspoon dried basil
- 1½ pounds linguini, cooked and drained

Lamb Chops with Dried Cherries

For years my wife, Neva, has had different dried fruits—cherries among them—shipped to us from a "crack-seed" shop (Hawaiian expression for a store specializing in preserved and dried fruit) in her hometown of Honolulu. Now they are available in fine supermarkets everywhere. They go very well with lamb.

- ½ cup boiling water
- ½ cup dried cherries
- 4 lamb chops
- Salt and pepper to taste
- ½ cup red wine
- ¼ teaspoon crushed fresh mint

≈

1. Pour the boiling water over the cherries and let stand while the chops are cooking.

2. Season the chops with salt and pepper and pan-fry them in a nonstick skillet to desired doneness. Remove from the skillet and keep warm.

3. Add the cherries in their liquid and the red wine to the skillet. Scrape up any browned bits of lamb from the pan. Bring the liquid to a boil and reduce it by half. Stir in the crushed mint. Serve the chops topped with the cherry sauce.

Serves 2.

Lamb Rib Chops with Tarragon Mousse

TARRAGON MOUSSE

2 medium chicken breasts (trimmed, and with skin removed)
½ cup fresh tarragon leaves
½ teaspoon salt
½ teaspoon black pepper
1 egg white
1 cup heavy cream
2 tablespoons dry vermouth

12 2-ounce lamb rib chops, "Frenched" (completely trimmed and with bones scraped clean)
4 tablespoons butter
4 tablespoons olive oil
Salt and pepper
½ pound caul fat*

* Caul fat is the thin, fatty membrane that lines the abdominal cavity of pigs and sheep. The caul resembles a lacy net and is used to wrap forcemeat. The fatty membrane melts during the cooking process. Caul fat can be ordered from your local butcher.

This recipe is based on a dish that I had as part of a fabulous seven-course dinner prepared by Chef John Johnston at the Greenbrier Hotel in White Sulphur Springs, West Virginia. It's marvelous for elegant entertaining, because it can be prepared ahead up to the point of encasing the chops with caul fat, then refrigerating them to be finished off when needed. It's kind of a complicated recipe, and caul fat may not be easily available, but if you have the time, order the caul fat and enjoy. It's worth it!

≈

1. Make the Tarragon Mousse. Dice the chicken, place in a food processor with the tarragon leaves, and process for 30 seconds. Add the salt and pepper and blend for 30 seconds more. Slowly drizzle in the egg white and then the cream. Pulse to combine. Remove from the bowl and beat in the vermouth. Taste for seasoning and add more salt and pepper as needed.

2. Quickly brown the lamb chops on each side in half the butter and olive oil. Season with salt and pepper and allow to cool.

3. When the chops are cool, place 1 tablespoon of Tarragon Mousse on top of each and wrap with the caul fat to encase the mousse. Gently pan-fry only on the meat side in the remaining butter and oil. Place the chops, mousse side up, in a preheated 350-degree oven to finish, 3 to 4 minutes.

Serves 6.

Put a Little Lamb in the Freezer

Lamb freezes well, so if you like lamb you can often save a little money if you put a little in the freezer.

There are several ways to do that. You can simply take advantage of the specials on lamb, buying a leg or two when the price is right, or a few extra chops when they are on sale. But if you have the freezer space, buy a whole lamb. A whole lamb provides a great variety of different meals, and most places that sell carcass lamb will cut to your specifications. Following are a few ideas for having a lamb cut to provide all manner of great meals for months to come.

A carcass of lamb will yield two legs (the front legs are called shanks). Have the butcher remove three or four sirloin steaks from each leg, leaving you with two three-quarter legs. These are the classic "legs of lamb," marvelous roasts for special occasions. You may want one leg boned and rolled to provide additional variety.

Have a loin section of lamb cut into chops as thick or as thin as you like. The loin is the tenderest section and yields mouth-watering chops. Depending on how thick you have them cut, you can get twelve to sixteen chops from the loin. With the six or eight sirloin steaks that were cut from the leg, you have a good collection of lamb chops and steaks for a lot of great meals.

The other loin can be cut for chops, or left whole for a roast, or boned-out and then cut up as you please for steaks and cutlets.

The rib section of the lamb yields two "racks," each with seven or eight ribs. These, I think, are best left whole. Have the butcher remove the "chine bone" from them so you can either roast them whole for a rack-of-lamb roast or cut them into chops yourself.

The two shoulders of lamb can be cut into chops if you like, but I would recommend having them boned and rolled. They make better roasts than they do chops, and, should you decide that you want a pot of lamb stew, you can easily cut one into cubes yourself.

The shanks can be left whole, or they and the neck can be cut into cubes with the bone left in for a meal or two of the most flavorful lamb stew that you will ever taste.

Put a Little Lamb in the Freezer (continued)

The breast can be trimmed for lamb ribs for the barbecue, or cut into tidbits for braising. Have any trimmings ground into ground "lamburger."

Have the cuts wrapped for the freezer in serving-size portions appropriate for your family, and you have in your freezer a treasure of good eating for months.

Hazelnut Lamb Cutlets

2 pounds boneless lamb cutlets, cut approximately ½ inch thick
½ cup flour mixed with ½ teaspoon salt and ¼ teaspoon pepper
1 cup milk
1 egg
½ cup finely crushed toasted hazelnuts*
½ cup freshly grated Parmesan cheese
¼ cup Rye Crisp crumbs
2 tablespoons butter
1 tablespoon olive oil

* Toast the hazelnuts in a 200-degree oven for 20 minutes before crushing them.

Here is a recipe that I got from another butcher, Stuart McGrath, an Englishman who sells packing-house equipment all over the world. He got it when he was cutting meat in the Pacific Northwest, where hazelnuts (filberts) are abundant. Hazelnuts must be toasted to develop their flavor.

≈

1. Trim all of the fat and any gristle from the lamb. Pound each cutlet to expand its diameter and reduce its thickness to about ¼ inch.

2. Dust the cutlets with the seasoned flour and dip each into a wash made by whipping the milk and egg together.

3. Mix the hazelnuts, Parmesan cheese, and Rye Crisp crumbs together. Coat both sides of each cutlet with the mixture, pressing the coating well into the meat.

4. Sauté the cutlets in the butter and olive oil over moderately high heat for only a couple of minutes on each side, until nicely browned. Serve immediately.

Serves 4 to 6.

Lemon-Honey Lamb Cutlets

The amount of lemon juice in this recipe makes a fairly tart sauce. You may want to start with half the quantity called for, adding more at the end to suit your own taste. These cutlets are great served with steamed asparagus spears, new potatoes, and carrots.

8 lamb cutlets
1 tablespoon olive oil
½ cup fresh lemon juice
1 teaspoon fresh tarragon leaves or ½ teaspoon dried tarragon

HONEY SAUCE

1 tablespoon honey
½ teaspoon salt
¼ teaspoon black pepper
1 teaspoon mustard

2 tablespoons butter

≈

1. Trim all the outer fat from the cutlets. Cook in a skillet in the olive oil for 3 to 6 minutes on each side, depending on the thickness of the cutlets. Remove them from the pan and pour off and discard the cooking juices.

2. Add the lemon juice and tarragon to the pan. Boil, stirring and scraping up the browned bits from the bottom and sides, until ¼ cup is left. Add the Honey Sauce ingredients and mix thoroughly. Swirl in the butter. Return the cutlets to the pan and heat through.

Serves 4.

LAMB ROASTS—LEG, RACK, ROLLED, AND STUFFED

A roasted leg of lamb makes a marvelous meal for entertaining family and friends. However, for the greatest success in cooking and carving there are a few don'ts and dos that you should be aware of.

Leg of Lamb Don'ts and Dos

Don't buy a full leg. The full leg of lamb has the hip section left intact, making it a pain to carve. It is also long and ungainly looking, and difficult to get in a roasting pan. To solve the problem, some butchers cut off the hind shank, making what is called an "American leg," or they cut the leg in half.

Don't buy an "American leg." It still has the hip section and is therefore no easier to carve than a full leg. And it doesn't look the way a leg of lamb should look.

Don't buy a half leg. At best, it's a bad buy. If you buy the sirloin half, you get all of the hip-section bone. If you buy the shank half, carving is easier but the best meat is on the other half.

Do buy a "short leg" (sometimes called a three-quarter leg). The short leg has the sirloin section with most of the hip bone removed, leaving a leg of lamb with a classic look to it that will also fit in most roasting pans. Have the butcher remove the tail bone and the "aitch bone," the small portion of the hip bone left in the three-quarter leg. With the aitch bone gone, carving the leg is so much easier. You may want to ask the butcher to cut an inch or so of meat away from the bone at the shank end (that's called "Frenching" the leg), to make a nice handle for carving. It's a good idea to tie a string around the leg at the sirloin end, to hold the meat firmly together where the aitch bone was removed.

So much for preparing the leg for the pan; now about the roasting.

Don't pay any attention to instructions that tell you to remove the "fell," a tissue-paper-like membrane covering the leg. To do so is totally unnecessary, as is removing any "gland" from the middle of the leg.

Don't roast a leg of lamb at a temperature above 350 degrees unless you have trimmed away most, if not all, of the fat. Lamb has what is termed "hard fat," which means that the fat burns at a lower degree of heat than most other fats. Keep the temperature low. I prefer 325 degrees. In some recipes the oven is preheated to 450 degrees to "jump-start" a roast, but the temperature is immediately or shortly lowered.

Don't cook a leg of lamb until well done! Even if you like your lamb well done, don't follow the instructions in most books that tell you to cook the meat to an internal temperature of 180 degrees. Meat that "well done" is bound to be dry and stringy.

Do roast a leg of lamb to an internal temperature of 135 degrees for rare, 145 for medium, and, if you must, no more than 165 for well done. Always let the leg rest on the cutting board for 10 minutes before carving.

The traditional way of carving a leg of lamb across the grain down to the bone, as recommended in most books, is unnecessarily cumbersome. My thanks to James Beard for introducing me to the French method of carving a leg. It is simple and neat and makes much nicer slices. Just hold the leg by the bone or put a fork into the meat of the leg bone and carve off nice thin slices, *with* the grain. Lamb is so young and tender that you needn't worry about the direction of the grain.

Neva's Honey-Glazed Lamb

My wife, Neva, does real magic with a leg of lamb, making what is left after a great meal of roast leg of lamb with honey glaze even *better* than a roast leg of lamb with honey glaze. Neva's Lamb Curry proves that there is a big difference between leftovers and "planned-overs." These are the recipes that made a lamb lover of my dad! We didn't tell him it was lamb until two days later, after he'd cleaned up the curry.

A 5-to-7-pound leg of lamb
1 teaspoon salt
½ teaspoon black pepper
½ cup honey
Water
6 tablespoons soy sauce

≈

1. Trim off as much of the fat as possible from the leg. Sprinkle on and rub in the salt and pepper. Place on a rack in a shallow roasting pan. Then, with a pastry brush, smear on the honey.

2. In the bottom of the pan, below the rack, pour about a quart of water, or enough to be ¾ inch deep. Put the leg, uncovered, in a preheated 450-degree oven for 30 minutes.

3. Immediately reduce the heat to 325 degrees. Pour on 3 tablespoons of soy sauce and continue roasting until the internal temperature of the leg reaches 140 degrees for medium rare. Use a meat thermometer to check; that's the only way to be sure. The total roasting time will be approximately 1½ to 2 hours.

4. While the leg roasts, baste it every 30 minutes with the liquid in the bottom of the pan. About halfway through, pour on the remaining 3 tablespoons of soy sauce.

5. When the lamb is done, remove it to your serving platter; pour the juices into a bowl and let them stand for 2 minutes. Then spoon off as much of the fat as possible.

6. Serve the lamb, carved in thin slices, with a splash of pan juices on each serving. *Save* both the leftover lamb and the leftover juice to make Lamb Curry (page 166).

Serves 4 to 6 (but don't let folks eat too *much—you need 2 cups leftover for the Lamb Curry!).*

Lamb Curry

- 1 onion, chopped
- 2 cloves garlic, minced
- 1 stalk celery, chopped
- 4 tablespoons butter
- 2 tablespoons flour
- 2½ cups leftover lamb broth from the Honey-Glazed Lamb (page 165)
- ¼ cup dry white wine
- 1 tart apple, chopped
- 1 dried red pepper, crumbled, or ½ teaspoon dry red-pepper flakes
- ¼ cup currants
- 2 tablespoons curry powder
- ½ teaspoon dried thyme
- 1 teaspoon powdered ginger
- 1 teaspoon ground coriander
- 1 cup milk
- 1 12-ounce package shredded coconut
- 2 cups leftover cubed lamb

Provide condiments of chopped onion, raisins, mango chutney, sour cream, and anything else you like.

≈

1. Sauté the onion, garlic, and celery in butter until they are just tender. Then stir in the flour.
2. Add all the remaining ingredients except the milk, coconut, and lamb. Cover and simmer over low heat for 30 minutes while you make the final ingredient, coconut cream.
3. Heat the milk until hot but not boiling and pour it over the shredded coconut. Let steep for 20 minutes, then strain. Save the coconut so you can toast it and use for a garnish on another recipe.
4. Add the coconut cream to the curry sauce. Toss in the lamb; heat through and serve on a bed of rice.

Serves 4.

Bert Greene's Roast of Lamb

Bert Greene was one of the best cooks this country has known. Like James Beard, Bert had the motto "good food, simply prepared." This recipe is both! He prepared it for Neva and me the first time we visited him in New York. I couldn't see how he did it; Bert was a big man, and the kitchen in his New York flat was tiny. I asked him for the recipe and he kindly sent it to me.

- A 4-to-6-pound leg of lamb
- 2 cloves garlic
- 1 small piece (approximately 1 inch square) fresh ginger root
- ⅓ cup Dijon mustard
- 1 teaspoon honey
- ½ teaspoon crushed dried rosemary leaves
- ½ teaspoon crumbled dried thyme leaves
- 2 tablespoons olive oil
- 2 tablespoons soy sauce

≈

1. Using an ice pick, pierce holes in a lattice pattern over the top and sides of the lamb. Cut 1 clove of the garlic and the ginger into slivers. Insert the garlic in some holes, ginger in others, about evenly distributed.

2. Crush the remaining garlic. Combine it, the mustard, honey, rosemary, and thyme in a small bowl. Slowly beat in the olive oil until the mixture thickens. Add the soy sauce. Spread the sauce over the lamb. Let stand for 3 to 4 hours.

3. Preheat the oven to 450 degrees. Place the lamb on a rack in a roasting pan. Roast for 15 minutes. Reduce the heat to 350 degrees and roast 10 to 12 minutes per pound for medium rare.

Serves 4 to 6.

Mint-Roasted Leg of Lamb

A 5-pound short leg (three-quarter leg) of lamb (see page 164)
Salt and pepper to taste
1 stick (4 ounces) butter
½ cup white-wine vinegar
½ cup sugar
1 tablespoon Worcestershire sauce
½ cup finely chopped fresh mint leaves or ¼ cup crumbled dried mint leaves

Somewhere along the line it became tradition to serve roast lamb with mint jelly. It is this butcher's opinion that mint jelly has destroyed more good lamb than the coyotes. However, this lamb roast basted in a glaze made from fresh mint is a different story; it's delicious! Skip the mint jelly!

≈

1. Place the lamb on a rack in a roasting pan. Season with salt and pepper. Combine the remaining ingredients in a small saucepan and heat, stirring, until the sugar dissolves.

2. Place the lamb in a preheated 325-degree oven and roast for 10 to 12 minutes per pound for medium rare. Thirty minutes before the lamb is done, baste it with half of the butter-mint sauce. Serve the remaining sauce with the lamb.

Serves 6 to 8.

VARIATIONS

Various fruit glazes are also good with roast lamb. Here are a few you might like to try.

Apricot Glaze

≈

½ cup apricot preserves
2 tablespoons sherry
1 tablespoon Dijon mustard
1 teaspoon fresh lemon juice

Combine all the ingredients in a saucepan and heat thoroughly. Use the glaze to baste the lamb during the last 30 minutes of cooking time. Serve the remaining glaze with the lamb.

Apple Rosemary Glaze

≈

Mix all ingredients together in a saucepan. Proceed as described above.

½ cup apple jelly
1 teaspoon fresh rosemary
1 tablespoon fresh lemon juice

Ginger Pineapple Glaze

≈

1. Drain the pineapple and reserve the syrup. Combine the cornstarch, ginger, and sugar in a small saucepan and mix well. Gradually add the reserved pineapple syrup and water. Cook over medium heat, stirring constantly, until the sauce is thickened and clear.

2. Use the glaze on the lamb during the last 30 minutes of roasting. Add the pineapple tidbits to any remaining glaze and serve with the lamb.

1 9-ounce can pineapple tidbits
1 tablespoon cornstarch
1 teaspoon grated fresh ginger
¼ cup sugar
½ cup water

Buckingham Glaze

I don't know why they call it that. Neva and I had lamb served with this glaze at a little bed-and-breakfast in the English Cotswolds, and that's what they called it. It was very tasty and it's very simple.

≈

Mix all the ingredients in a small saucepan and heat until the jelly melts. Brush on the lamb during the last 30 minutes of cooking time. Heat the remaining sauce and serve with the lamb.

1 cup dry sherry
½ cup currant jelly
½ cup catsup
1 tablespoon fresh marjoram leaves or ½ teaspoon crumbled dried

Leg of Lamb on the Grill

A leg of lamb boned and butterflied (cut partially open to lie flat) is a great meat for grilling. Ask the butcher to butterfly a leg for you, then fire up the coals and invite the neighbors. Because the muscles of a butterflied leg of lamb vary in thickness, it will come off the grill with something cooked to everyone's taste—well done, medium, and rare.

Barbecued Lamb, Sonoma Style

- ¾ cup olive oil
- ½ cup red-wine vinegar
- ½ cup dry red wine
- 1 4-ounce can chopped green chilies
- 6 cloves garlic, minced or mashed
- 4 teaspoons Italian seasoning
- 2 tablespoons hot mustard
- 1 leg of lamb, 6 pounds or more, boned and butterflied

Sam and Vickie Sebastiani own Viansa Winery in Sonoma, California. Not only do they produce some of the finest wines in the region, but Vickie is one of Sonoma's best cooks. Together they also do a great "Q." Here is a sample.

≈

1. Combine the oil, vinegar, wine, chilies, garlic, Italian seasoning, and mustard. Mix well. Place the lamb in a shallow dish and pour the mixture over it. Turn to coat the topside. Cover and marinate overnight in the refrigerator, turning once more.

2. To barbecue: Prepare and preheat barbecue grill. Remove the meat from the marinade and prepare a basting sauce by blending the tomato sauce and honey into the marinade, stirring well. Cook the marinated lamb over hot coals for 8 to 20 minutes on each side, depending on the thickness, basting frequently until done.

Serves 6 to 8.

Chinese Marinade for Lamb

My Polynesian bride has another wonderful way with butterflied leg of lamb on the grill.

- **¼ cup soy sauce**
- **¼ cup lemon juice**
- **¼ cup honey**
- **1 teaspoon ground black pepper**
- **1 fresh ginger root (1½ inches long), peeled and sliced, or ½ teaspoon ground ginger**
- **1 clove garlic**
- **1 6-to-9-pound butterflied leg of lamb**

≈

1. Place all the ingredients except the lamb in a blender or food processor and blend until smooth. Place the meat in a glass casserole and pour the marinade over the lamb. Refrigerate, covered, up to 12 hours; baste occasionally.

2. Grill the lamb 4 to 6 inches over charcoals or another source of heat for 10 to 20 minutes per side, depending on the degree of doneness you desire, basting occasionally.

Serves 6 to 8 generously.

Lamb Rack

Properly prepared and presented, a rack of lamb is the perfect romantic meal for two with candlelight and wine. The rack is the seven-rib-chop combination on one side of the animal; it is the ultimate in ease of preparation if the butcher has done his job well. Racks must be thoroughly trimmed.

At a market where I once worked, lamb racks poorly trimmed were "backing up" and turning dark in the case and cooler. We just couldn't sell them, even at $3.29 per pound—a very reasonable price at the time. As butchers often do when something doesn't sell, I took a few racks home for dinner. But before I did, I trimmed them the way that I wanted them on my plate. I totally removed the chine bone and all of the back fat clear down to the lean rib-eye. The rib bones were "Frenched"—exposed—clear down to a quarter-inch from the rib-eye. What I took home looked very like the raw version of a rack of lamb presented to you in a fine restaurant. Elegant!

When I went back to the market the next day, I decided to do a cutting test on a couple of racks still turning dark in the cooler. I trimmed them up the way I had the ones I had taken home the night before, and then weighed them to see how much we would have to charge to make the same profit that we made on the traditional trim at $3.29. The price difference was rather staggering. Not counting the extra labor cost required for the full trim, we needed to charge $9.89 a pound just to make the same profit margin. We put the trimmed racks in the case in a wine marinade for $10.99 a pound. And we developed such a demand for lamb racks that we had to order extras just to keep up.

Broiled and Roasted Rack of Lamb

A 2-to-2½-pound rack of lamb
1 cup dry white wine
1 cup Basic Lamb Broth (page 184) or canned chicken broth
¼ cup white-wine vinegar
2 teaspoons dried mixed herbs (rosemary, thyme, oregano, dill, marjoram)
1 clove garlic, crushed
¼ cup grated onion
1 tablespoon brown sugar
1 teaspoon salt
½ teaspoon black pepper
½ cup olive oil
1 teaspoon soy sauce

Cooking a rack of lamb is simplicity itself. I have developed a foolproof way. Marinate the rack in the refrigerator for an hour or two or overnight, if you like, in a simple wine vinaigrette with your favorite herbs. Mine are rosemary and thyme.

≈

1. Have your butcher remove the chine bone and "French" the rack.

2. Mix together all of the remaining ingredients to make a marinade, using 2 or 3 of your favorite herbs. Pour the marinade over the rack of lamb in a glass dish or plastic bag and marinate in the refrigerator for several hours or overnight.

3. Preheat the oven for broiling (500 degrees). Put the lamb rack under the broiler, rib side up, and broil for 5 minutes. Turn the rack rib side down and broil for an additional 5 minutes. Then turn the oven control from "broil" to "bake." Leave the temperature at 500 degrees and continue cooking for an additional 10 to 12 minutes. The rack comes out beautifully medium rare all the way through. An absolutely delicious dish, and it only takes 20 to 25 minutes.

4. The marinade can be reduced down over high heat to use as a sauce for the meat.

Serves 4.

VARIATION

Rack of lamb is also great meat for the barbecue. Grill the racks over coals to the desired degree of doneness, basting the last few minutes of cooking time with the marinade reduction or with any of the glazes recommended for leg of lamb (see pages 168–69). Be sure to heat any leftover glaze to serve as a sauce.

Rack of Lamb with Herb Crumb Crust

When preparing this recipe, I often buy an extra rack and roast it for fifteen minutes, as described in step 1. Then I let it cool and refrigerate it. Two or three days later, I carve the half-cooked rack into chops, and coat them with a mixture of equal parts of prepared mustard and cream. Then I dip them in finely crushed cracker crumbs and sauté them in butter until crisp and golden brown.

Here is a recipe for rack of lamb that makes a beautiful presentation and a delicious dinner. Have the butcher remove the chine bone and "French" the rack of lamb. Trim off any excess fat.

- A 2-to-2½-pound rack of lamb
- ¼ teaspoon salt
- ¼ teaspoon black pepper
- 2 cloves garlic, minced
- 1 cup soft bread crumbs
- ¼ cup minced parsley
- ¼ teaspoon crumbled dried thyme
- ¼ cup melted butter

≈

1. Preheat the oven to 375 degrees. Season the rack with salt and pepper and rub well with the minced garlic. Place in the oven and roast for 15 minutes.

2. Meanwhile, combine the bread crumbs, parsley, thyme, and melted butter. Remove the rack from the oven and press the crumb mixture firmly into the top, meaty side of the lamb, covering completely. Return the lamb to the oven and roast 20 minutes more, until the crumbs are golden brown. Carve into chops between the ribs and serve.

Serves 4.

Stuffed and Rolled Lamb Roasts

Both the leg and shoulder of lamb are good candidates for boned, rolled, and stuffed lamb roasts. They make elegant presentations, and they make carving a simple task.

Ask your butcher to "bone-out" either a "short leg" (three-quarter leg) of lamb or a "square-cut" lamb shoulder. Ask him also to give you the bones; they make marvelous soups and sauces (see pages 184–87). If you are having a leg of lamb boned, you may want to ask the butcher to separate out the top-round muscle. That's the most tender muscle of the leg, and it can be sliced into steaks or cutlets for a separate meal. It is also the thickest muscle of the leg, and removing it makes stuffing the leg easier and the results more uniform in thickness and appealing in final presentation.

Jay's Lamb Roast

A 5-to-7-pound boned "square-cut" shoulder or leg of lamb
2 teaspoons Greek seasoning mix, available in the spice section of most markets*
1 8-ounce jar marinated artichoke hearts

* If you can't find Greek seasoning mix in your local supermarket, you can order it from Arkansas (you can find most anything in Arkansas): Cavender's All Purpose Greek Seasoning,

Jay Jones, a butcher whom I worked with years ago at the Mill Valley Market in Mill Valley, California, prepared a simple stuffed rolled lamb shoulder roast that became very popular with his customers. He called it a "Greek lamb roll"; everybody else called it "Jay's Lamb Roast."

≈

1. Lay the boned shoulder or leg on a cutting board and pound it to flatten the thicker muscles. Sprinkle half of the Greek seasoning mix over the meat and pour on a tablespoon or two of the marinade from the artichokes.
2. Rub the seasoning and the marinade well into the meat. Then lay the artichokes down the center of the lamb. Roll and tie securely with kitchen twine.
3. Rub any remaining marinade over the outside of the roll and sprinkle on the remaining Greek seasoning mix.
4. Roast in a preheated 325-degree oven for approximately 1½ hours, until an instant-read meat thermome-

ter inserted into the center of the meat reads 145 to 150 degrees for medium rare.

5. Remove the strings, carve the lamb, and serve with a simple Greek salad of tomatoes, onions, and feta cheese.

Serves 6 to 8.

S-C Seasoning Co., Inc., P.O. Box 1296, Harrison, AK 72601.

Roast Lamb with Ham and Rice Pilaf Stuffing

This is one of my favorite rolled stuffed lamb roasts. We usually use the shoulder of lamb—it has just a bit more fat and, as a result, a bit more flavor—but a boneless leg can also be used.

- 3 tablespoons butter
- ¼ cup chopped onion
- 3 cloves garlic, minced
- 1 cup raw long-grain rice
- ½ pound ham (or smoked sausage), diced
- 2 cups lamb or beef stock
- A 5-to-7-pound boned "square-cut" shoulder of lamb
- ½ teaspoon salt
- ¼ teaspoon fresh-ground black pepper
- 1 cup coarsely chopped onion
- 1 cup coarsely chopped carrot
- 1 cup coarsely chopped celery
- ½ cup dry white wine
- 1 teaspoon arrowroot dissolved in 1 tablespoon water

≈

1. Melt the butter in a heavy saucepan over moderate heat. Add the onion and garlic and cook for a few minutes. Stir in the rice and continue cooking until the rice browns slightly and the onion is limp. Stir in the ham.

2. Pour in the stock, stir once or twice, cover, and reduce the heat to low. Simmer until all of the liquid in the pan is absorbed and the rice is tender—about 15 minutes.

3. Lay out the boned shoulder on a cutting board and pound it to flatten the thicker muscles. Sprinkle with the salt and pepper and spread on a layer of the rice mixture. You'll only need about a third of it for stuffing. Reserve the remainder to serve with the roast. Roll the roast and tie with string.

4. Make a bed of the chopped vegetables in the bottom of a roasting pan or ovenproof casserole dish. Place the roast on the vegetables and pour in the white wine. Roast in a preheated 325-degree oven for approximately 1 hour, until a meat thermometer inserted in the center of the roll reads 145 to 150 for medium rare.

5. Transfer the roast to a warm serving platter and let

Roast Lamb with Ham and Rice Pilaf Stuffing *(cont.)*

sit for 10 minutes before carving. Strain the pan juices into a saucepan, pressing the vegetables to extract some of their juices. Bring to a simmer and thicken slightly with the arrowroot mixture.

6. Reheat the reserved rice mixture with a tablespoon or two of the pan juices to moisten. Fluff with a fork as you heat it through over low heat. Remove the strings, carve the lamb, and serve on a warm platter with the extra rice pilaf. Serve the sauce separately.

Serves 6 to 8.

Spinach-Stuffed Braised Lamb Roast

- 1 bunch (about 1 pound) fresh spinach
- 6 ounces prosciutto, thinly sliced
- 3 cloves garlic, minced
- ¼ cup pine nuts
- 2 tablespoons water
- A 5-to-7-pound boned "square-cut" shoulder or leg of lamb
- ½ teaspoon salt
- ¼ teaspoon fresh-ground black pepper
- 2 tablespoons olive oil
- ¼ cup dry white wine
- ¼ cup lamb or beef stock
- 1 teaspoon arrowroot dissolved in 1 tablespoon water

Lamb roasts are often overlooked for pot roasting. This recipe proves they deserve consideration in that category. A delicious and attractive meal for family and friends.

≈

1. Rinse and coarsely chop the spinach. Cut the slices of prosciutto into ½-inch strips.

2. Put the spinach, prosciutto, and garlic in a good-sized saucepan, add the pine nuts, and toss together. Sprinkle on the water, cover, and "sweat" over low heat just until the spinach turns limp.

3. Lay out the boned shoulder or leg on a cutting board and pound it to flatten the thicker muscles. Spread on the spinach mixture. Roll and tie with string. Rub with salt and pepper.

4. Heat the oil in a Dutch oven and brown the lamb well on all sides. Add the wine and cook for a minute to reduce a little, while scraping up any meat particles in the bottom of the pan. Pour on the stock, reduce the heat to low, cover, and simmer for about 1 hour, until tender. Add more stock if necessary.

5. Remove the meat to a warm serving platter and thicken the pan juices slightly with the arrowroot mixture. Remove the strings from the lamb and slice the meat. Arrange on a serving platter with some of the pan juices. Serve with any extra sauce on the side.

Serves 6 to 8.

STEWS, CASSEROLES, AND SOUPS

Lamb Stews

A good stew is such a wonderfully hearty dish. It's a big hug of a meal that makes you feel good all over. For us the most popular stews are those made with lamb. Cuts from the neck and shoulder with the bone make the best lamb stew for my money, and fortunately those cuts cost the least. One of the best buys for lamb stew, should you happen to find them, are called "lamb blocks." These are the portion of the lamb shoulder left after the shoulder chops have been removed. They are often sold at a bargain price, just to get rid of them, the money having been made on the chops.

If you must have boneless lamb stew, ask for boneless shoulder. A boneless leg (except for the shank portion) is much too lean for a good stew. Fat is where the flavor is in any meat, so for a good stew don't be afraid of a little fat. But once it has made its contribution to flavor in the cooking process, it's a good idea to remove any excess before serving. There are a couple of ways to "degrease" a stew. Most stews lend themselves to advance preparation. Make the stew a day ahead, then refrigerate it. All the waste fat will come to the top and can easily be removed before reheating. Or allow the stew to sit for just a few minutes before the final step. The excess fat will come to the top and can easily be skimmed off.

There are as many recipes for lamb stew as there are cookbooks that mention meat; here are a few from our family collection.

Irish Stew

2 tablespoons vegetable oil
2 to 2½ pounds lamb neck or shoulder, cut into 1½-to-2-inch cubes
2 medium onions, coarsely chopped
4 medium potatoes, peeled and quartered
½ teaspoon crumbled dried thyme
Salt and pepper to taste
2 cups lamb or beef broth

This is unquestionably the simplest of lamb stews. Rich and hearty, it makes a great family dinner on a chilly night.

≈

1. Heat the oil over medium heat in a heavy pot. Add the lamb and brown well on all sides. Stir in the onions and cook them till limp. Skim off any excess fat and discard.

2. Add the potatoes, thyme, salt, and pepper. Add the stock, cover, and simmer for 1 hour more.

Serves 4 to 6.

Scotch Lamb Stew

The Scots make marvelous use of barley and "neeps," as they call turnips. Both of those items are inexpensive and underutilized in our country. We could learn something from the Scots. This recipe uses both.

≈

2 to 2½ pounds lamb stew meat cut into 1½-inch cubes
1 tablespoon cooking oil (or, if there is some trimmed fat from the lamb, render that)
1 medium onion, chopped
½ cup pearl barley
4 cups lamb or beef broth
¼ cup chopped parsley
2 teaspoons salt
½ teaspoon freshly ground black pepper
4 carrots, cut into 2-inch pieces
4 turnips, peeled and quartered

1. In a large pot brown the meat on all sides in hot fat. Add the chopped onion and barley and continue cooking

until the onion is soft and the barley somewhat browned. Add the beef broth, parsley, salt, and pepper.

2. Cover the pot tightly and simmer for 1 hour. Skim off the fat. Add the turnips and carrots, cover, and continue cooking for 30 minutes, or until the vegetables are tender.

Serves 4 to 6.

Creamy Lamb Stew

This makes a delicate yet hearty lamb stew that is great served over noodles. If you're planning to serve this dish to company, you may want to use boneless stew meat and cut it into smaller cubes.

- 2 pounds lamb neck, cut into 1½-inch cubes
- 2 tablespoons cooking oil
- 1 large onion, chopped
- 3 to 4 cloves garlic, minced
- 2 tablespoons minced parsley
- ½ cup dry sherry
- ½ cup chicken stock
- 3 or 4 carrots, sliced
- 1 cup sour cream
- Salt and pepper to taste
- Chopped parsley (optional)
- Sprinkling of paprika (optional)

≈

1. In an ovenproof pan, brown the lamb cubes in oil. When the meat is brown, add the onion and garlic and cook for 3 minutes, stirring. Add the parsley, sherry, stock, and sliced carrots. Cover and bake in a preheated 350-degree oven for 1 hour; add more chicken stock if necessary.

2. When the meat is tender, skim off the fat, stir in the sour cream, and season to taste with salt and pepper. Garnish with bits of chopped parsley or a sprinkling of paprika and serve with buttered noodles.

Serves 4 to 6.

Neva's Lamb Stew with Tomatoes

- 2 tablespoons cooking oil
- 1 cup flour
- Salt and pepper
- 2 pounds lamb neck or shoulder, cut into 1½-to-2-inch cubes
- 1 large onion, sliced
- 3 to 4 cloves garlic, minced
- 1 29-ounce can whole tomatoes
- 4 carrots, cut into 1-inch pieces
- 4 stalks celery, cut into 1-inch pieces
- 3 potatoes, cut into 1½-inch cubes

This is a family favorite not only around our house but also for a family in Oakland, California. The recipe first appeared in my column, "The Butcher," years ago in the San Francisco *Chronicle*. After the terrible "fire storm" that destroyed so many homes in the Oakland hills in 1991, I received a letter from a family who had lost everything in the fire except their St. Bernard dog and were trying to put their lives back together. They'd had a recipe of ours that they loved and wanted to get another copy of it. Neva was, to say the least, very flattered, and sent off a copy the next day. It is a good stew. I hope it becomes a favorite around your house too.

≈

1. In a heavy pot or Dutch oven, heat the oil over medium-high heat. Put the flour, salt, and pepper in a paper bag, add the lamb, and shake the bag to dust the meat with seasoned flour. Brown the meat in the hot oil, turning frequently to brown well on all sides.

2. Stir in the sliced onion and minced garlic. Continue cooking until the onion is limp. Add the tomatoes (juice included) and stir. Reduce the heat to the point where the sauce is gently simmering, cover, and cook for 1 hour. Skim off the fat.

3. Add the carrots, celery, and potatoes. Add a bit of hot water, beef, or chicken broth if the sauce becomes too thick. Cover and continue cooking for 30 to 40 minutes, until the vegetables are tender. Taste and correct the seasoning before serving. This dish freezes well.

Serves 4 to 6.

Spanish Lamb Stew with Olives

Add a few pimento-stuffed olives to almost anything and you can call it Spanish. This very good stew has the qualifications to be called Spanish. If you want to go all the way, substitute one cup of rice for the potatoes, add a pinch of saffron, and you have a variation on the national dish of Spain—paella.

- 2 tablespoons olive oil
- 2 to 2½ pounds lamb stew meat (neck or shoulder) cut into 1½-inch cubes
- 2 tablespoons flour
- ½ teaspoon salt
- ¼ teaspoon freshly ground black pepper
- 2 medium onions, sliced
- 3 to 4 cloves garlic, minced
- 2 cups lamb or beef broth
- 1 cup red wine
- 4 tomatoes, peeled and quartered
- ½ teaspoon crumbled dried thyme
- 1 cup pimento-stuffed olives
- 4 large potatoes, peeled and quartered
- 1 tablespoon arrowroot dissolved in 2 tablespoons water (optional)

≈

1. Heat the oil in a large covered kettle or Dutch oven over medium heat. Dust the meat with a mixture of flour, salt, and pepper.
2. Brown the meat in the hot oil. When well browned on all sides, remove the meat from the oil and set it aside. Add the onions and garlic and cook until tender and light brown. Add the broth, wine, tomatoes, and thyme. Add the browned meat, cover, and simmer for 30 minutes.
3. Add the olives and potatoes and continue cooking for an additional 30 minutes. Remove the meat and vegetables to a serving dish and keep warm.
4. Drain the cooking liquid into a saucepan and skim off the fat. Bring the cooking liquid to a boil. Reduce the liquid slightly, and thicken if you like with the arrowroot mixture. Pour the sauce over the stew and serve.

Serves 4 to 6.

Lamb Casseroles

Casserole cookery is very convenient, because everything is usually cooked and served in the same pot and can most often be made ahead to a certain point and finished off just before guests arrive. A "casserole dish" usually refers to a deep round or oval ovenproof container of glass, ceramic, metal, or other heatproof materials with a tight-fitting lid.

The following are a few classic casserole dishes modified slightly to make marvelous use of lamb.

Haricot of Lamb

- 2 cups dried lima beans
- ½ cup chopped onion
- 1 pound lean boneless lamb, cut into cubes
- 1 cup drained canned tomatoes
- 1 teaspoon salt
- ½ teaspoon black pepper
- 2 cups boiling water

"Haricot" (pronounced "*ah*-ree-koh") is French for "bean," but it also means a mutton or lamb stew. This simple casserole is delicious in any language.

≈

1. Rinse the lima beans, then soak overnight in water to cover by 2 inches. Drain and place in a kettle, cover with fresh water, and cook 1 hour, or until nearly tender.
2. Place the cooked beans in a casserole and add the remaining ingredients. Cover tightly and cook in a preheated 350-degree oven for 2 hours. Remove the cover after 1 hour.

Serves 6 to 8.

Greek Lamb and Mixed Fruit Pilaf

Neva and I and three other couples once chartered a seventy-two-foot sailboat for a two-week cruise in the Greek isles. It was a marvelous vacation with a lot of great Greek food. George, the cook on board, prepared this recipe using *katsike,* or goat. Neva, with the aid of an interpreter, talked him into giving her the recipe. When we got home we had a hard time finding goat meat, so Neva made the casserole with lamb. Should you get to Piraeus to sail on the *Doxa,* don't tell George, but this casserole is better with lamb.

- **¼ pound butter**
- **1 medium onion, thinly sliced**
- **1¾ pounds lean boneless lamb, cut into cubes**
- **½ cup dried apricots, soaked overnight in cold water, drained and halved**
- **3 tablespoons seedless raisins**
- **2 teaspoons salt**
- **½ teaspoon ground cinnamon**
- **¼ teaspoon black pepper**
- **3¾ cups water**
- **1½ cups long-grain rice, washed, soaked in cold water for 30 minutes, and drained**

≈

1. Melt the butter in a large, deep skillet. When the foam subsides, add the onion and cook until soft and translucent but not brown. Add the lamb and cook for 5 minutes, stirring until browned.

2. Stir in the apricots, raisins, 1 teaspoon of the salt, the cinnamon, and pepper. Pour in 2 cups of the water and bring to the boil, stirring occasionally. Reduce the heat, cover the pan, and simmer for 1 hour, or until the meat is tender.

3. Put the rice in a medium saucepan. Pour the remaining water over the rice and add the remaining salt. Bring to a boil, reduce the heat, cover, and simmer for 15 to 20 minutes, or until all the liquid is absorbed.

4. Place a third of the cooked rice in a medium-sized ovenproof casserole. Cover with a layer of half the cooked meat mixture. Top with another third of the rice. Continue making layers until all the ingredients have been used, finishing with rice. Cover the dish and place in the center of a preheated 350-degree oven. Bake for 20 minutes and serve from the casserole.

Serves 4 to 6.

Lamb Soups

Beef and chicken broth can be bought in cans at the supermarket, but lamb broth you must, I fear, make for yourself. It's a simple process and well worth the effort.

Lamb broth will add additional flavor and richness to the sauces and gravies that you serve with lamb chops and roasts. It is also the base for many hearty meal-in-a-bowl soups, classic among them Scotch Broth.

Following is a recipe for preparing Basic Lamb Broth along with a few lamb-soup recipes that will make the process more than worth the effort.

Basic Lamb Broth

2 to 2½ pounds lamb bones
1 onion, stuck with a couple of cloves
1 stalk of celery
1 carrot
3 bay leaves
6 peppercorns
2 quarts cold water

The bones that you save when you have your butcher bone-out a shoulder, leg, or rack of lamb can be turned into many a tasty bonus with lamb broth.

≈

1. In a 4-quart saucepan, put the lamb bones, onion, celery, carrot, bay leaves, and peppercorns. Cover with cold water and bring to a boil. Reduce the heat and simmer, covered, for 2 hours, or until any meat falls from the bones.

2. Strain the broth into a large bowl and cool in the refrigerator. Save any bits of meat if you want to make Scotch Broth. The lamb broth may be frozen in small containers to use in sauces and gravies as needed, but for a real treat make a big pot of Scotch Broth.

Makes approximately 2 quarts.

Scotch Broth

Scotch Broth is a soup that freezes well, so if it's too hot for a hearty soup, freeze it for a cooler time. Start with one recipe of Basic Lamb Broth (preceding recipe).

2 quarts Basic Lamb Broth
Meat scraps from Basic Lamb Broth*
3/4 cup pearl barley
1/2 teaspoon Italian seasoning
1/2 teaspoon cayenne pepper
1/4 pound butter
1 small onion, chopped
1/2 cup chopped celery
1/2 cup chopped carrot
1/2 cup fresh or frozen peas
Chopped parsley, for garnish

≈

1. Put the lamb broth and meat back in the saucepan, add the barley, Italian seasoning, and cayenne, and simmer for 1 hour.

2. Melt the butter in a heavy skillet and sauté the chopped onion, celery, and carrot until just limp. Add the sautéed vegetables to the lamb broth. Cover and simmer until the barley is nice and tender, for another 10 to 20 minutes. Add the peas and heat through. Garnish with chopped parsley and serve.

Serves 6 to 8.

* If you are using lamb broth from your freezer and have no meat scraps, a half or three-quarters of a pound of lean lamb diced and sautéed in a bit of the butter will add a pleasing meatiness to the broth.

Greek Lamb and Vegetable Soup

- 1½ pounds stewing lamb, cut into 1½-inch cubes
- 2 tablespoons olive oil
- 2 or 3 large garlic cloves, minced
- 2 teaspoons salt
- ½ teaspoon white pepper
- 12 cups Basic Lamb Broth (page 184)
- 1 medium potato, diced
- 1 cup green beans, cut into 1-inch pieces
- 1 medium-sized onion, chopped
- 1 cup fresh or frozen peas
- 1 large ripe tomato, peeled, cored, and coarsely chopped
- ½ cup tomato juice
- 2 cups broccoli florets
- 1 small zucchini, diced
- 1 tablespoon chopped flat-leaf parsley
- Chopped flat-leaf parsley for garnish

The Greeks are lovers of lamb, and they do some hearty, economical, and delicious dishes with the meat. This is a good example. The recipe is based on one from a friend, Holly Garrison, a great cook and writer, who recently co-authored *The Periyali Cookbook: New Classic Greek Cooking.*

≈

1. Lightly brown the lamb in olive oil in a Dutch oven or heavy saucepan over medium heat, stirring occasionally to brown evenly.

2. Stir in the garlic, salt, pepper, and lamb broth. Bring to a boil and reduce the heat. Simmer gently, uncovered, for 45 minutes.

3. Add the potato and green beans and simmer for 10 minutes more. Add the onion, peas, tomato, and tomato juice. Simmer 10 minutes more. Add the broccoli, zucchini, and 1 tablespoon of parsley and continue simmering for 5 minutes. Taste and adjust the seasonings, if necessary.

4. Ladle into warm shallow soup bowls and sprinkle with parsley. Serve with warm bread.

Serves 6 to 8.

Bonanza Lamb Chowder

This is a wonderful way to use any leftover roast lamb. It makes a hearty chowder. Simply take the "c" out of "clam" and add on a "b" (for "bonanza").

- 2 cups water
- 2 medium-sized potatoes, diced
- ¼ cup sliced celery
- ¾ cup sliced carrots
- 1 teaspoon salt
- ¼ teaspoon black pepper
- 6 tablespoons butter
- ½ cup sliced scallions
- ¼ cup flour
- 1¼ cups milk
- 2 cups sharp Cheddar cheese
- About 3 cups cooked lamb, cubed
- ¼ teaspoon hot-pepper sauce
- 1 teaspoon Worcestershire sauce

≈

1. Place the water, potatoes, celery, carrots, salt, and pepper in a saucepan. Bring to a boil and cook for about 10 minutes, or until the vegetables are tender. Remove from the heat but do not drain; set aside.

2. Meanwhile, melt 4 tablespoons of the butter in a large saucepan. Add the scallions and cook until limp. Add the remaining 2 tablespoons butter and heat until melted. Blend in the flour, stirring well.

3. Gradually add the milk, stirring constantly. Continue stirring until the milk mixture boils about a minute. Gradually add the cheese, stirring until it is melted and well blended with the mixture.

4. Add the vegetables and their liquids to the lamb. Stir in the hot-pepper sauce and Worcestershire sauce. Heat through, stirring constantly.

Serves 4 to 6.

SPECIAL CUTS—BREASTS, SHANKS, AND BLOCKS

Lamb Breast

Breast of lamb, in most markets, is displayed and labeled in one of two ways: as the whole breast trimmed of its outside fat, left in one piece, and sold as "lamb spareribs," or as the trimmed breast cut between each two ribs and with the pieces sold as "riblets."

The lamb spareribs are great on the barbecue grill, glazed with your favorite barbecue sauce. Or they can be simply boned-out and the meat rolled into "pinwheel" lamb chops for some of the cheapest lamb chops you'll ever eat. The whole breast is also great for stuffing to make "Scotch lamb chops." Cut away any fat. Make a pocket in the breast by cutting along the rib bone, but leaving the meat attached to the bone on three sides. Stuff with ground lamb, tie with a string at one-inch intervals, then cut between the strings to make chops.

Cut into "riblets," the breast of lamb can be turned into some wonderful and wonderfully simple quick-to-fix dishes. If the butcher doesn't offer lamb breast already cut into riblets, it's a simple matter to do it yourself. Simply cut through the meat between the ribs. There may be a bit of cartilage to cut through, but if you use a good sharp cook's knife to do the job, it's not difficult.

Grilled Lamb Spareribs Dijon

4 racks (approximately 5 pounds) of lamb spareribs
2 lemons, halved
3 teaspoons ground coriander
3 teaspoons ground cumin
2 teaspoons freshly ground black pepper
4 large garlic cloves, minced or crushed through a press
¾ cup Dijon mustard

This recipe took second place at the first Sizzlin' Lamb Barbecue Contest in Chicago. It won its creator, Bettie Brown of Casa Grande, Arizona, $1,000!

≈

1. Rub the racks with cut sides of lemons. Combine the coriander, cumin, and pepper; sprinkle equal amounts on both sides of the racks. Place the seasoned racks in plastic bags. Close the bags securely and refrigerate for 1 hour or overnight.

2. Prepare and preheat a kettle grill.

3. Combine the garlic with the mustard. Brush both sides of the racks with the mustard mixture, reserving about ¼ cup.

4. Place the racks on the grill over medium coals. Grill 15 minutes, turning once. Cover the kettle grill with the lid and continue cooking until the lamb is tender. Remove the cover, brush on more marinade, and cook until heated through, 1 to 2 minutes.

Serves 8.

Barbecued Lamb Spareribs Hawaiian

This is another super-simple recipe from the files of my Hawaiian bride.

- 5 pounds lamb spareribs
- Salt and pepper to taste
- ½ cup catsup
- ¼ cup soy sauce
- ½ cup canned sweetened pineapple juice
- 3 tablespoons honey

≈

1. Place the ribs in a large pot. Cover with water, add a teaspoon of salt, and simmer for 30 minutes. Drain and rinse. Trim off any excess fat and sprinkle the lamb lightly with salt and pepper.

2. Prepare and preheat a barbecue grill. Mix the catsup, soy sauce, pineapple juice, and honey in a saucepan; simmer for 5 minutes. Brush some of the marinade over the lamb. Grill the ribs until browned on both sides (only a minute or so on each side), brushing frequently with the sauce. Serve with extra sauce on the side.

Serves 6.

Neva's Quick Lamb Riblets

One of the easiest recipes for riblets comes from my wife's "Quick" file. We're talking real convenience food here.

- 2 pounds lamb riblets
- Salt and pepper
- 2 tablespoons soy sauce
- 1 8-ounce jar orange marmalade

≈

1. Preheat the oven to 350 degrees. Trim the riblets of any excess fat and cut into 2-rib serving pieces. Salt and pepper them. Bake for 20 minutes. Pour off the excess fat.

2. Sprinkle the meat with soy sauce and spread the marmalade over it. Bake for an additional 15 minutes, until warmed through.

Serves 4 to 6.

Sweet and Sour Lamb Riblets

- 2 pounds lamb riblets
- 1 onion, sliced
- 2 garlic cloves, minced
- 2 tablespoons honey
- 1 tablespoon peanut oil
- 4 tablespoons soy sauce
- ½ cup dry sherry
- 1 tablespoon freshly grated ginger
- 2 tablespoons brown sugar
- 1 teaspoon ground allspice

This recipe could be made with ground ginger, but fresh-grated ginger is, in my opinion, much better. If you can't find fresh ginger in your supermarket, substitute one teaspoon of ground ginger.

≈

1. Put the lamb riblets in a large bowl. Add the sliced onion, garlic, honey, oil, soy sauce, sherry, ginger, sugar, and allspice. Mix together well, cover and marinate at room temperature for 2 hours or refrigerate overnight.

2. Put the meat in a baking dish and pour over the marinade. Bake, uncovered, in a preheated 375-degree oven for 30 minutes, basting occasionally with the marinade. Serve with rice.

Serves 4.

Lamb Shanks

Lamb shanks are the front legs of the lamb, and in many markets it is a cut that is not easy to "move." Because of this they're usually a pretty good lamb buy.

There are dozens of delicious things to do with lamb shanks. Because they are a part of the animal that gets plenty of exercise in the process of moving from one side of the mountain, pasture, or pen to the other, they develop a good amount of connective tissue, which makes them perfect for simmering with all manner of wonderful sauces. Yet, because lamb is a young animal, lamb shanks are tender enough for simple roasting, even grilling on the barbecue grill.

Curried Lamb Shanks in Wine

From the McNab Ranch in Mendocino County, California, where sheep have been raised for generations, comes a very tasty recipe. Nice with rice, fruit salad, and hard rolls.

- **4 tablespoons cooking oil**
- **4 lamb shanks**
- **4 tablespoons flour**
- **1½ teaspoons curry powder**
- **1 cup water**
- **1 cup dry white wine**
- **Salt and pepper**
- **2 cloves garlic, minced**
- **1 onion, sliced thin**

≈

1. Heat the oil in a heavy skillet with a tight-fitting lid, add the shanks, and brown slowly on all sides. Remove from the pan.
2. Add the flour and curry powder to the drippings and blend well. Add the water and wine, stirring well as the sauce cooks until thickened. Place the shanks in the sauce, season with salt and pepper, and add the garlic. Top with the onion slices and cover. Simmer gently for 1 hour, or until the meat is tender. Serve with Spinach Rice (recipe follows).

Serves 4.

Spinach Rice

- **3 cups fresh spinach, thoroughly rinsed**
- **½ cup chopped onion**
- **2 tablespoons butter**
- **3 tablespoons tomato paste**
- **1½ cups chopped fresh tomato**
- **¼ cup chopped fresh dill**
- **3 tablespoons crushed dried mint leaves**
- **Salt to taste**
- **½ cup uncooked rice**
- **1 cup water**
- **1 tablespoon olive oil**
- **1 tablespoon fresh lemon juice**

1. Boil the spinach in water for just a few minutes, until limp. Drain and chop coarsely. Place in a large bowl.
2. Sauté the onion in the butter until translucent. Add to the spinach along with the tomato paste, chopped tomato, dill, mint, salt to taste, rice, and water. Pour everything into a baking dish. Drizzle with the olive oil and lemon juice.
3. Bake in a preheated 400-degree oven for 35 to 40 minutes, until the rice is tender. Serve with lamb shanks.

Serves 4.

Twenty Garlic Cloves Lamb Shanks

4 lamb shanks
2 tablespoons cooking oil
1 cup finely chopped onion
1 cup finely chopped carrots
1 cup finely chopped mushrooms
1 cup dry white wine
½ cup finely chopped green pepper
1 teaspoon ground cumin
½ teaspoon salt
¼ teaspoon black pepper
20 unpeeled garlic cloves
Hot cooked couscous

At an American Lamb Council–sponsored recipe contest for food editors, I found a great recipe for lamb shanks. Surprisingly, it came from Iowa, and I know lamb is not a favorite back there. It's nice to see that folks seem to be beginning to appreciate lamb. Diana McMillen, with *Midwest Living Magazine,* took second place with her recipe for "Twenty Garlic Lamb." It's absolutely delicious.

≈

1. In a skillet, brown the meat in the hot oil. Drain off the fat. Add the onion, carrots, mushrooms, wine, green pepper, cumin, salt, and pepper to the skillet. Top with the unpeeled garlic. Bring to a boil and reduce the heat. Cover and simmer the mixture for 1½ hours.

2. Transfer the meat to a serving platter. Skim the fat from the juices and discard. Spoon the vegetables and juices over the meat. Serve with couscous.

Serves 4.

Brandied Lamb Shanks

This is a wonderfully simple recipe that goes so well with Barley Pilaf (recipe follows this one).

- 4 lamb shanks
- ½ cup brandy
- ½ cup soy sauce
- ½ cup honey
- 2 tablespoons vegetable oil
- 2 tablespoons butter
- 1 large onion, thickly sliced

≈

1. Marinate the lamb shanks overnight in a mixture of the brandy, soy sauce, and honey. Remove the shanks from the marinade and reserve it. Brown the shanks in the hot oil in a heavy skillet, turning often to brown evenly on all sides. Remove from the skillet and set aside.

2. Pour off the oil. Add the butter to the skillet and cook the onion slices over low heat until golden. Return the shanks to the pan and pour in the reserved marinade. Cover and simmer over medium-low heat for 1½ hours, until tender.

Serves 4.

Barley Pilaf

The James Beard Cookbook has been Neva's constant kitchen companion. One of the many family favorites adapted from his book is this excellent barley dish.

- 1 large onion
- ½ pound fresh mushrooms
- 4 to 5 tablespoons butter
- 1 cup pearl barley
- 2 cups of broth (meat or chicken)

≈

1. Peel and chop the onion. Wipe the mushrooms with a damp cloth and slice them. Melt the butter and sauté the onions and mushrooms until they are soft.

2. Add the barley and brown it lightly. Add the broth and test it for seasoning. Add salt and pepper if necessary. Bring to a boil; lower the heat and cover, simmering for about 20 minutes. Remove the cover and continue cooking until the liquid is absorbed and the barley is tender.

Serves 4 to 6.

Lamb Shanks with Fresh Tomatoes

- 5 to 6 pounds lamb shanks
- 1 medium onion, chopped
- 1 tablespoon butter
- 1 tablespoon olive oil
- 2 cups chicken broth
- ½ cup tomato paste (optional)
- 2 cups chopped fresh tomatoes or 2 cups drained canned tomatoes
- Salt and pepper

Greektown in East Detroit is a great place for lamb lovers. Lamb is a featured meat in many of the restaurants there. This recipe is based on one from the Pegasus Tavern on Monroe Street, just a few blocks from Detroit's famed Renaissance Center.

≈

1. Simmer the lamb shanks in water to cover for 30 minutes. Drain and rinse. Place the lamb shanks in a baking pan.
2. Sauté the onion in butter and olive oil until translucent. Stir in the chicken broth, tomato paste, and chopped tomatoes; mix well. Add a little salt and pepper.
3. Pour the tomato mixture over the shanks. Add just enough water to cover and bake, covered, in a preheated 325-degree oven for 1 hour. Taste, and add more seasoning if needed. Serve with steamed rice, rice or barley pilaf, or pasta.

Serves 4.

Lamb Blocks

Lamb blocks are one of those cuts of meat that—like "London broil"—seem to change from one market to the next. One never knows for sure what one is apt to buy when one buys one, does one? They are, nonetheless, often a very good buy.

Lamb blocks are usually some portion of the shoulder of lamb, cut thick. In some markets, the round bone or arm portion of the lamb is cut into 1- or 1½-inch-thick slices and called lamb blocks. In others, it's thick slices of the blade portion of the shoulder. And in many markets, what's left of the shoulder of lamb after the round-bone arm chops and the blade chops have been removed is labeled "lamb blocks."

No matter which portion of the shoulder of lamb the "blocks" come from, they are very likely to be one of the least expensive cuts of lamb in your butcher's meat case. They are also one of the most versatile.

During the summer, when folks are thinking barbecue, lamb blocks are often featured as inexpensive cuts for the grill, and they are adequate for that. But to my mind, when lamb blocks are at their best is midwinter, prepared Moroccan style. Moroccan food has, like so many other foods from other cultures, become a delicious addition to the total American food picture.

Lamb and Onions

A favorite restaurant for the Ellis family is the Mamounia in San Francisco. Mehdi Ziani, the chef-owner, does marvelous things with lamb blocks. This recipe and the one that follows are good examples. Both are surprisingly similar in their simplicity of preparation, but are totally different in the taste of the finished dish.

- 3 tablespoons olive oil
- 2 pounds lamb shoulder blocks
- 1 teaspoon salt
- 1 teaspoon black pepper
- 1 teaspoon powdered ginger
- 1 teaspoon ground coriander
- 1 pinch saffron
- 2 cups water
- 2 medium white onions, sliced ½-inch thick
- 1 teaspoon cornstarch
- 1 tablespoon water

≈

1. Heat the oil in a heavy pot. Add the lamb, salt, pepper, ginger, coriander, and saffron. Brown the meat well on all sides over medium heat.
2. Pour the water over the meat, cover, and simmer (do not boil) for 1½ to 2 hours.
3. Before adding the onions, skim off any excess oil that has risen to the top and discard. Add the onions to the pot when the meat is half cooked.
4. When the meat is tender, remove meat and onions to a warm platter. Thicken the juices slightly with a teaspoon of cornstarch dissolved in a tablespoon of cold water. Cook until slightly thickened. Adjust the seasonings if necessary. To serve, pour the sauce over everything. Do not be afraid to use your fingers to eat the tender meat. They do in Morocco!

Serves 4.

Lamb with Honey and Almonds

≈

- 2 pounds lamb shoulder blocks
- 4 tablespoons olive oil
- 1 teaspoon salt
- 1 teaspoon black pepper
- 1 pinch saffron
- 1 teaspoon powdered ginger
- ½ teaspoon powdered cinnamon
- 1 onion, minced
- 1 tablespoon butter
- 2 cups water
- 2 ounces blanched almonds
- 1 cup honey
- ½ teaspoon nutmeg

1. Brown the lamb in 3 tablespoons of hot oil in a heavy pot. Add the salt, pepper, saffron, ginger, cinnamon, minced onion, and butter. Continue cooking over medium heat until the onion is soft and lightly browned. Add the water, cover, and simmer for 1½ to 2 hours, until the lamb is tender.

2. Meanwhile, sauté the almonds in 1 tablespoon olive oil over low heat until they turn a nice golden brown. Drain on paper towels and set aside.

3. When the meat is cooked, remove it to a large platter and keep warm. Pour off all but approximately ½ cup of the sauce. Add the honey and stir in the nutmeg and the sautéed almonds. Pour the sauce over the lamb and serve.

Serves 4.

MISCELLANEOUS—KABOBS, STRIPS, AND GROUND LAMB

Lamb Kabobs

Shish kabobs, the classic of kabob cookery, are traditionally made with lamb. But there are lots and lots of ways to go about making them. The kabob custom originated in the Middle East, where nomadic people began cooking their meats—mostly lamb—on swords over the campfire. Today shish kabobs are much more sophisticated and take many forms.

You can stick most any cut of lamb on a skewer and call it a kabob, but the best cuts I have found are pieces of the boneless leg cut into 1-to-1½-inch cubes.

For accompaniments you can choose from an array of vegetables and fruits, whatever your imagination suggests.

One important thing to remember is that many fruits and vegetables cook in less time than the meat. It's a good idea, therefore, to consider skewering the fruits and vegetables separately instead of arranging them alternately with the meat on the same skewer. Also, meats skewered between vegetables or fruits tend to steam rather than broil or grill, and the desired texture and appearance of the meat is lost. Keep the meat on a separate skewer.

Classic Lamb Shish Kabob

This recipe I call "classic," but, then, I wasn't there when kabobs began. It just seems as if it might be much like the original. It is in any case a delicious point of kabob departure.

MARINADE

- ¼ cup olive oil
- ¾ cup dry red wine
- 1 onion, chopped
- 1 clove garlic, minced
- ¼ teaspoon crumbled dried basil
- ¼ teaspoon crumbled dried marjoram
- ¼ teaspoon crumbled dried rosemary
- 1 teaspoon salt
- ¼ teaspoon black pepper

KABOBS

- 2 pounds lamb, cut into 1-to-1½-inch cubes
- 1 large green pepper, cut into 12 pieces
- 16 medium-sized mushrooms
- 1 pound small white onions
- 1 dozen cherry tomatoes

≈

1. Combine the oil, wine, and marinade seasonings and mix thoroughly. Add the lamb cubes and marinate overnight, covered.
2. Prepare and preheat an outdoor grill. Place the lamb on four skewers. Cook on the outdoor grill 4 inches from the coals for about 20 minutes, turning occasionally.
3. Arrange the vegetables on 4 other skewers and cook alongside the lamb for the last 10 minutes, turning occasionally. Baste the meat and vegetables frequently with the remaining marinade.

Serves 4.

BULGUR WHEAT PILAF

Bulgur wheat, a Middle Eastern favorite, is best when cooked in a meat broth with onion and seasonings. The nutritious whole wheat makes a moist, rich, nutty accompaniment for meat. At our house we like bulgur wheat as a pilaf. It's good with shish kabob, curry, other broiled meats, and roasts. Middle Eastern and specialty stores carry bulgur.

≈

4 tablespoons cooking oil or butter
2 cups bulgur wheat, uncooked*
½ cup chopped onion
1 teaspoon salt
½ teaspoon black pepper
1 teaspoon crumbled dried oregano (optional)
4 cups beef broth

1. Heat the oil in a saucepan and add the bulgur wheat. Stir constantly to brown, about 5 minutes. The wheat will smell nutty. Add the onion and stir an additional minute, until limp. Add the seasonings and the broth. Cover and bring to a boil.

2. Lower the heat and continue cooking for 30 minutes until all the liquid is absorbed and the wheat is tender.

Serves 6 to 8.

* White rice can be substituted, or you can use a combination of white and brown rice and bulgur wheat.

Curried Kabobs with Peanut Butter Sauce

This recipe is another example of what has become a family truism—"Put peanut butter on it and the kids will love it!"

≈

1. Mix all the Marinade ingredients together, toss the lamb cubes to coat well, and let marinate for an hour or two. Thread the meat on skewers and grill or broil to the desired degree of doneness.

2. Mix together all the Peanut Butter Sauce ingredients and let stand at room temperature for an hour or two, so the flavors blend. Serve on the kabobs, accompanied by a rice pilaf.

Serves 4 to 6.

MARINADE

- 1 tablespoon curry powder
- 1 tablespoon sugar
- 1 tablespoon tomato sauce
- 1 tablespoon wine vinegar
- 1 tablespoon Worcestershire sauce
- 1 tablespoon olive oil
- Dash Tabasco sauce

- 2 pounds lean boneless lamb, cut in 1-inch cubes

PEANUT BUTTER SAUCE

- ¼ cup tomato sauce
- ¼ cup chunky peanut butter
- 2 tablespoons mayonnaise
- 1 tablespoon vinegar
- Dash Tabasco sauce

Lamb Teriyaki Kabobs

This recipe is influenced by my wife's Hawaiian heritage. In Hawaii, kabobs are often made with strips of meat rather than with cubes. Strips can be threaded on the skewers, ribbon style, with pieces of fruit and vegetables between the folds so they don't fall off in the grilling process.

≈

- 2 pounds boneless lamb, cut into 5-by-1-inch strips
- 1 cup soy sauce
- ½ cup brown sugar
- ¼ cup peanut oil

(recipe continues)

Lamb Teriyaki Kabobs *(cont.)*

- ¼ cup white-wine vinegar
- 3 cloves garlic, minced
- 2 teaspoons toasted sesame seeds
- 1 teaspoon ground ginger
- 1 teaspoon salt
- ⅛ teaspoon red-pepper flakes
- Approximately 1 cup water chestnuts
- Approximately 1 cup pineapple chunks

1. Place the strips of lamb in a shallow glass baking dish. In a bowl combine the soy sauce, brown sugar, peanut oil, vinegar, garlic, sesame seeds, ginger, salt, and red-pepper flakes. Pour over the lamb. Marinate the meat for several hours in the refrigerator, turning occasionally.

2. Preheat the broiler, or prepare and preheat the grill. Remove the meat from the marinade and thread the strips on bamboo skewers, ribbon fashion, with water chestnuts and pineapple chunks skewered between the folds. Broil or grill for 5 to 6 minutes, turning once, until the desired degree of doneness, brushing occasionally with the marinade. Do not overcook. Serve immediately.

Serves 4 to 6.

Ground Lamb

You won't find it in every meat market in the country. A pity, because ground lamb makes wonderful meat loaves and meatballs and hamburgers. It can be substituted for beef or pork in most recipes.

The best cut by far for grinding is the boneless lamb shoulder. Ask the butcher to grind it for you. Or, better yet, grind it yourself. That way you know for sure what goes into and comes out of the grinder.

Lamb Meatballs with Water Chestnuts

- 1 egg, beaten
- 1½ cups milk
- ¼ teaspoon ground mace

These make a hearty main course or can be served as appetizers. They can also be made ahead through step 1, then individually frozen on a cookie sheet and kept frozen in a plastic bag, so you have them ready to finish off whenever needed.

≈

1. In a large mixing bowl, combine the egg, 1 cup of the milk, the mace, allspice, salt, bread crumbs, water chestnuts, parsley, onion, and lamb. Mix everything very well. Shape the lamb mixture into ¾-inch balls.

2. In a skillet, brown the meatballs in batches on all sides. Remove them from the skillet with a slotted spoon to a casserole with a tight-fitting lid.

3. Drain off all the drippings, reserving 3 tablespoons. Add the flour to the reserved drippings and stir until smooth. Gradually add the consommé, wine, and the remaining ½ cup milk.

4. Cook over medium-low heat until thickened, stirring constantly. Add the pepper and additional salt if needed. Pour the gravy over the meatballs. Cover and cook in a preheated 350-degree oven for 45 minutes.

Serves 4 to 6.

¼ teaspoon ground allspice
1 teaspoon salt
1 cup fresh bread crumbs
1 5-ounce can water chestnuts, drained and finely chopped
2 tablespoons chopped fresh parsley
1 tablespoon grated onion
1½ to 2 pounds lean ground lamb
3 tablespoons flour
1 10½-ounce can consommé or bouillon
1 cup dry white wine
¼ teaspoon ground black pepper

Stuffed Acorn Squash

Acorn squash and lamb make a delicious fall or winter dish. Easy too!

≈

1. Lightly mix together the ground lamb, onion, eggs, Worcestershire sauce, and oatmeal. Divide the mixture into quarters and mound it in the acorn-squash cavities.

2. Top with bacon strips, making an X over each mound of lamb. Bake in a preheated 350-degree oven for 1 hour, or until the lamb is done and the squash is tender.

Serves 4.

1½ pounds ground lamb
1 medium onion, very finely chopped
2 eggs
1 tablespoon Worcestershire sauce
1 cup uncooked oatmeal
2 acorn squash, cut in half lengthwise, seeds removed
4 slices bacon, cut in half crosswise

The Vanishing Shepherd

World War II ushered in yet another problem for the sheep industry. The manpower requirements of war created what has become a long-lasting labor problem for sheep rearing in the West. During the conflict, many laborers left the rural areas to join the army or to work in war plants. And when the war finally ended, the laborers did not return. For the rangeland sheep industry, which relies heavily on experienced shepherds, this caused a major problem.

To deal with the continuing labor problem, Congress in 1957 passed legislation allowing the import of labor on a temporary basis. Shepherds were brought in from other parts of the world, predominantly Basques. A unique race of people who populate the Pyrenees on both sides of the French-Spanish border, the Basques have a long history as excellent shepherds. On the Western ranges of the United States, you're likely to hear the guttural sound of the Basque language as often as English or Spanish. The Basques who migrate today to America's sheep country come as contract herders, through the help of the Western Range Association.

Albert Pouquette, an Arizona sheep man whose ancestors were Basque, talks about his peers in the language of the range and the shearing shed: "Sheep men are a special breed of people. They are gentle because their sheep require it. They are fierce because conditions are almost always adverse. They are rugged because they are outdoorsmen. They are businessmen because sheep are their livelihood. They are good providers because they have the welfare of their families and employees at heart. Perhaps more than anything else, they are fighters. They fight droughts, predators, bad feeding grounds, inflation, depression, and every kind of sickness and disease known to sheep."

Sheepdogs

The sheep industry in this country—indeed, in the world—would likely not exist were it not for dogs. Dogs have been the true guardians of the flock for centuries.

If you have never watched a Border collie move a flock of a thousand sheep gently and quietly across a grassy meadow high in the Colorado Rockies, you have indeed missed a beautiful sight. With a few soft-spoken commands—"way-to-me," "go-by," or "there"—one man, or even a young boy or girl, can gently move a flock of sheep wherever he or she wants them to go, with the help of a good sheepdog.

The most common herd dog used in the sheep industry is the Border collie. A breed that originated in the British Isles, it is noted for its intelligence and the ability to keep sheep in line by "skirting them," systematically going back and forth behind the flock and moving them in the desired direction. The dog responds readily to oral commands and is prized by sheep men for a gentle disposition coupled with a never-quit-moving work ethic.

Sheepdogs (continued)

In northern Mendocino County, in northern California—prime sheep country—there is another type of herd dog, developed by Alexander McNab. Mr. McNab left Scotland in 1868 to settle in California, where he continued his life as a shepherd. He developed a particularly smart breed of dog, known today as the McNab shepherd. It's a cross between a Border collie and the local dogs from Mendocino County. The long-haired Border collie is comfortable in the severe Scottish Highland weather. The McNab is a short-haired breed, better suited to the hot, dry ranges of northern California, where there are a lot of burrs and stickers in the fields.

McNab shepherds are alert and intelligent, and have the stamina to work sheep all day. How smart are they? O. E. Chambers, a relative of the McNab family, tells the tall tale of one proud owner of a McNab shepherd who, after working long hours, decided to go fishing. "He was hustling around getting a lunch and his gear together, and thought he'd take his dog along. He searched everywhere but couldn't find the animal. Finally, as he passed the back of the barn on his way to the lake, he spotted him. You know what that dog was doin'? Diggin' worms!"

In recent years another type of sheepdog has become important to the sheep industry in America—the guard dog. The wily coyote has always been and will undoubtedly continue to be a problem to sheep men, but in the past twenty years the problem has become much more serious. Early in 1972, President Nixon signed into law an order banning the use of predator-control poisons in public lands. Many of the sheep raised in the Western part of this country graze at least part of the year on public lands—they always have. Without any effective means of control, the coyote has been free to multiply and to increase his take of the yearly lamb crop in those areas. Coyotes do not just kill for food—they kill for fun, and they can devastate a sheep herd overnight.

To provide some protection to their flocks, American sheep men in the early 1970s turned to guard dogs: breeds like the Great Pyrenees, used for centuries by Basque shepherds in the mountains between Spain and France. These dogs live among the sheep, and their size and strength tend to intimidate would-be predators, including bobcats and coyotes, even bears.

The dogs literally live with the lambs almost from the time of birth. By the time a pup is seven or eight weeks old, it has bonded more with sheep than with people. Guard dogs can then be trained to work together with the herd dogs, as long as both animals understand their respective roles. By the time the young guard dog is four to six months old, it is ready to go live with the flock. According to sheep men I have talked with, there is nothing better than a well-trained guard dog to protect sheep around the clock.

Shepherd's Pie

MASHED POTATOES

4 potatoes, peeled
½ cup milk
1 egg, beaten
Salt and pepper

2 pounds ground lamb
2 medium onions, chopped
1½ teaspoons salt
½ teaspoon black pepper
1 8-ounce can tomato sauce
1½ cups lamb or beef stock
1 cup frozen peas
1 cup diced carrots
½ cup diced celery
8 ounces shredded Cheddar cheese

One of the most delightful culinary adventures in England is found in the neighborhood pubs. Most every pub has some version of Shepherd's Pie. It's a simple, hearty dish consisting of some sort of ground-meat stew topped with a layer of mashed potatoes. In many pubs ground beef is used, but shepherds don't herd cows! The best Shepherd's Pie I had in the pubs of Devon, Cornwall, and the Cotswolds was made with ground lamb.

≈

1. Boil the potatoes until cooked. Mash the potatoes and add the milk and beaten egg. Season to taste with salt and pepper and whip until fluffy.

2. Brown the lamb in a large skillet. Add the onions and cook until tender. Spoon off the excess fat. Add the remaining ingredients except the cheese and mix well. Taste, and add more salt and pepper if needed. Place in a 2-quart baking dish or casserole.

3. Drop the mashed potatoes in fluffs over the top of the meat mixture and sprinkle with the cheese. Bake in a preheated 350-degree oven for 30 to 35 minutes, until lightly browned.

Serves 6 to 8.

Veal

≈

THE HISTORY OF VEAL

Calves of course turned up in America as a result of the cows and bulls that came with Columbus. However, veal in America, as we know it today, dates back only to the early 1960s.

Veal is a by-product of the dairy industry. In order to continue to give milk, dairy cows must be "kept fresh," meaning they must give birth to a calf once each year. Most female calves, called heifers, become replacements—each destined to take her place in the dairy herd when an old cow stops producing and goes on to become hamburger. But the bull calves were, until the early 1960s, considered a waste product. Because there was no economic incentive to raise them, most male calves were slaughtered within a few days of birth. The mother cow was needed back on the production line at the dairy. Feed costs money, and the meat of dairy calves wasn't worth much. They were marketed at under one hundred pounds as "drop calves," "cull calves," or "bob veal." The meat they provided was bland and tasteless, and there was little demand for it. Many, in fact, never made it to market. They were "done in" and buried out behind the barn they were born in.

Such was not the case in Europe. In Holland, France, Germany, and Italy, veal was a delicacy, expensive but prized. There young bull calves were fed, to an age of two and a half to three months, a diet of milk, with some eggs toward the end. The whitish-pink meat that resulted, with its firm white fat smelling of milk and its bland flavor ready to absorb any flavor added to it, became the creative canvas for the gastronomic artists of Europe. Many of the recipes for veal that we enjoy in America today had their origin in the kitchens of the great chefs of France and Italy.

After World War II, in the early 1950s, the United States had a surplus of dry skim milk, a by-product of modern butter-and-cheese production. Much of it was shipped to Holland, "the veal capital of the world," at low prices. The Dutch discovered that feeding calves exclusively on skim milk, whey powder, and fat led to heavier weights and very much improved the quality of the veal.

The technology for producing fancy-fed, special-fed, or "Dutch-process" veal, as it became known, soon spread from Holland to France, Italy, and Germany. Chefs and gourmets all over Europe found that the meat of calves raised by the Dutch process to weights over three hundred pounds was far superior in flavor, texture, and appearance to any veal available at the time. American tourists came home with a taste for the veal they had eaten in the restaurants of Europe. I can't count the times customers asked me over the meat counter when I was working as a butcher, "Why can't we get veal here like that nice white veal they have in Europe?" Well, now we can!

The Dutch process was first introduced in America in 1963, when Aat Groenevelt, a young Hollander, came to America to establish Provimi, Inc., USA, a feed company producing milk-replacer feed for the Dutch-process veal industry that Aat felt certain would develop in America. Many people thought that "Provimi" was some exotic foreign word. Actually it's contrived from the first letters of the words "*pro*tein," "*vi*tamin," and "*mi*neral," which make up a large part of the diet of calves raised on feed produced by Provimi.

Provimi located its first plant and headquarters in Saddle Brook, New Jersey, a few miles from New York City, to develop a market with the fancy restaurants of the Big Apple. The Provimi-fed veal caught on! Within two years, not only were Dutch-process veal calves, nine to twelve weeks old and weighing three hundred pounds plus, welcomed by the chefs and diners of New York, but the farmers were making a forty-cents-a-pound premium on their calves.

The East Coast led in the production of fancy-fed veal until 1968, when Aat's brothers Eric and Robert Groenevelt came from Holland to open a second feed plant, in Wisconsin. Being the country's largest dairy state, Wisconsin has an ample supply of calves.

In 1973, Provimi took a dramatic step to become the first feed company to enter the meat business. "Delft Blue" became the trademark for Provimi veal. According to Guy Tober (then the vice-president of Provimi and today the owner of Grober Feeds), the company felt the meat industry was overlooking potential markets, including the home cook and restaurants outside of the New York metropolitan area. During the 1970s, Provimi became involved with all facets of the veal industry. They packaged, marketed, advertised, and sold vacuum-packed veal all across America. They made the name Provimi synonymous with veal. Delft Blue commissioned the first cookbook devoted entirely to veal, *Veal Cookery*, by Craig Claiborne and Pierre Franey, published by Harper & Row. I highly recommend it!

Today dozens of companies across the country produce Dutch-processed veal, and hundreds (if not thousands) of dairy farms in America—mostly small family operations—give tender loving care to the calves that provide it.

CUTS OF VEAL

The cuts of veal that you will find in the supermarket may be a bit confusing. This is partly due to differences in handling and packaging. One meat seller may be handling small "drop calves," weighing only about sixty-five to seventy pounds, which come in carcass form and are divided into retail cuts at the market, usually with the bone left in. Lamb is marketed in much the same way (see chart on page 152). Another market (or even the same market) may be handling Dutch-processed veal, which is much larger and is usually divided into small boneless "sub-primal" cuts at the packing house and shipped to the market in boxes, each cut and vacuum-packed in Cryovac, a special plastic packaging material.

The shoulders of Dutch-processed veal come to market boneless as two separate cuts, the "Veal Square Cut Chuck Neck Off, Boneless" and the "Veal Chuck Shoulder Clod Roast." These are further divided at the retail level into cubes for stew and kabobs, rolled into veal roasts, or cut into cutlets. Similarly, the leg and sirloin sections of Dutch-processed veal arrive at the market as "Leg, Shank Off, Boneless," there to be cut into retail cuts, mostly cutlets.

The only cuts of Dutch-processed veal apt to reach the retail market with the bone left in are the rib and the loin, which are usually cut into chops; the shank, the cut called for in the classic Osso Buco (see page 236); and the breast, the best cut of veal for any veal lover on a budget.

Many of the various cuts of veal are interchangeable, depending on the cooking method used in any given recipe, so let's talk a bit about cooking veal.

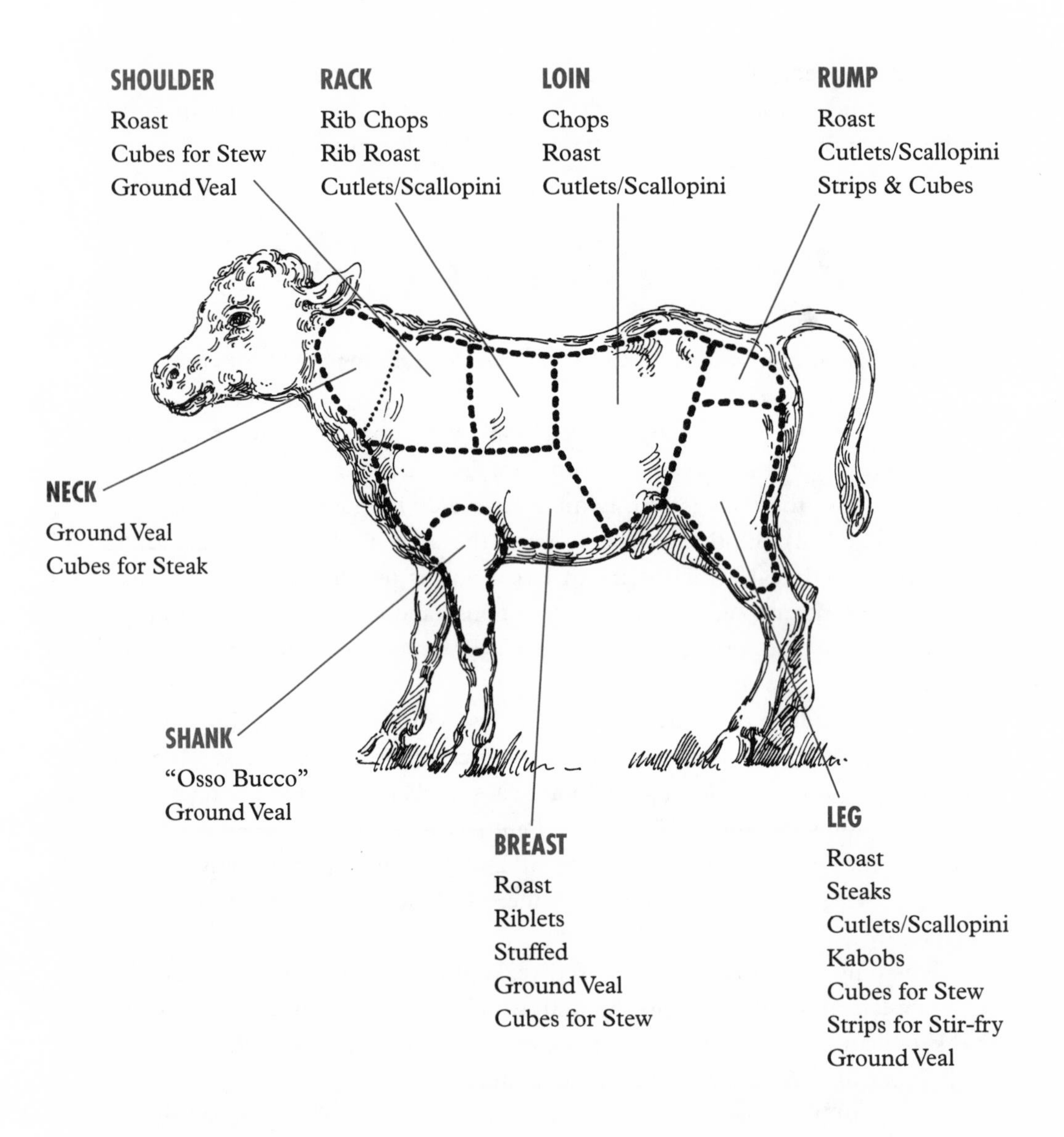
SHOULDER
Roast
Cubes for Stew
Ground Veal
RACK
Rib Chops
Rib Roast
Cutlets/Scallopini
LOIN
Chops
Roast
Cutlets/Scallopini
RUMP
Roast
Cutlets/Scallopini
Strips & Cubes
NECK
Ground Veal
Cubes for Steak
SHANK
"Osso Bucco"
Ground Veal
BREAST
Roast
Riblets
Stuffed
Ground Veal
Cubes for Stew
LEG
Roast
Steaks
Cutlets/Scallopini
Kabobs
Cubes for Stew
Strips for Stir-fry
Ground Veal

"Cruelty to Calves!"

Animal-rights activists have caused a fire storm of controversy over how veal is raised. They've picketed restaurants, sported chilling posters, and placed strident ads in newspapers and magazines. They've been so effective that people have felt guilty buying veal. But here's the story, and it answers the activists' objections.

"Veal Calves Are Raised in the Dark"

Today it is well known that veal calves develop best in well-lighted barns. However, in the early years of the veal industry, calves were raised in modified dairy barns that had been used, not as the cows' home, but as a place to bring them for milking twice a day. The barns had no insulation, and any windows were open or fitted with cold-admitting simple glass panes. To flourish, veal calves need a draft-free ventilation system; the raised, slatted floors common to old dairy barns kept them clean and dry, but compounded the draft problem. Winters in the veal country of Wisconsin and New York can get mighty cold, down to twenty below. To keep the adapted dairy barns at a comfortable sixty-five degrees, windows were covered and sealed over with insulating tape. As new veal raisers checked out the remodeled barns, they assumed the calves *needed* a dark environment. Eventually veterinarians and scientists found that those "pioneers" who had kept their windows raised healthier calves. Today veal barns have supplemental heating systems for cold weather and ventilation, and cooling systems for warm weather. And most of the growers now have barns with windows or skylights.

"Calves Are Anemic from an Iron-Free Diet"

Anti-veal activists say that formula-fed calves are purposely deprived of iron in order to produce light-pink meat. Nothing could be further from the truth, which is that their diet is very similar to that of milk-fed calves. The composition of cow's milk is the criterion used to establish the nutritional requirements of the milk-substitute diet. All milk replacements duplicate as closely as possible the taste and texture of cow's milk. These products are designed to be reconstituted with water, since calves inher-

"Cruelty to Calves!" (continued)

ently prefer milk over dry feeds and grasses. In most cases, they drink from a bucket during twice-daily feedings. According to experts in ruminant nutrition, it is natural for young calves to consume only a liquid diet, because their digestive systems must mature before they can handle solid food.

A calf needs iron to produce two oxygen-containing proteins: hemoglobin, which carries oxygen to the bloodstream, and myoglobin, which takes oxygen to the muscle tissues. Once the calf has enough iron in his diet to maintain healthy hemoglobin levels, excess iron goes toward myoglobin production.

Veal calves need a healthy level of blood hemoglobin, but since myoglobin produces an undesirable red pigment, farmers control the amount of iron carefully to keep myoglobin to moderate levels. They take care to ensure that their formula-fed calves are not anemic; anemia leads to reduced appetite and poor growth.

"Calves Are Cruelly Penned So They Cannot Move"

Animal-rights groups claim that confining the animals in individual stalls is inhumane. These stalls usually have slats on sides and front, and a slatted wooden floor. Actually, calves in these stalls are able to stand, stretch, lie down, and interact with neighboring calves. The veal industry maintains that these stalls provide positive health benefits. They allow the farmer easy access for inspection and care, and ensure that each calf gets its allotment of food and water without having to fight with more aggressive animals. The stalls keep them from sucking on each other, a habit that can cause skin lesions or can lead to urine drinking, and from turning around and defecating where they eat. Because the floor is slatted, the calves do not lie in their own excrement, and cleaning is easier. In other words, stalls reduce the treatment of disease. (An experiment in the early 1980s, of the "loose" housing of twenty calves in large pens with ten square feet or more per calf, led to the problems mentioned above. The experiment was ultimately rejected because of the dramatic increase of disease.)

So far, the best way to raise veal calves is in individual pens. If research shows a better way, the veal industry, I feel sure, will change.

Unfortunately, the controversy over veal in the diet will probably last as long as certain vegetarians and animal-rightists continue with untrue and misleading rhetoric and write "Meat Is Murder" on the sides of veal barns. Fortunately, knowledgeable doctors, nutritionists, consumers, and particularly creative young chefs have ignored the controversy and have greatly increased their acceptance and demand for formula-fed, pen-raised veal.

To quote a friend for whom I have the greatest respect: "If it isn't raised in confinement, it isn't veal." So sayeth Julia Child.

VEAL COOKERY

Because of its youth, veal is naturally more tender from one end to the other than older, more mature beef. There is, however, a great deal of difference in the tenderness of different muscles within any individual carcass. The difference in the natural degree of tenderness in the various muscles of a beef animal is largely attributed to use: the muscles that get used get tough; those that get little use stay tender.

However, with modern veal-production methods, no muscle of the veal animal gets much use. In veal, the toughness or tenderness of any cut is related to the amount of connective tissue contained therein. A cutlet from the tenderloin that has not been trimmed of connective tissue may be no more tender than one cut from a solid muscle of the shoulder or the leg that has had all of the connective tissue trimmed away. Connective tissue is like a thin membrane that surrounds and separates individual muscles and groups of muscles.

In dry-heat methods of cooking, such as you would use for veal chops or cutlets, this connective tissue toughens, making the meat a little hard to chew. But that same connective tissue in a cut cooked with moist heat—that is, braised or stewed—dissolves into a very desirable rich, thick, gelatinous substance that adds much to the consistency of a sauce.

So the real secret to satisfaction in buying veal is to match the cut—with or without connective tissue—to the cooking method. Use cuts with little or no connective tissue—the tenderloin; top loin; top, bottom, or eye of round; or shoulder clod—for dry-heat cooking. The rest of the critter—the shoulder, shank, breast, and rib—is loaded with connective tissue and is best braised or stewed.

In the following recipes, I have recommended the cuts most appropriate to each cooking method.

VEAL ROASTS

There is no easier piece of meat to prepare than an oven roast of veal. It is sure to be tender—veal is too young to be tough; it requires little attention, just an occasional basting with pan juices; and it lends itself to all manner of seasoning variations. A veal roast is to a cook what a blank canvas is to an artist.

For oven roasting, or any dry-heat method of cooking—spit-roasting or barbecue—a veal roast from the leg, loin, or rib is preferable. Those cuts have the least connective tissue and tend to be the most tender. They also have very little fat, and many cooks add flavor by adding a bit of fat by "larding"—inserting slivers of fat into slits in the meat.

For pot roasts, slowly cooked in liquid, cuts from the shoulder work well. The connective tissue in shoulder cuts adds much to the sauce in the cooking process. The breast is good for pot roasting, but the breast works for so many things it deserves its own section (see pages 216–21).

Roast Loin of Veal

Craig Claiborne and Pierre Franey's excellent book *Veal Cookery* has this simple roast recipe. A roast is so easy to cook; season it the way you want, baste it occasionally, don't overcook it—then enjoy!

- A 5-to-6-pound veal loin
- 2 to 3 tablespoons softened butter
- Salt and pepper to taste
- ½ cup diced carrot
- ½ cup diced celery
- ½ cup diced onion
- 1 clove garlic, chopped
- 1 cup chopped fresh or canned tomatoes
- 6 sprigs parsley
- 3 sprigs fresh thyme or ½ teaspoon dried
- 1 bay leaf

≈

1. Preheat the oven to 425 degrees. Rub the meat thoroughly with butter. Season with salt and pepper. Place the loin in a shallow roasting pan, fat side up. Bake for 15 minutes, basting occasionally.
2. Turn the meat fat side down and scatter the carrot, celery, onion, and garlic around it. Bake for 15 minutes, basting once.
3. Turn the meat fat side up and scatter the tomato bits around it. Tie the parsley, thyme, and bay leaf in cheesecloth and add to the pan. Reduce the heat to 400 degrees and bake for 15 minutes.
4. Cover the meat with foil and bake 30 minutes longer. Total baking time is about 1 hour and 15 minutes or less. It is advisable always to use an instant-read thermometer for a successful roast. A veal roast is ready at 160 degrees.
5. Strain the pan juices and remove any excess fat. Carve the roast and serve with the pan juices.

Serves 6 to 8.

VEAL BREAST

The breast of veal is the best cut of veal for my money. Most cuts of top-quality veal are pretty expensive; veal cutlets and chops are often the most expensive cuts in the meat case. Breast of veal, however, is often a very good buy, and there are so very many, varied things to be done with it. You can bone it and roll it, put a pocket in it, stuff it, sauté it, and sauce it up with dozens of delightful sauces. With a breast of veal, you can serve veal, even fancy French "veau," without going broke!

When you run across one at a reasonable price, buy it. Take it home and do something with it! See "Boning the Breast" (below).

Boning the Breast

Boning the breast of veal is an easy task. The marvelous things that can be done with a boneless veal breast are limited by little more than your imagination. To bone one, put it on the cutting board with the meaty side down so the rib bones are on top and easy to get at. On top of the rib bones is the diaphragm muscle, the skirt steak. It is a long, thin flap of lean meat that extends nearly the length of the breast. Use that as a handle. Lift up on the "skirt" and cut under it along the rib bones to loosen the meat from the bone all the way down to where the bone becomes a soft white cartilage connecting the ribs to one another. The French would leave some of the white cartilage in the breast—the *tendron*—and relish its crunchy texture and the beautiful gelatinous quality it adds to the sauce. But if the idea of crunching on cartilage turns you off, leave it attached to the rib bones.

Now turn the whole breast over so that it is resting on the rib bones and continue trimming along to the bones, lifting the meat as you go. Don't worry about the little bit of meat between the ribs. This can be trimmed off later, or left on the bones to go into the stock pot (see page 237); it's not worth the time and effort necessary to leave it on the breast. I often make a point of leaving extra meat on the bones; veal ribs are great cooked up in a barbecue sauce (see page 221). After removing the ribs, you have easy access to and can easily trim away any excess fat that lies between the bones and ribs.

When you have finished, you'll have a great huge slab of lean boneless breast of veal that can be made into all manner of marvelous meals. With the breast of veal it is possible to feed a small army a feast for less than a fortune. Your boneless breast of veal can be sliced, diced, or cubed for quick-cooking dishes, or stuffed with a variety of things for an elegant boneless stuffed veal roast. For stuffing, the breast works best and looks most elegant if it is first butterflied.

Butterfly the boneless breast by cutting horizontally through the meat, leaving a half-inch-thick uncut "hinge" so that you can open out the meat like a book. Flatten the opened meat with a mallet as thin as possible, approximately a half-inch. Spread whatever stuffing ingredients your recipe calls for, then roll the breast up jelly-roll fashion and tie with string at one-inch intervals. The end result, whatever the stuffing, makes an attractive presentation, and we taste things first with our eyes!

Stuffed Breast of Veal

1 cup seedless black raisins
½ cup cooked rice
2 slices rye bread soaked in ½ cup milk
¼ pound salt pork, finely diced
2 egg yolks
1 10-ounce package frozen chopped spinach, thawed and drained
¼ teaspoon freshly grated nutmeg
1 teaspoon dried basil
Salt and pepper
3 to 4 pounds boneless breast of veal, butterflied (see page 217)
1 tablespoon vegetable oil
2 bay leaves
1 cup white wine

A boneless veal breast can be stuffed with all manner of tasty ingredients. Try this recipe, or make whatever variations you like. Serve hot or cold with a sauce of sour cream mixed with raisins.

≈

1. Mix the raisins, rice, bread, salt pork, egg yolks, spinach, nutmeg, basil, and salt and pepper to taste. Spoon the mixture into the center of the butterflied veal breast. Then roll the meat around the stuffing and tie with kitchen twine at 1-inch intervals.

2. Brown the breast on both sides in the oil in a roasting pan. Season with salt, pepper, and a little nutmeg and top with the bay leaves. Add the wine, cover, and bake in a preheated 350-degree oven about 1½ hours, until tender. Remove the string and discard the bay leaves.

Serves 6.

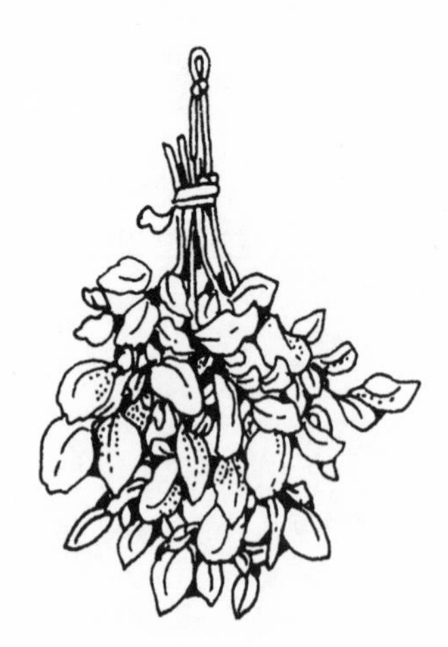

Italian-Style Rolled Veal with Hazelnuts

Hazelnuts are "big" in Italy, which is why this recipe is tagged "Italian-Style." I first had this dish in Portland, Oregon. Hazelnuts are big in that part of the world as well, but they call them "filberts" there.

≈

3 cloves garlic, minced
A 2-to-3-pound boneless veal breast, butterflied (see page 217)
Salt
¼ teaspoon freshly grated nutmeg
¼ pound prosciutto or cooked ham, sliced thin
⅓ cup shelled hazelnuts, toasted and chopped
2 eggs
2 tablespoons milk
2 tablespoons butter
1 tablespoon freshly grated Parmesan cheese
1 tablespoon olive oil
2 tablespoons brandy
¼ cup beef broth

1. Spread the minced garlic over the meat and season evenly with salt and nutmeg. Lay on the ham slices and sprinkle with the hazelnuts.

2. Beat the eggs and milk together. Heat 1 tablespoon of the butter in a 12-inch nonstick pan and make a thin omelette. Lay the omelette on the veal. Sprinkle the Parmesan cheese on the omelet. Roll up the breast jelly-roll fashion and tie with string at 1-inch intervals.

3. Heat the remaining butter and the olive oil in a heavy casserole over high heat and brown the roll well all over. Pour on the brandy and cook until evaporated. Reduce the heat to medium low, add the beef broth, cover, and simmer for about an hour, basting occasionally with pan juices. Add more broth if necessary.

4. When the meat is cooked, transfer it to a carving board and allow to cool to room temperature. When it is cool (not before, or it will fall apart!), remove the string and carve into ½-inch slices. Arrange the slices on a heatproof serving dish into which you have poured the pan juices. Reheat in a 300-degree oven for 10 minutes and serve.

Serves 6 to 8.

Lemon Veal Roast with Rosemary

- 2 ounces pancetta (unsmoked Italian bacon)
- 1 large clove garlic
- ¼ cup chopped Italian parsley
- 2 tablespoons fresh lemon juice
- 1½ to 2 pounds boneless veal breast, butterflied (see page 217)
- 2 tablespoons extra-virgin olive oil
- Salt and freshly ground pepper
- 3-inch sprig fresh rosemary or 1 teaspoon dried
- ⅔ cup dry white wine
- ½ cup veal stock or chicken broth
- Rosemary sprigs for garnish

This recipe is based on one from a marvelous book by a friend of mine. I'm having a wonderful time cooking my way through *The Splendid Table,* by Lynne Rosetto Kasper.

≈

1. With a sharp knife mince together the pancetta, garlic, and parsley. Add 1 tablespoon of the lemon juice. Spoon the mixture into the center of the butterflied veal breast, then roll the meat around the stuffing and tie with string at intervals. Set the roast on a platter, cover lightly with plastic wrap, and refrigerate for 24 hours to allow the flavors to blend.

2. Preheat the oven to 350 degrees. Rub the veal with the olive oil and season lightly with salt and pepper. Set the roast in a shallow roasting pan with the rosemary. Roast for 20 minutes, then pour half of the wine over the meat. Baste with the pan juices. Continue roasting, basting, and adding small amounts of wine, until an instant-read thermometer inserted into the center of the meat reads 150 degrees (the roast takes approximately 1 to 1½ hours). Remove the roast to a warm platter and keep warm.

3. Skim the fat from the pan juices and discard it. Set the roasting pan on a burner over high heat. Bring the juices to a boil and stir in the stock. Boil, scraping up the brown glaze in the pan with a wooden spatula, for 2 minutes, or until the sauce has thickened slightly and is full-flavored. Season with salt and pepper and stir in the remaining tablespoon of lemon juice.

4. Keep the sauce warm as you carve the meat into ¼-inch slices. Garnish the platter with a few sprigs of rosemary, and pass the sauce separately.

Serves 4.

Barbecued Veal Breast Ribs

There are those (I am one of them) who would argue that this is not true BBQ, since it's not cooked long and slow over coals—I would classify it as a "barbesauce." But it is delicious, well worth leaving a little extra meat on the bones when you bone out a veal breast.

- 1 pound smoked bacon, chopped
- 2 medium onions, chopped
- 4 garlic cloves, minced
- 3 stalks celery, finely chopped
- 6 ounces (½ of a 12-ounce can) dark beer
- 2 8-ounce cans tomato sauce
- 1 cup tomato catsup
- ½ cup brown sugar
- 1 tablespoon Worcestershire sauce
- 3 tablespoons prepared brown mustard
- 2 pounds meaty veal rib bones
- Salt and pepper
- ½ cup vegetable oil
- 3 scallions, finely chopped

≈

1. Preheat the oven to 325 degrees. Sauté the bacon in a large saucepan until browned. Add the onions, garlic, and celery. Cook until the onions are translucent, drain off the fat, and deglaze the pan with the beer, scraping up any browned bits. Add the tomato sauce, catsup, brown sugar, Worcestershire sauce, and prepared mustard. Cover and simmer for 30 minutes.
2. Season the veal ribs on both sides with salt and pepper; heat the oil, and brown well on both sides. Cut the veal between the ribs. Place the ribs in a heavy casserole, pour on the sauce, cover, and cook in a preheated 325-degree oven for 30 minutes. Sprinkle with the chopped scallions before serving.

Serves 6.

VEAL CHOPS

Chops are cut from the loin or rack of veal. They can be grilled, broiled, pan-fried, sautéed, or braised. For dry-heat cooking, the nice big chops from Dutch-processed veal are the best. Look for a light-pink color with a smooth firm texture and creamy white fat. For braising, I find the smaller chops of "bob veal" every bit as good.

Veal Chops with Tarragon Sauce

4 veal rib chops, cut ¾ inch thick
3 tablespoons butter
Large clove garlic, peeled
¾ cup chicken broth
¼ cup brandy
1½ teaspoons chopped fresh tarragon or ½ teaspoon dried
½ cup heavy cream
Salt and pepper to taste

Any chop can be enhanced with a simple sauce. Tarragon, which is widely used in classic French cooking, is the herb of choice with this recipe, but you can use whatever you like, since we have so many wonderful fresh herbs available to us today.

The cream also reflects the rich French way with veal. A lighter variation can be made by eliminating the cream and thickening the sauce at the end with a half-teaspoon cornstarch dissolved in a tablespoon of chicken broth.

≈

1. Score the fatty edges of the chops at ½-inch intervals to avoid curling.

2. Heat a large skillet over medium heat and add the butter. Add the garlic, lower the heat, and cook for 2 minutes. Do not let the garlic brown. Discard the garlic.

3. Increase the heat to high, add the chops, and brown quickly on both sides. Lower the heat to medium and cook for 15 minutes, turning once. Transfer the chops to a platter, cover with aluminum foil, and keep warm in a preheated 200-degree oven.

4. To make the sauce, pour off the oil and add the broth, brandy, and tarragon to the skillet. Over high heat, deglaze the pan by scraping the brown bits from the bottom. Add the cream, lower the heat to medium, and reduce the liquid to ¾ cup. Season with salt and pepper. Pour the sauce through a fine strainer. Keep warm.

5. Spoon some sauce onto plates and top with a veal chop. Serve the rest of the sauce on the side.

Serves 4.

Veal Chops Supreme

16 small boiling onions
12 medium mushrooms
¼ pound thickly sliced smoked bacon, finely chopped
½ cup flour
Salt and freshly ground pepper
4 veal loin chops, cut ¾ inch thick
⅓ cup brandy
2 tablespoons Dijon mustard
1 cup heavy cream

Once the onions are prepared, this is almost like a stir-fry recipe: one pan and quick. For a lighter variation, use three-quarters of a cup of beef or chicken broth in place of the cup of heavy cream.

≈

1. In a medium saucepan cover the unpeeled onions with water and boil for 10 minutes. While the onions are cooking, clean the mushrooms and trim the stems level with the cap. Drain the onions in a colander. Trim off the roots and slip off the skin.

2. Cook the bacon in a large skillet over medium heat until crisp. Remove the bacon with a slotted spoon and transfer to paper towels. When cool enough to handle, chop and set aside. Leave the fat in the pan and keep it hot.

3. Mix the flour, salt, and pepper in a pie dish. Dredge the chops in the mixture to cover lightly. Shake the chops to remove excess flour.

4. Add the chops to the bacon fat and brown evenly, about 3 minutes on each side. Remove the chops, set aside, and keep warm. Add the onions and brown evenly on all sides.

5. Push the onions to the side of the pan and add the mushrooms. Brown, stirring frequently. Transfer the onions and mushrooms to the warmed platter with the chops.

6. Stirring with a wooden spoon, add the brandy and deglaze the skillet, scraping up brown bits from the bottom of the pan. Whisk in the Dijon mustard. Add the cream, chopped bacon, and salt and pepper to taste, and stir well. Cook until the mixture thickens, about 3 to 5 minutes. Pour the sauce into a warmed sauce boat.

7. Spoon some of the sauce onto 4 dinner plates and place on each a chop and some mushrooms and onions. Serve the extra sauce separately.

Serves 4.

Veal Chops with Berry Sauce

- 6 veal loin or rib chops, cut 1 inch thick
- ¾ teaspoon salt
- ¼ teaspoon freshly ground black pepper
- 3 tablespoons oil
- 2 cups fresh or thawed frozen red raspberries or blackberries
- 3 tablespoons sugar
- 3 tablespoons sherry
- ¼ teaspoon dry mustard
- ¼ teaspoon powdered ginger

My wife loves this recipe. It's tasty and *quick*!

≈

1. Season the chops with the salt and pepper. In a large skillet, brown the chops in the hot oil, turning once. Remove from the pan and keep warm.
2. Stir the berries, sugar, sherry, mustard, and ginger into the drippings in the pan. Cook over medium heat until thickened, about 5 minutes.
3. Return the chops to the pan and baste them with the sauce. Cover, lower the heat, and simmer for about 20 minutes, stirring occasionally. Serve the chops with the sauce.

Serves 6.

Veal with Pepper Pear Relish

Simply grilled chops get a zing of flavor with this relish.

≈

- 4 veal loin or rib chops, cut 1 inch thick
- 1 tablespoon olive oil
- 1 large red bell pepper, cut into ½-inch pieces (about 1 cup)
- 1 large green bell pepper, cut into ½-inch pieces (about 1 cup)
- 1 small or medium onion, chopped (about ½ cup)
- 2 tablespoons seeded, minced jalapeño pepper
- 1 tablespoon minced fresh ginger root
- 1 large firm bosc pear, peeled, cut into ½-inch pieces (about 1 cup)
- 6 tablespoons fresh lemon juice
- 3 tablespoons firmly packed brown sugar
- 1 teaspoon grated lemon peel
- ¾ teaspoon salt
- 2 tablespoons chopped cilantro
- ¼ teaspoon coarsely ground black pepper
- Cilantro sprigs and lemon twists, for garnish

1. Heat the broiler to its highest point. Place the chops on the rack of the broiler pan. Broil 4 inches from the heat, 5 minutes on each side, for medium (150 degrees), or to desired doneness.

2. Meanwhile, heat the oil in a large skillet over medium heat. Add the bell peppers, onion, jalapeño, and ginger. Cook, uncovered, 10 minutes, stirring occasionally. Stir in the pear pieces, 4 tablespoons of the lemon juice, the brown sugar, lemon peel, and ½ teaspoon of the salt. Simmer uncovered until the pear is tender, about 5 minutes. Remove from the heat.

3. Stir in the remaining 2 tablespoons of lemon juice and the chopped cilantro. Season the broiled chops with the remaining salt and the pepper. Arrange on a platter and keep warm. Spoon the relish over the chops. Garnish with cilantro sprigs and lemon twists.

Serves 4.

Neva's Quick Veal Chops with Almonds

My wife would prefer not spending a whole lot of time in the kitchen. She's a great cook, but most of her recipes are "Neva's Quick."

- **4 veal rib chops, cut ¾ inch thick**
- **2 tablespoons vegetable oil**
- **½ cup sliced fresh mushrooms**
- **½ cup sliced celery**
- **¼ cup chopped onion**
- **½ cup chicken broth**
- **2 tablespoons soy sauce**
- **2 teaspoons cornstarch**
- **2 tablespoons toasted almonds**

≈

1. In a large skillet, brown the chops in the hot oil. Add the mushrooms, celery, and onion (it is not necessary to stir), ¼ cup of the chicken broth, and the soy sauce. Cover, lower the heat, and simmer for 20 minutes, or until the veal is tender.

2. Remove the chops and keep warm. Stir the remaining broth into the cornstarch; blend into the mixture in the skillet. Cook, stirring constantly, until the mixture thickens and bubbles. Stir in the almonds. Drizzle a little sauce over the meat, and pass the remaining.

Serves 4.

VEAL CUTLETS AND PATTIES

Veal Cutlets

Cutlets are thin slices of veal taken from the leg or loin. They are, to be sure, one of the most versatile cuts of meat. There seems to be no limit to the variations of their preparation, and almost no limit to the variety of terms used to describe them. Depending upon how well your butcher speaks a foreign language, cutlets may be called "escalopes," "médaillons," or "noisettes" (French); "schnitzel" (German); or "scaloppine" (Italian). In English, ask for cutlets, scallops, medallions, or thin slices. Cutlets can also be stuffed and rolled and called paupiettes, roulades, or veal birds.

Veal Piccata with Pistachios

1 pound veal leg cutlets
1 teaspoon lemon pepper
1 tablespoon butter
2 tablespoons dry white wine or water
2 teaspoons fresh lemon juice
2 teaspoons horseradish mustard
1 teaspoon honey
½ teaspoon grated lemon peel
2 tablespoons chopped toasted pistachio nuts
4 large romaine-lettuce leaves
Lemon slices, for garnish

I was a judge at the 1990 Veal Cooking Contest in Wisconsin. The second-place winner, Tillie Astorino from North Adams, Massachusetts, won $750. It was my favorite recipe.

≈

1. Pound the cutlets to ⅛-inch thickness. Sprinkle with the lemon pepper. Heat the butter in a 10-inch nonstick skillet over medium heat. Cook the cutlets in two batches until cooked through, 2 to 3 minutes, turning once. Remove from the skillet and keep them warm.

2. Add the wine, lemon juice, mustard, honey, and lemon peel to the skillet. Heat through, stirring. Stir in the nuts. Arrange the cutlets on the lettuce leaves. Spoon the nuts and remaining liquid in the skillet over them. Garnish with the lemon slices.

Serves 4.

Veal Birds with Ham and Cheese

Although this is a recipe for four, it can easily be expanded to make an excellent entrée for a buffet.

≈

- 4 thin slices veal (about 1 pound), pounded thin
- 3 teaspoons Dijon mustard
- 4 thin slices boiled ham
- 4 thin slices cheese (Swiss, Monterey Jack, or American)
- 3 scallions, chopped
- Fresh herbs: thyme, tarragon, rosemary
- Salt and pepper
- 1 tablespoon butter
- ½ cup white wine
- 2 tablespoons flour
- 1 cup milk
- 2 tablespoons grated cheese (same kind as above)

1. Spread the cutlets with the mustard and cover with the slices of ham and cheese. Sprinkle with the chopped scallions, your choice of herbs, and salt and pepper. Roll up the cutlets and secure them with toothpicks.

2. Heat the butter in a skillet and brown the "birds." Add the wine and simmer, covered, for 20 to 30 minutes, or until the meat is tender. When the birds are cooked, remove them to a warm platter.

3. Blend the flour into the pan juices. Gradually add the milk and the grated cheese, stirring until the sauce is smooth and thick. Add more salt and pepper if needed. Pour the sauce over the birds and serve.

Serves 4.

VARIATION

For a lighter sauce, use beef or chicken broth in the final step and skip the extra cheese.

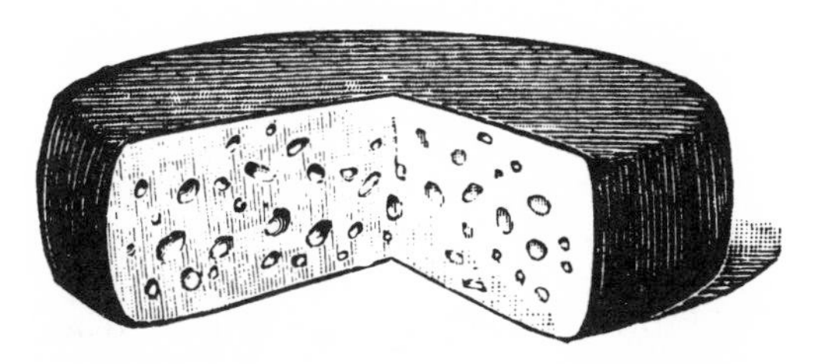

Veal Scaloppine with Capers

2 tablespoons capers
1 pound thin veal cutlets (12 slices, each about ¼ inch thick)
½ cup flour
2 tablespoons butter
2 tablespoons olive oil
1 cup dry white wine
¼ teaspoon black pepper
Juice of ½ lemon
1 tablespoon tomato paste
1 tablespoon chopped fresh oregano
½ lemon, thinly sliced

"Scaloppine" is Italian for "scallops" in English, "escalopes" in French, or just plain "cutlets" in America. Sliced thin and pounded, as they should be, they cook fast and lend themselves to all manner of flavorings. This dish is a favorite around our house, but a few of many variations follow. Use your imagination.

Quick cooking is the key to good scaloppine. They should be sautéed very quickly in a mixture of butter and oil (the oil helps keep the butter from burning) until just cooked through and lightly browned.

≈

1. Rinse and drain the capers. Set aside.

2. Dredge the veal in flour to coat lightly. In a large skillet, heat the butter and oil over medium-high heat. When the butter foams, add the meat to the pan and sauté, about 1 minute on each side. (You will have to cook the cutlets in batches.) Transfer the meat to a platter and keep warm in a preheated 200-degree oven.

3. Add the white wine, pepper, and lemon juice to the skillet, stirring up the brown bits from the bottom of the pan. Add the tomato paste and capers, and whisk until blended. Pour the sauce over the veal, sprinkle with the oregano, and garnish with the lemon slices.

Serves 4.

VARIATIONS

Scaloppine with Pine Nuts Omit the capers and tomato paste. Sauté ½ cup of pine nuts in 2 tablespoons of butter in the pan after you remove the cutlets and before adding the wine and other ingredients. Or use almond slivers and create another variation.

Scaloppine with Fresh Herbs Fresh herbs are increasingly available in America today. They're in the produce departments of fine supermarkets, in farmers' markets, and, for many of us, in backyards and in pots on windowsills. They go wonderfully with veal.

Cook the veal cutlets as described in step 2. Then add a tablespoon or two of your favorite herb—parsley, chives, tarragon, rosemary, or a combination—and ⅔ cup of dry white wine. Bring to a boil and cook for a couple of minutes to reduce the liquid slightly. Pour over the veal and serve.

Veal Patties

Any cut of veal can be ground to make patties. The shoulder or breast is most often used. All the dos and don'ts of making good hamburger (page 72) apply to making good veal patties: do grind some fat with the meat, and don't overhandle the patty.

Veal Patties with Mustard Sauce

1 pound ground veal
1 egg, beaten
¼ cup fresh bread crumbs
2 tablespoons milk
1 clove garlic, minced
2 tablespoons chopped parsley
¼ teaspoon salt
¼ teaspoon ground sage
⅛ teaspoon white pepper
⅛ teaspoon freshly grated nutmeg
1 tablespoon butter
½ cup plain yogurt
1 tablespoon coarse-grain mustard
1 tablespoon cornstarch
Parsley, for garnish (optional)

A simple recipe, but a tasty way to enjoy the delicate flavor of ground veal.

≈

1. In a large bowl, combine the veal, egg, bread crumbs, milk, garlic, chopped parsley, salt, sage, pepper, and nutmeg; mix thoroughly but gently. Divide the mixture into 4 equal portions; shape into ¾-inch-thick patties.

2. Heat the butter in a large skillet over medium-high heat. Place the patties in the skillet; cook 5 to 6 minutes on each side, just until cooked through. Transfer patties to serving plate and keep warm.

3. Mix together the yogurt, mustard, and cornstarch. Add to the skillet; cook, stirring over medium heat, until bubbly and thickened, about 2 minutes. Serve the sauce over the patties. Garnish with parsley, if desired.

Serves 4.

Hidden Treasure Veal Patties

½ cup cracker crumbs
¼ cup sour cream
½ teaspoon Dijon-style mustard
½ teaspoon salt

Blue cheese is the hidden treasure, and, coming from Iowa as I do, I believe it has to be Maytag Blue!

≈

1. In a large mixing bowl, combine the cracker crumbs, sour cream, and mustard. Allow to stand for 10

minutes. Stir in the salt, pepper, onion, 1 tablespoon parsley, and egg. Mix well.

2. Add the veal and mix thoroughly. Shape the mixture into 4 patties. Press one piece of blue cheese into the center of each patty. Fold the meat over the cheese and reshape the patties to be certain the cheese is completely encased in the meat. Chill for 1 to 2 hours.

3. Lightly dust each patty with flour. In a shallow pan, melt the butter. Brown the patties over medium heat for 2 minutes per side. Place in a preheated 350-degree oven for 20 minutes.

4. Garnish each patty with a lemon slice and sprinkle with chopped parsley.

Serves 4.

¼ teaspoon lemon pepper
1 tablespoon chopped onion
1 tablespoon chopped parsley
1 egg, lightly beaten
1 pound ground veal
2 ounces blue cheese, cut into 4 equal pieces, chilled
Flour
3 tablespoons butter
4 lemon slices
1 tablespoon chopped parsley

VEAL SAUTÉS, STEWS, AND STOCK

"Sauté" is a generic cooking term that applies to the preparation of any meat cut into small equal-size pieces which are sautéed—that is to say, cooked quickly in a small amount of oil in a skillet or sauté pan over direct high heat. It's a preparation technique that's close kin to stir-fry. Many different vegetables, mushrooms, etc., can be added to the pan after the meat is browned; then the dish is cooked until done and finished off with some sort of sauce.

Sauté is also step one in the preparation of a good veal stew. After the meat is browned, the vegetables are added and the ingredients are covered with a broth and simmered slowly to make a rich, delicious stew. Following are a few of my family's favorites in this category.

Also included here is veal stock, without which no refrigerator is well stocked.

Veal and Eggplant Sauté

TOMATO SAUCE

1 medium onion, chopped
2 cloves garlic, minced
3 tablespoons olive oil
2 tomatoes, peeled and chopped
1 tablespoon tomato paste
¼ teaspoon dried basil
¼ teaspoon dried rosemary
¼ teaspoon salt
¼ teaspoon black pepper
¼ cup dry white wine

SAUTÉ

1 medium eggplant
Salt
⅓ cup olive oil
1½ pounds boneless veal breast or shoulder
Chopped parsley

The zesty Tomato Sauce adds a little zip to the veal and eggplant.

≈

1. Make the sauce. Cook the onion and garlic in the oil until soft. Add the tomatoes and the remainder of the sauce ingredients and bring to a boil. Lower the heat and cook uncovered until thickened, about 30 minutes.

2. Meanwhile, remove the stem from the eggplant; do not peel. Slice crosswise into ½-inch-thick slices, then cut into ½-inch-wide strips. Spread the strips on several paper towels. Sprinkle liberally with salt and let stand 20 minutes. The eggplant will exude liquid; blot it with paper towels.

3. Heat the olive oil in a large skillet and add the eggplant. Cook until brown and tender. Remove from the pan.

4. Cut the veal into bite-size pieces. Cook them for about 5 minutes, turning often to brown all sides. Return the eggplant to the pan and stir in the Tomato Sauce. Simmer for 8 to 10 minutes until the veal is done. Sprinkle with parsley.

Serves 4 to 6.

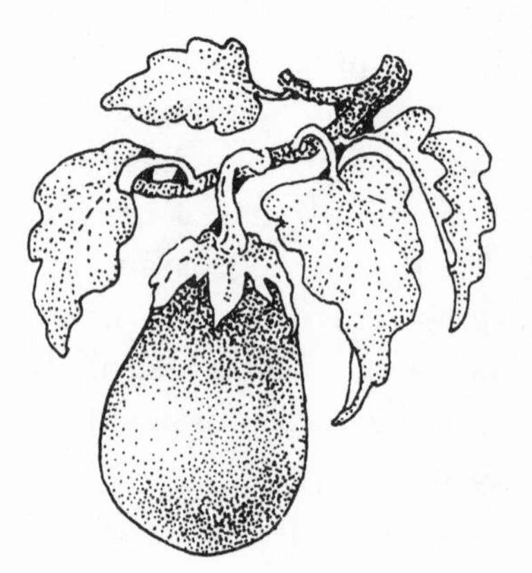

Veal Bontemps

Guests dining at The Old Plank Depot in High Point, North Carolina, find this dish, served in individual casseroles, a special treat.

- 2 sticks (16 tablespoons) butter
- ⅔ cup flour
- 1½ cups chicken broth
- 1½ cups beef broth
- 1½ cups apple juice
- 2 medium tart apples, peeled, cored, and finely chopped
- ¼ cup Dijon mustard
- 2 pounds lean boneless veal breast or shoulder, cut into thin strips
- 10 medium mushrooms, sliced
- Salt and freshly ground pepper, to taste

≈

1. Melt 8 tablespoons of the butter in a large saucepan. Stir in the flour and cook, stirring, until the mixture begins to brown. Whisk in the chicken broth, beef broth, and apple juice. Increase the heat and simmer the mixture for 5 minutes. Add the apples and blend in the mustard; cook for another minute. Set aside.

2. Melt the remaining 8 tablespoons of the butter in a large skillet. Add the veal and mushrooms and season with salt and pepper. Sauté for about 3 minutes, stirring. Stir in the sauce and simmer until the mushrooms are tender, about 3 minutes. Serve immediately.

Serves 8.

Pasta with Veal Sauce

This is a wonderful sauce to serve with all types of pasta. Keep in mind that veal is a very delicate-tasting meat that lends itself to all kind of imaginative seasonings. So create!

- ½ cup dried porcini mushrooms
- 2 cups chicken broth
- ¼ cup olive oil
- 2 pounds lean boneless veal breast or shoulder, cut into 1-inch cubes
- 1 onion, chopped
- 1 cup white wine
- 4 bay leaves
- Salt and pepper to taste

≈

1. Soak the mushrooms in the chicken broth for 30 minutes. Drain the mushrooms, strain the liquid through cheesecloth, and reserve. Chop the mushrooms, and set aside.

2. Heat the oil in a large skillet. add the veal, and cook quickly over moderately high heat until browned. Add the onion and cook until golden.

3. Add the wine and bay leaves, season with salt and

(recipe continues)

Pasta with Veal Sauce
(cont.)

1 celery rib, chopped
1 carrot, chopped
¼ cup chopped parsley
1 cup canned tomatoes, drained and chopped
2 cups (approximately ½ pound) uncooked pasta (shells, corkscrews, or bows)
½ cup grated Parmesan cheese

pepper, and cook until the alcohol evaporates, about 5 minutes. Lower the heat and add the celery, carrot, parsley, mushrooms, tomatoes, and 1 cup of the reserved liquid. Cover and cook over low heat for 45 minutes. Remove and discard the bay leaves.

4. Cook the pasta and drain it. Toss the pasta with half of the sauce. Place on a warmed serving plate and pour the remaining sauce over the top. Sprinkle with cheese and serve.

Serves 6.

Dad's Veal Marengo

2 to 3 pounds lean boneless veal breast or shoulder, cut into 1½-to-2-inch pieces
Salt and pepper
2 tablespoons olive oil
1 cup chopped onion
1 cup diced carrots
3 cloves garlic, finely chopped
1 bay leaf
½ teaspoon crumbled dried thyme
2 tablespoons chopped parsley
¼ cup tomato paste
1 cup dry white wine
1½ to 3 cups veal stock or chicken broth
2 teaspoons arrowroot dissolved in 1 tablespoon cold water

I first made this dish years ago, when I ran across veal breast in the market at a bargain price. Not being one to pass up a bargain, I took it home. The result of a little cutting up and cooking in my kitchen was this dish I called Veal Marengo. The kids loved it and the name stuck. It is not, I'm sure, anything remotely resembling the original dish prepared by Napoleon's chef near the village of Marengo in northern Italy in 1800, but my kids, who are adults now, still love it. So will yours! Call it what you will.

≈

1. Season the veal cubes with salt and pepper. Heat the oil in a large, heavy skillet; add the veal cubes and brown over high heat, tossing to brown evenly on all sides.

2. Transfer the veal to a heavy casserole or Dutch oven with a lid. Pour off any fat in the skillet and discard it. Place the skillet over low heat and add the onion, carrots, garlic, bay leaf, thyme, parsley, tomato paste, wine, and veal stock. Cook, stirring briefly to blend and to loosen and incorporate any browned particles of veal that have stuck to the pan. Pour the mixture over the veal in

the casserole, and stir to blend. Cover and bake in a preheated 350-degree oven for 1 hour.

3. Transfer the veal cubes with a slotted spoon to another casserole or serving dish and keep warm. Some of the carrots and onion can go with the veal to provide a bit of garnish to the finished dish, but try to leave most of them in the cooking liquid.

4. Strain the sauce through a sieve into a saucepan, pressing out as much liquid as possible. Discard the solids in the sieve. Place the saucepan over high heat and thicken slightly with the arrowroot mixture. Add more salt and pepper if needed, and pour the sauce over the veal cubes.

Serves 6 to 8.

Veal Stew

Here's a tasty stew in less than an hour!

≈

- 1 to 1½ pounds boneless veal breast or shoulder, cut into 1-inch cubes
- ½ cup flour seasoned with 2 teaspoons salt and grindings of fresh pepper
- ¼ cup olive oil
- ½ cup chopped onion
- 1 teaspoon crushed dried rosemary
- 1 cup dry white wine
- ½ cup chicken broth
- 10 small boiling onions, peeled
- ¼ pound fresh mushrooms, quartered
- 2 carrots, sliced
- 2 stalks celery, sliced
- 2 teaspoons arrowroot or cornstarch dissolved in ¼ cup water (optional)

1. Dredge the veal cubes in seasoned flour and brown on all sides in hot oil. Add the onion, rosemary, white wine, and chicken broth. Cover and simmer for 30 minutes.

2. Add the vegetables, cover, and simmer 15 to 20 minutes, until just tender. Thicken the sauce, if desired, with the arrowroot mixture. Add more salt and pepper if needed, and serve.

Serves 4.

Osso Buco

6 pounds veal shanks, cut into 2-inch pieces
¼ cup flour
½ teaspoon salt
¼ teaspoon black pepper
½ cup olive oil
1 medium onion, finely chopped
1 medium carrot, finely chopped
1 rib celery, finely chopped
2 cloves garlic, minced
1 cup dry white wine
1 cup beef broth
2 1-pound-13-ounce cans whole tomatoes, drained
½ teaspoon dried basil
½ teaspoon dried rosemary

GREMOLATA

6 cloves garlic, minced
2 tablespoons grated lemon rind
½ cup chopped fresh parsley

Meat from both the fore and hind shanks of veal has a great deal of connective tissue and is therefore one of my favorite cuts for long, slow, moist-heat cooking. The connective tissue dissolves in the cooking process, contributing to a rich, delicious sauce, so desirable in most stews and casseroles. I very often add a bit of cubed veal-shank meat to a pot of beef chili for the richness it adds to the pot. Veal shank sliced into two-inch-thick pieces with the shank bone left in is the cut for the classic Italian dish Osso Buco.

Osso Buco, which originated in Milan, has become very popular in America since northern-Italian cooking has become such an important part of the restaurant scene in the past twenty-five years. The name of this dish means "hollow bone." But the marrow is the best part, so warn your guests not to overlook this delicacy. Gremolata, the recipe for which follows, is the traditional garnish.

≈

1. Have the shanks sawn into 2-inch pieces, and tie each with string. Coat the chunks of veal with the flour seasoned with the salt and pepper. Heat ¼ cup of the oil in a heavy skillet. Add a few pieces of veal at a time and brown them till dark and crusty.

2. While the veal is browning, sauté the onion, carrot, celery, and garlic in the remaining oil in a large casserole or Dutch oven. Cook, stirring occasionally, until the vegetables are tender.

3. When all the veal is browned, arrange it on the vegetables. Stand the pieces up to preserve the marrow inside the bones. Add the wine, beef broth, tomatoes, and herbs to the pan used for browning the veal. Cook, stirring, until the mixture boils.

4. Pour the mixture over the veal. Cover the casserole and bake in a preheated 325-degree oven for 1½ hours, or until the veal is very tender. Spoon off any visible fat. Place the veal on a platter and remove the strings. Taste

the sauce for seasoning. Ladle the sauce over the shanks and serve with Gremolata.

5. While the meat is cooking, make the Gremolata: mix the garlic, lemon, and parsley together and sprinkle over the Osso Buco.

Serves 4 to 6.

Quick Veal Stock

If you saved those bones from your cutting up in the kitchen, find your pressure cooker and make a quick stock to use for future recipes. If you don't have a pressure cooker, do not despair. You can make the same stock using the same ingredients in a stock pot on top of the stove, but it won't be "quick." It will take 3½ to 4 hours to cook at a slow simmer.

Veal stock is great to have on hand to add a wonderful richness to sauces and gravies to accompany most any meat dish.

- Bones from a veal breast, shank, or other cuts, about 2 pounds
- ½ onion
- 1 stalk celery
- 1 carrot, cut in half crosswise
- 1 bay leaf
- 2 cloves garlic
- 4 to 6 peppercorns
- ½ teaspoon dried thyme
- 2 tablespoons chopped parsley
- Water to cover

≈

1. Cut the veal bones into manageable-sized pieces by cutting between the ribs with a heavy knife. Put the bones in a 4-to-6-quart pressure cooker. Add the remaining ingredients and enough cold water to cover. Lock on the lid, put the pressure regulator in place, and bring to pressure over high heat. Cooking time begins at this point. Adjust the heat to the medium setting until the pressure regulator maintains a slow, steady rocking motion.

2. Cook for 30 minutes. Remove the pressure cooker from the heat and allow pressure to drop of its own accord. The pressure is completely reduced when the regulator is lifted and no steam escapes. Remove the regulator and open the pressure-cooker cover. Strain the stock; discard the bones and vegetables. Return the stock to the pressure-cooker pot and cook over high heat, without the cover, until it is reduced to 2½ to 3 cups.

Makes approximately 2½ to 3 cups.

Odds 'n' Ends and Innards

≈

The English call them "offal," but something seems to get lost in the translation. Far too many Americans call them "awful." In cookbooks, they're listed as "variety meats." They include brains, hearts, kidneys, livers, tails, tongues, tripe, and a variety of other miscellaneous parts, "odds 'n' ends," that are nutritious, delicious, and, in some cases, relatively cheap.

Any conscientious would-be gourmet should spend at least as much time learning to appreciate all of these odds 'n' ends and innards as he does developing a taste for escargots (snails) and caviar (fish eggs). If the term must be French, call them *abats de boucherie*. That doesn't sound so awful.

These items of meat have been an important part of man's diet since the beginning of recorded history. Being the most perishable parts of the animal, they were traditionally eaten first, often at some great feast to celebrate the success of a hunt, or for dinner on the farm following hog-killin' time. Unfortunately, in America in recent years, they seem to have fallen from favor. In far too many markets in this country today you won't find them at all.

There are, I think, two major reasons for the disappearance of so many of these delicious delicacies. In the first place, most of us have lost touch with where our food comes from. We are not hunters or farmers. We have become a nation of "city folks," and we have forgotten the "waste-not-want-not" philosophy of our farming forefathers. At the turn of the century, over 95 percent of the American population was involved in agriculture. Folks back then knew that, come hog-killin' time, the only thing that went to waste was the squeal. Today, 2 percent of our population feeds us all, and does it better than in any other

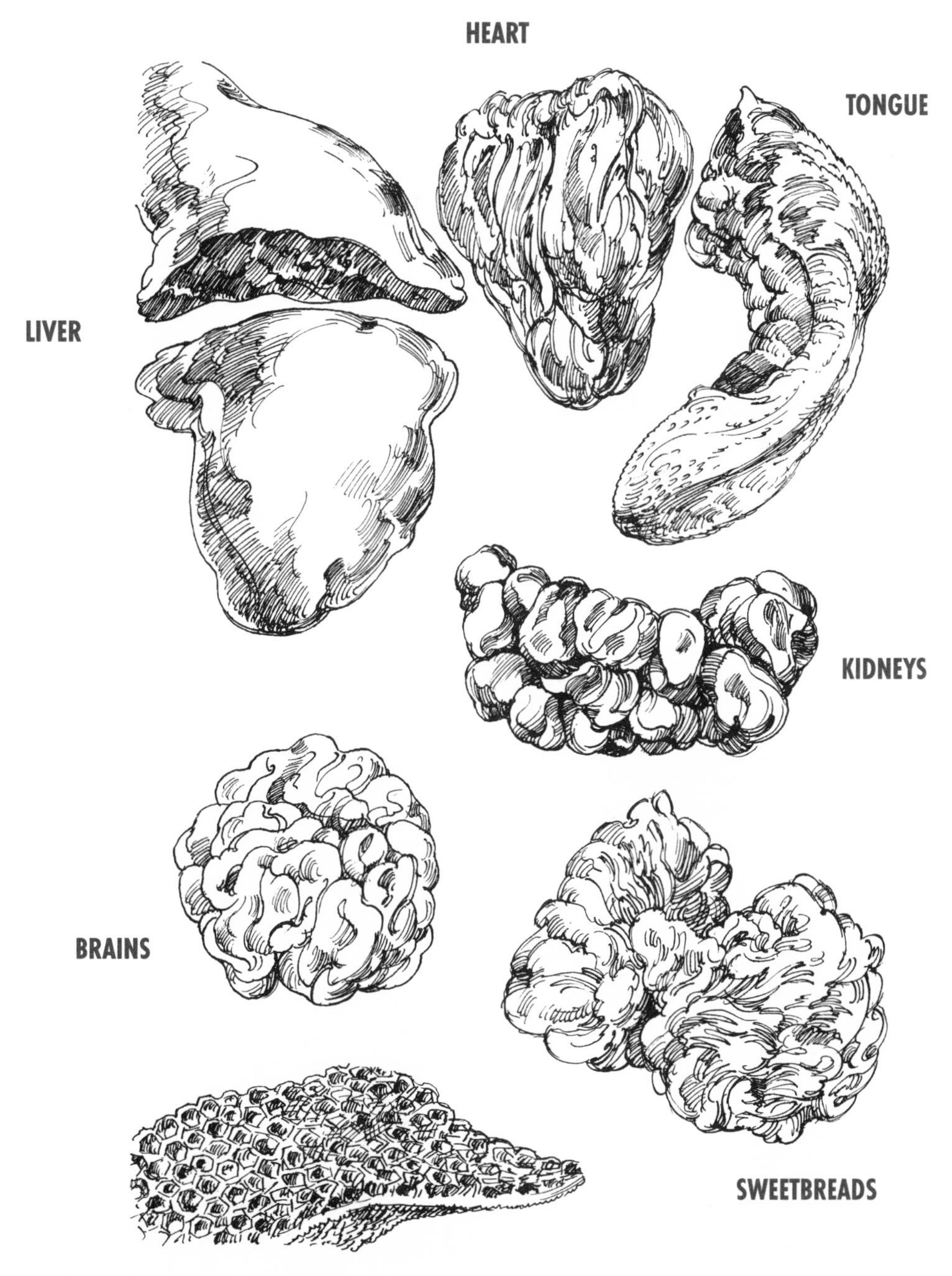
HEART
TONGUE
LIVER
KIDNEYS
BRAINS
SWEETBREADS
TRIPE

nation on the face of the earth. We're spoiled. In a land of abundance we have come to wrinkle our noses at that offal stuff. It really is too bad; we're missing some great eating.

Such is not the case in much of the rest of the world. Which brings me to the second reason for the disappearance of this whole category of good food in America. In Europe, particularly in France, *abats de boucherie* are very much in demand, and the French care little where they came from. The import restrictions placed on most meat to protect local production do not exist for *abats.* They'll take all we'll ship them, and we ship them a lot.

Another factor that may be adversely affecting the availability of all this good meat is the cholesterol scare. Now, I'm not a registered dietitian, but it seems to me that we have become a nation of hypocritical hypochondriacs convinced that most of what we put in our mouths is going to kill us. Whatever happened to common sense and moderation? Nobody, not even the French, eats sweetbreads, brains, or liver every day. But Europeans enjoy them all occasionally, and so should we.

Try some of these odds 'n' ends and innards. You may find that you like them!

TONGUE

Tongue is one of the easiest of all variety meats to learn to like. All you have to do is get it past your mind and into your mouth, and the rest will take care of itself.

Tongue is available fresh, smoked, or cured; it can be served hot or cold, plain or with a number of sauces. The recipes I've included here call for beef tongue, which is the most readily available, but calf, lamb, or pork tongues can be prepared in the same manner.

A nice bright surface is an indication of quality and freshness in a fresh tongue, so look for one that glistens. But don't worry too much about color: tongues range in color from light grayish-pink to black, and are often multicolored. Don't shy away from a tongue with black spots, as long as the black spots sparkle. But stay away from a dull tongue.

Tongue freezes well, so, if you see a nice bright one but can't use it for a while, buy it and freeze it just as you would any fresh meat. Wrap it well in a good moisture-proof freezer wrap and stick it in the freezer, or cook it first and then freeze it.

To freeze a tongue after it has been cooked, first skin it (instructions follow; every tongue must be skinned before it can be eaten), then put it in a container of sufficient size, cover it with some of the liquid in which it was cooked, and freeze the whole works. That way, the tongue stays nice and moist, and when you are ready to serve it, you have some broth from which to make a sauce.

Tongue is much easier to skin if you do it while it is still hot. After cooking, plunge the tongue into cold water to cool it just enough so you can handle it comfortably. Also, if you add a tablespoon or two of vinegar to the cooking water, the skin will readily slip off the tongue. Start at the root end with a small incision, then peel off the skin as you would peel an orange.

Basic Tongue Preparation

All tongue, fresh or packaged, needs this first basic preparation before use in a recipe. I often prepare several tongues ahead and freeze them for later use. Once you're past the basic preparation, so many delicious things can be done with this cut. Though different in size, beef, veal, pork, and lamb tongues can all be used interchangeably, with only slight adjustments in cooking time based on size.

A tongue (1 beef or 2 veal or 4 pork or up to 6 lamb)
1 onion, stuck with 2 whole cloves
1 carrot
1 stalk celery
2 bay leaves
¼ teaspoon black peppercorns
2 tablespoons white vinegar
Water to cover

≈

1. Rinse the tongue(s) under cold water. Place in a large heavy pot. Add all the remaining ingredients, cover, and simmer over moderately low heat for about 2 hours for large tongues, somewhat less for smaller tongues.

2. Remove from the heat and allow to cool in the stock. Drain and reserve the stock for use as a soup base or in a sauce to accompany the finished dish.

3. Remove the skin, gristle, and any excess fat from the "root" end of the tongue. Slip the skin off the tongue (see above).

4. Trim the root end, removing any small bones and excess fat. Proceed with recipes using the meat, or refrigerate for later use. If you plan to keep the tongue for longer than a day or two before serving, freeze it. Tongue freezes very well, but be sure to freeze it in the stock to keep moist.

Serves 6.

Tongue Servings and Leftovers

The recipes that follow call for beef tongue, to serve six people, but veal, pork, or lamb tongues can also be used. If you're serving fewer than six people, plan on leftovers. There are so many things to do with leftover tongue: slice it for sandwiches; cut it into julienne strips to toss on a salad; or cut little cubes, stick them with toothpicks, and serve them with a dipping sauce at a cocktail party.

Braised Tongue

- 12 to 18 tiny pearl onions, peeled
- 2 large carrots, sliced
- 1 beef tongue, cooked, peeled, and trimmed (see Basic Tongue Preparation, page 241)
- 4 tablespoons butter
- 2 tablespoons flour
- 1 cup white wine
- ½ cup beef tongue stock (see Basic Tongue Preparation)
- Salt and pepper
- 1 tablespoon arrowroot dissolved in ⅓ cup water (optional)

This is a hearty dish, perfect for chilly winter days. Once you are past the basic preparation, the rest of the work can be done in a matter of minutes. The dish can also be made a day ahead up to the point of baking and kept in the refrigerator overnight.

≈

1. Cook the onions and carrots in a small amount of water until just half done; drain and set aside.
2. Brown the trimmed tongue in the butter in a large skillet, turning often so that all sides are evenly browned. Remove to a casserole and set aside.
3. Over moderate heat, add the flour to the pan and stir to loosen any pan drippings; brown the flour, stirring constantly. Add the wine and stock; season to taste with salt and pepper and bring to a boil.
4. Arrange the carrots and onions around the tongue in the casserole and pour the sauce over all. Bake, covered, in a preheated 350-degree oven for 30 minutes, or until the tongue is very tender. Baste occasionally with the sauce to give both the tongue and the vegetables a nice even glaze.
5. To serve, slice the tongue and arrange on a warm platter, surrounded by the carrots and the onions. Thicken the sauce, if necessary, with the arrowroot mixture, and correct the seasonings. Serve the remaining sauce on the side. Serve with mashed potatoes or parsley-buttered noodles.

Serves 6.

Grilled Tongue with Mustard

With a crisp salad and a cold beer, this makes a marvelous summer lunch!

≈

1 beef tongue, cooked, peeled, and trimmed (see Basic Tongue Preparation, page 241)
2 tablespoons prepared mustard, smooth or grainy
4 tablespoons butter
½ cup toasted bread crumbs

1. Preheat the broiler to its highest point. Slice the tongue and arrange the slices in a shallow casserole. Spread the top generously with the mustard. Melt the butter and drizzle over the slices.

2. Sprinkle on the crumbs and broil until hot and bubbling.

Serves 6.

Tongue with Onion Sauce

This is one of my favorite tongue recipes. Served with a salad, rice pilaf, and a nice steamed vegetable, it can qualify as company fare.

≈

2 onions, thinly sliced
1 teaspoon sugar
3 tablespoons butter
3 tablespoons flour
2 cups reserved tongue stock (see Basic Tongue Preparation, page 241)
¼ cup dry white wine
Salt and freshly ground pepper to taste
1 beef tongue, cooked, peeled, trimmed, and sliced (see Basic Tongue Preparation)

1. Gently cook the onions with the sugar in the butter for 10 to 12 minutes, stirring often. Add the flour, stir

Tongue with Onion Sauce *(cont.)*

well, and cook for 5 minutes. Add the stock, wine, and seasonings; simmer for 10 minutes.

2. Arrange the slices of tongue in an ovenproof casserole; pour the sauce over them and bake, uncovered, in a preheated 350-degree oven for 20 to 25 minutes.

Serves 6.

Sweet and Sour Tongue

- 4 or 5 slices bacon, chopped
- 3 onions, chopped
- 1 bay leaf
- 1 tablespoon grated lemon rind
- 4 black peppercorns
- 4 cups beef tongue stock (see Basic Tongue Preparation, page 241)
- 1 tablespoon cider vinegar
- 1 tablespoon sugar
- 2½ cups gingersnap crumbs
- 6 to 8 prunes, cooked, pitted, and pressed through a sieve
- Salt and pepper to taste
- 1 tablespoon arrowroot dissolved in ⅓ cup water (optional)
- ½ cup raisins
- ½ cup sliced almonds
- 1 beef tongue, cooked, peeled, trimmed, and sliced (see Basic Tongue Preparation)

This dish almost certainly had its origin in a Jewish kitchen. The gingersnaps are reminiscent of the flavoring in Sauerbraten, a dish we have shared many times with Jewish friends during Hanukkah. The recipe is based on one that I got from a great Jewish cook, food writer, and friend, Ethel Hofman. Ethel's recipe calls for "schmaltz" (chicken fat), but I didn't have any handy, so I used bacon fat. It came out great, but it ain't kosher. The dish can be made ahead up to the point of the final reheating, and kept in the refrigerator for a few hours.

≈

1. Fry the bacon in a large heavy skillet over moderate heat for 5 minutes; add the onions and continue cooking for another 5 minutes, until the onions are limp.

2. Add the bay leaf, lemon rind, and peppercorns and cook an additional 5 minutes. Pour in the stock; add the vinegar, sugar, gingersnap crumbs, and prune puree. Simmer for 15 minutes.

3. Taste the sauce and correct the seasoning, adding salt and pepper to taste and, if necessary, adding more sugar or vinegar. You may want to thicken the sauce with the arrowroot mixture, or thin it with more stock. Strain the sauce and add the raisins and almonds.

4. Slice the tongue and arrange in a heatproof serving dish or saucepan. Cover with the sauce and heat over moderate heat. Serve with steamed rice.

Serves 6.

LIVER

The lack of liver in local supermarkets is lamentable. There was a day when every butcher shop offered not one type of liver but several. Calf's liver was the most favored. It still is, but it is very scarce. Most of the really good calf's liver goes to the white-table restaurant trade. I don't know where the pork liver goes, but I never see it anymore. Too bad, too! It used to be the cheapest; a bit stronger in flavor than other liver, but perfect for making pâtés.

Lamb's liver! I don't know how long it's been since I have had, or even seen, lamb's liver, and yet it is, to my taste, on a par with calf's liver for mild-flavored tenderness. I once worked at a market that sold lamb's liver labeled, and priced, as calf's liver, and nobody knew the difference.

About the only liver that you see in most markets these days is beef liver and, unfortunately, all too often that is presliced, dumped into plastic trays, and presented as if it were only good as cat food. When liver is sold like that in self-service meat cases, it is extremely difficult to know what you're getting. The size of the liver is the best indication of the age of the beef from which it came: the smaller, the younger. Obviously you can't tell what size the liver was before it was sliced, and therefore the best criterion for judging its probable quality is not available to you.

The next-best thing, and in most cases the only thing, you have to go on is color. At best, color is a second-rate factor in determining quality, but it can provide some general guidelines. I have seen huge old beef livers that were light in color, and calves' livers that were comparatively dark. Generally, however, calf's liver is lighter in color than beef liver, usually a light reddish-brown color. In young beef, the liver is a darker reddish-brown; in a more mature animal, it may become a deep purplish-brown.

In shopping for liver in your local supermarket, check the color. If the little plastic package labeled "calf liver" is exactly the same color as the little (and less expensive) plastic package labeled "beef liver," it may be that the butcher gave in to that uncontrollable urge to sell the small end of a beef liver at calf's-liver prices.

One way to be more certain that you are getting what you pay for is to buy it in the piece and slice it yourself. If you ring the bell and ask the butcher for a "piece of calf's liver to bake," at least you'll get a look at the size of the liver he's cutting. If it looks like the small end of a much larger piece, it probably is, so change your mind and buy beef liver. Don't pay the calf's-liver premium unless you are sure that you are getting the real thing. Even then, I'm not convinced it's worth the difference in price.

Basic Liver Preparation

Liver doesn't need the advance preparation that many of the meats in this chapter require. The little that it does need should have been done by the butcher, but these days it often isn't. Liver has a thin membrane that encases it. This toughens in the cooking process and should be removed before cooking. If it has not been removed, simply loosen the membrane with the tip of a sharp knife and peel it off.

Also, if it hasn't been done by the butcher, trim around and remove any sinew surrounding any large veins in the liver.

Cooking Liver

Liver is best cooked over fairly high heat for a short period of time. No matter how you cook it—fried, broiled, sautéed, or grilled—it will be best if it is still a little pink in the center. Don't overcook it!

The following recipes are good with any kind of liver—beef, pork, lamb, or calf.

Liver and Mushrooms

Liver may well have been the original "convenience food." It doesn't take long to cook. This recipe proves it.

- 1 pound beef liver, thinly sliced
- ½ cup flour, seasoned with salt and pepper
- 1 tablespoon butter
- 1 small onion, chopped
- 2 cloves garlic, minced
- 6 to 8 mushrooms, thinly sliced
- ¼ cup dry white wine
- 1 tablespoon lemon juice
- 1 tablespoon chopped parsley
- Salt and pepper to taste

≈

1. Cut the liver into ¾-inch strips. Dust lightly with seasoned flour.

2. Melt the butter in a heavy skillet over medium-high heat. Add the liver strips, onion, and garlic. Cook, stirring, for 3 minutes. Add the mushrooms and continue cooking and stirring for another 3 minutes.

3. Add the wine, lemon juice, and parsley. Continue cooking for 2 or 3 more minutes, until the sauce thickens slightly. Adjust the seasonings. Serve with boiled rice.

Serves 4.

Liver with Onion and Pepper

This is a recipe I like to use for pork liver, when I can find it. The onion and pepper hold up well to the rich flavor of the pork liver. Serve with a rice pilaf.

½ cup vegetable oil
1 pound liver, sliced ¾ to 1 inch thick
1 onion, sliced in ¼-inch rings
1 bell pepper, seeded, sliced into ¼-inch rings
2 tablespoons flour
1 cup beef stock
Salt and pepper

≈

1. Heat the oil in a heavy skillet over medium-high heat. When the oil is hot, put in the liver slices and fry for 2 to 3 minutes; turn and fry for 2 or 3 minutes more. Remove the liver to a warm platter.

2. Add the sliced onion and pepper to the hot pan, lower the heat, and cook gently for 2 to 3 minutes until tender. Remove from the pan and set aside.

3. Pour off and dispose of all but 2 tablespoons of the oil. Mix the flour into the remaining oil and cook the flour and oil together over moderate heat until the flour turns a nutty brown. Then slowly pour in the beef stock, stirring to make a nice sauce.

4. Return the liver, sliced onion, and pepper to the sauce and continue cooking for 5 to 6 minutes. Season to taste with salt and pepper.

Serves 4.

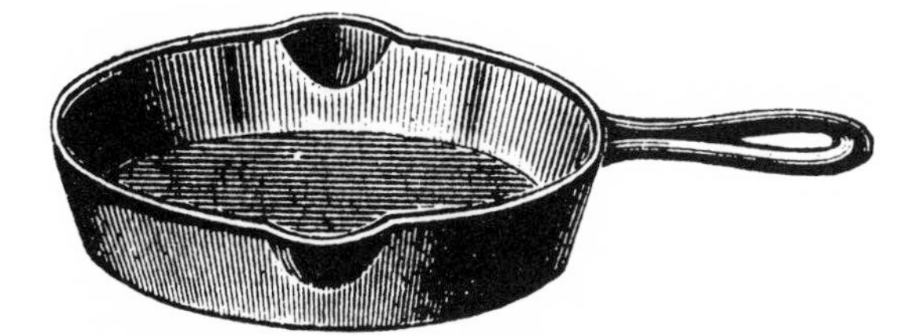

Deviled Liver

- 1 teaspoon salt
- ½ teaspoon black pepper
- 1 teaspoon dry mustard
- ¼ teaspoon hot red pepper (cayenne)
- ¼ teaspoon paprika
- 3 tablespoons melted butter
- 2 teaspoons vinegar
- 1 teaspoon Worcestershire sauce
- 2 egg yolks
- 1 pound liver, sliced ¾ to 1 inch thick
- ¾ cup dry bread crumbs
- ½ cup vegetable oil

Deviled Liver is another recipe that works well with the stronger flavor of pork liver, but any liver will do. This is also a good recipe for those who may not yet have decided they like liver. I think they will like this.

≈

1. Combine the salt, pepper, dry mustard, cayenne pepper, paprika, melted butter, vinegar, Worcestershire sauce, and egg yolks. Mix well. Dip the liver slices into the mixture, then coat the slices with the bread crumbs and set aside.

2. Heat the oil in a heavy skillet over medium-high heat. Cook the liver slices, turning frequently, until the meat is browned and tender, about 4 to 6 minutes. Don't overcook—liver is more tender if not cooked to death. This dish goes well with buttered mashed potatoes.

Serves 4.

Liver in Sour Cream

- 1 pound liver, sliced thin
- 1 large onion, thinly sliced
- 4 tablespoons butter
- 2 teaspoons paprika
- Salt and pepper to taste
- ½ cup sour cream

This recipe has an air of "Stroganoff" about it, but liver is a lot less expensive than beef tenderloin.

≈

1. Cut the liver slices crosswise into narrow strips about 2 or 3 inches long and the thickness of a pencil. Gently cook the onion in 2 tablespoons of the butter until golden. Remove from the pan and set aside.

2. Melt the remaining butter in the pan, add the liver, and cook for 3 or 4 minutes over medium-high heat, turning occasionally to brown the strips evenly on all sides.

3. Return the onion to the pan with the liver, add the seasonings, stir in the sour cream, and heat through. Serve on toast or with a rice pilaf.

Serves 4.

Liver in Wine Sauce

This is an interesting variation on the classic liver with bacon and onions.

- 1 pound liver, sliced thin
- ½ cup flour, seasoned with salt and pepper
- 4 tablespoons butter
- 4 slices bacon, cut in 1-inch strips
- 2 large onions, cut in half and sliced thinly
- ½ cup red wine
- ¼ cup Garlic-Flavored Croutons (see below)

≈

1. Dredge the liver in the seasoned flour and gently cook it in the butter over medium-high heat until nicely browned on both sides. Don't overcook; it should be pink in the center. Remove to a warm platter and keep warm.
2. Cook the bacon until almost crisp; add the onions to the pan and cook, stirring often, until the onions are soft and golden. Pour in the wine, cover, reduce the heat, and simmer for 5 minutes.
3. Return the liver slices to the pan and heat through. To serve, arrange the liver on a warm platter, pour on the sauce, and garnish with croutons.

Serves 4.

Garlic-Flavored Croutons

You can buy croutons at the supermarket, but it is a simple process to make your own, and they're better. Simply cut leftover French bread into ½-to-¾-inch cubes and cook them in butter into which you have crushed several cloves of garlic. When the bread cubes are nicely coated with the garlic-butter mixture, continue cooking, turning over very low heat, until the croutons are crisp.

KIDNEYS

It's really a shame that kidneys have fallen into such disfavor among so many in recent times. But it's not the first time. Kidneys passed through a period of rejection during the Italian Renaissance. Then folks thought that the consumption of kidneys caused ill humor.

Beef kidneys were once the most common kind available. Back in the days when beef came to market in carcass form, every carcass came with a couple. These days, the beef carcass is divided up at the packing plant and the component parts are shipped out separately. All the various parts go in a variety of different directions, depending on demand. A good percentage of the beef kidneys in this country go in the direction of Europe. They have developed a great appreciation for kidneys there—since the Renaissance.

Pork kidneys are available in some markets, and, on occasion, you may find a veal kidney or two.

But it's lamb kidneys that you are most likely to find today. Some lamb still comes to market in carcass form, and each lamb has two kidneys. In a market that handles lamb, you're apt to find a few. When you do, try them. You'll like them.

In selecting kidneys, look for those that have a fresh, glossy appearance. Avoid any that look dried out. If you have a real live butcher to whom you can talk, ask him to save you some lamb kidneys still encased in the fat that surrounds them. The fat helps keep the kidneys fresh until you're ready to use them.

Basic Kidney Preparation

Kidneys come in two different shapes. Beef and veal kidneys are multi-lobed and elongated, whereas the kidneys of lamb and pork have a single lobe that resembles a giant bean. They can be used interchangeably in any recipe, but they do require somewhat different treatment.

The outside membrane should be removed from all kidneys before cooking. This is a simple process for single-lobe pork and lamb kidneys; it's like peeling a peach. The procedure with the multi-lobed kidneys, beef and veal, is a bit more tedious, like peeling a bunch of grapes. Beef and pork kidneys, which tend to have a stronger flavor, need to be split in half lengthwise, and the white core and excess fat must be removed; this is not necessary for lamb and veal kidneys.

Beef and pork kidneys benefit from being soaked in acidulated water (one tablespoon of lemon juice or vinegar to two cups of water) or buttermilk for one hour, then drained and patted dry. Because of their milder flavor and texture, veal and lamb kidneys need no soaking. Like liver, kidneys should be cooked over fairly high heat, and not too well done. A touch of pink makes for a more tender kidney.

Grilled Kidneys

1 beef or veal kidney, cut into 1-inch-thick slices, or 2 pork or 4 lamb kidneys, split
¼ cup olive oil or melted butter
Salt and freshly ground pepper to taste
½ cup fine bread crumbs (optional)

The simplest and, to my mind, one of the best ways with kidneys is to grill them. Cut beef and veal kidneys into one-inch-thick slices. Pork or lamb kidneys need simply to be split in half. Use wood or metal skewers to keep the kidneys flat on the grill.

≈

1. Prepare kidneys according to appropriate procedure in Basic Kidney Preparation (page 250).
2. Prepare and preheat a barbecue grill. Skewer serving-size portions, 3 or 4 pieces, on wooden or metal skewers to keep edges from curling up in the grilling process.
3. Brush each side with oil or melted butter. Sprinkle with salt and pepper. Sprinkle on and pat in a coating of bread crumbs, if desired.
4. Place skewered kidneys on the grill over hot coals and cook for 3 to 4 minutes. Pork or lamb kidneys need to go on the grill cut side down first, to help prevent them from curling up.
5. Turn the kidneys and grill for about a minute or two on the other side. Don't overcook them!
6. Serve with lemon wedges, crisp bacon, and French-fries or boiled potatoes. Or serve on toast or a bed of risotto or pilaf.

Serves 2 to 4.

VARIATION

Blend the butter or olive oil with chopped herbs—such as parsley, tarragon, or chives—shallots, prepared Dijon-style mustard, or lemon juice.

Deviled Kidneys

- 6 to 8 lamb kidneys, drained and split
- 2 tablespoons butter
- 1 tablespoon white-wine vinegar
- 2 teaspoons Dijon mustard
- Salt and pepper
- Toast points
- 6 to 8 slices bacon, fried (optional)

My dad used to bring lamb kidneys home from the market still encased in their suet, and Mom would fry them up in the rendered leaf fat. Here is a simple recipe from my mother's file, using butter instead. Lamb suet is hard to find today.

≈

1. Prepare kidneys according to appropriate procedure in Basic Kidney Preparation (page 250).
2. Fry the halved kidneys quickly in the butter over medium-high heat for about 4 minutes, turning so both sides cook evenly. Stir in the vinegar and mustard.
3. Season to taste with salt and pepper. Cook for 2 minutes more. Serve on toast with fried bacon, if you wish.

Serves 4 to 6.

Kidneys in Red Wine Sauce

- 6 to 8 lamb kidneys (or 1 beef, 2 veal, or 3 pork kidneys)
- 2 tablespoons flour
- ½ teaspoon salt
- ¼ teaspoon freshly ground black pepper
- ½ teaspoon crumbled dried tarragon
- 2 tablespoons butter
- ¼ pound mushrooms, thinly sliced
- ½ cup chicken stock
- ½ cup red wine

This is a quick-and-easy simple supper dish that is just right served over toast or a rice pilaf with a simple salad.

≈

1. Clean the kidneys, removing any membranes (see Basic Kidney Preparation, page 250). Cut into ½-inch-thick slices.
2. Mix the flour, salt, pepper, and tarragon together in a small paper sack. Add the kidney pieces and shake to coat them. Cook the kidney pieces in the butter over medium-high heat for just a minute or two, until lightly browned.
3. Add the mushrooms and any seasoned flour left in the sack. Cook for another minute or two.

4. Stir in the stock and the wine. Bring to a boil, reduce the heat, and simmer gently for 3 to 4 minutes, until the sauce thickens slightly. Adjust the seasonings.

Serves 4 to 6.

Kidneys in Sherry Mustard Sauce

I enjoy this dish for breakfast served on toast, but it is equally good for lunch or dinner with rice or noodles.

6 to 8 lamb kidneys (or 1 beef, 2 veal, or 3 pork kidneys)
Salt and pepper to taste
4 tablespoons butter
⅓ pound fresh mushrooms, sliced
¼ cup chopped onion
¼ cup dry sherry
2 teaspoons Dijon mustard
½ cup sour cream
Toast
Chopped parsley

≈

1. Clean the kidneys, removing any membranes (see Basic Kidney Preparation, page 250). Cut into ½-inch-thick slices. Season with salt and pepper.

2. Melt half of the butter in a skillet over medium heat and cook the mushrooms and onion until the onion is soft; set aside. Add the remaining butter to the pan, raise the heat to medium-high, and cook the kidneys very quickly, stirring constantly, until just firm. Set aside with the mushrooms and onion.

3. Reduce the heat to medium, add the sherry and mustard to the pan, and stir until the mixture is smooth. Return the kidneys, mushrooms, and onion to the pan. Stir in the sour cream and heat through gently. Serve on buttered toast and garnish with parsley.

Serves 4 to 6.

TRIPE

In its broadest sense, the term "tripe" may refer to the edible stomach of any of the animals that we use for food. More specifically, and traditionally in America for generations, tripe refers to the lining of the stomachs of beef animals. There are two different kinds of tripe available. One is referred to as "smooth" or "flat" tripe. It comes from the walls of the rumen (the first compartment in the stomach of a ruminant). The second type comes from the reticulum, or second stomach. It has a honeycomblike appearance and for that reason has come to be called "honeycomb" tripe.

In the process of preparing tripe for the market, it is cleaned, soaked, and parboiled at the packing house. Tripe is therefore partially cooked when you buy it, but it still will require a lot of cooking before it's ready for the table. The exact amount of cooking time can vary, depending upon the extent of processing at the packing house.

Both types of tripe can be used interchangeably in any recipe, but I prefer the honeycomb, and that's what the following recipes use. Honeycomb is the more tender of the two and requires less cooking time. If you are using flat tripe, you'll need to add another thirty minutes or more to the cooking time.

Occasionally you will find what is called "pickled tripe" in those markets that have any kind of tripe at all. This has been brine-cured at the packing house, giving it a unique flavor. It is to any other tripe, by way of comparison, as corned-beef brisket is to fresh brisket. The finished dish will obviously have a different flavor, but pickled tripe can be used in any of the following recipes and is preferred for the recipe on page 260 for Pickled Tripe.

Basic Tripe Preparation

Tripe recipes fall into two different categories. There are those that are cooked long and slow, simmering for hours in a sauce, to make rich and hearty soups, stews, and casseroles. In these kinds of recipes the long, slow cooking is sufficient to tenderize the tripe. Tripe recipes in which the final step calls for some dry-heat cooking method, such as frying, broiling, or sautéing, require that the tripe be simmered long and slow before the final step.

Therefore, there are two steps to the basic preparation. All tripe recipes benefit from the cleaning and parboiling described in Basic Prep I, and recipes to be finished with dry heat demand Basic Prep II.

Basic Prep I: Wash the tripe well under cold running water, then sprinkle well with salt and rub it in. Rinse thoroughly with cold water. Put the tripe in a large stock pot and cover with salted water (1 tablespoon of salt for each quart of water). Bring to a boil, reduce the heat, and simmer for 15 to 20 minutes. Drain, and discard the water. The tripe is now ready for use in any recipe calling for long, slow moist-heat cooking. For use in recipes employing dry heat, proceed to Basic Prep II.

Basic Prep II: Prepare the tripe according to Basic Prep I above. Return the tripe to the pot and add: 1 onion stuck with 2 or 3 cloves, 1 carrot, 1 stalk of celery, 2 bay leaves, 10 peppercorns, and a few sprigs of parsley. Cover the tripe with water and bring to a boil. Reduce the heat to a gentle simmer, cover the pot, and cook for 1½ to 2 hours, or until the tripe is tender. Drain and reserve the stock, if it is needed in the final recipe, and discard the vegetables. The tripe is now ready for making fried tripe, broiled tripe, etc.

The basic preparation can be done ahead, and the tripe stored in the refrigerator for two or three days, or in the freezer for several weeks. Defrost slowly in the refrigerator.

Simmered Tripe

The classic French recipe for this dish is called *tripe à la mode de Caen,* as described in *Larousse Gastronomique.* It calls for ten to twelve hours of cooking along with a calf's foot and a pound of fat in a special sealed earthenware casserole. Because ten to twelve hours is a long, long time, and calves' feet are hard to find, and nobody today wants a pound of fat, I've modified this classic recipe somewhat.

Cider and calvados are the liquids called for in the French recipe, but tripe cooked in cider tends to turn an unappetizing brown. I've found that using white wine and beef or chicken stock makes for a more appealing color and doesn't change the flavor except for the better. Also traditionally, the dish was sealed for baking in an earthenware casserole with a thick paste of flour and water around the lid. Aluminum foil works fine.

≈

Simmered Tripe *(cont.)*

2 pounds honeycomb tripe (prepared as described in Basic Prep I, pages 254–55)
A 2-pound veal shank, cut into 1-inch pieces
2 onions, sliced
3 carrots, sliced
3 stalks celery, sliced
2 leeks, rinsed well, split in half and sliced
1 teaspoon crumbled dried thyme
2 bay leaves
3 to 4 garlic cloves, minced
1 teaspoon salt
10 to 12 black peppercorns
1 teaspoon allspice
2 cups dry white wine
Beef or chicken stock

1. Cut the tripe into 1½-inch squares and set aside.

2. Put the veal-shank pieces in a saucepan and cover with cold water. Bring to a boil, reduce the heat, and simmer for about five minutes. Drain and rinse with cool water. This step helps eliminate the scum that is an inevitable part of simmering most meat.

3. Layer the bottom of a good-sized covered casserole with the sliced onions, carrots, and celery. Lay the tripe over the vegetables and add the leeks, veal shank, and seasonings. Pour the wine over, and add enough stock to cover.

4. Seal the casserole with heavy-duty aluminum foil and top with a heavy lid. Bake in a preheated 250-degree oven for 3 or 4 hours, or until the tripe is tender. Check from time to time to make sure the mixture is covered with liquid, adding a bit more stock if necessary.

5. To serve, remove the foil. Drain the tripe, reserving the broth. Remove and discard the bones from the veal shanks and dice the meat. Put the tripe, veal, and vegetables in a serving dish and keep warm.

6. Strain the broth and remove any fat that rises to the top. Over high heat reduce the broth to approximately 2 cups. Pour it over the tripe and serve with a good crusty bread and a glass of hearty red wine. It will make you a lover of tripe.

Serves 6 to 8.

Papagayo's Menudo, Sonora Style

3 pounds honeycomb tripe (prepared as described in Basic Prep I, pages 254–55)
Water
2 pigs' feet, split
2 cloves garlic, crushed
2 bay leaves
1 large onion, diced or sliced thin
Salt and pepper to taste
1 or 2 sprigs fresh mint (optional)
2 jalapeño peppers (optional)
1 29-ounce can white hominy, drained

CONDIMENTS

Dried oregano, chopped onion, dried chili flakes, lemon wedges

Menudo is traditionally served in Mexico on New Year's Day. Some say it's for good luck; others credit it as a sure cure for a hangover.

I first tasted menudo and felt its sobering effects at Al Williams' Papagayo Room in San Francisco's Fairmont Hotel in the early 1950s. The Papagayo Room was the place to go in those days after a night on the town. Al Williams had "the cure." Since the fifties, menudo has become popular all over America, wherever there is even the smallest Hispanic community. Not, I think, for its medicinal value, but simply because it is good hearty fare and easy to prepare.

≈

1. Cut the tripe into 1-inch squares. Rinse the tripe well. Put it in enough water to cover.

2. Add the pigs' feet, garlic, bay leaves, and onion and about 1 tablespoon salt and a few grinds of pepper. A sprig or two of mint and a couple of jalapeño peppers can go in at this time, if you like.

3. Cover the pot and simmer for 1½ to 2 hours, until the tripe is done to your taste. I like mine still a bit on the chewy side, but it can be cooked tender or even mushy, if you prefer.

4. Remove the bay leaves, chilies, and mint. Add the hominy and simmer for an additional 15 minutes. Taste for seasoning and add more salt and pepper if needed.

5. Serve in large bowls, with small bowls on the side filled with the condiments, which can be sprinkled on top, and a bowl of lemon wedges for those who would like to squeeze on a little lemon juice.

Serves 10 to 12.

George Washington

Tripe is the cut of meat that has been credited by gastronomic historians with turning the tide of the American Revolution and helping secure freedom for us all. Maybe the story is apocryphal, but let's believe it is true!

It was the winter of 1777–78. Washington had made camp in a valley twenty-five miles north of Philadelphia. The valley was barren and the winter was severe. Washington's troops were in rags, without food, and living in crude huts. Many died of starvation and exposure. Desertion was frequent and morale was low. Something had to be done.

Washington called the company cook. "Cook," he said (if you'll excuse some light tinkering with quotations from the past), "you must create a meal to kindle the spirits of these men." "But, General, sir," the cook said, "there is nothing in the mess but a mess of scraps. A few hundred pounds of that awful tripe the local butcher gave us and a pile of peppercorns from a Germantown patriot. The rest, sir, is scraps and more scraps." "But," the general said, as generals will, "I want no excuses, man, I want a great meal. Now go make one!"

So the cook did. What else could he do? And the resulting dish was fantastic. It filled Chester County, Pennsylvania, with a heartwarming fragrance and brought not only full stomachs but new hope and, ultimately, victory to the ragged troops at Valley Forge.

The dish was dubbed "Philadelphia Pepper Pot" in honor of the cook's hometown. It makes a hearty winter meal any winter, with that rich stick-to-your-ribs goodness that helps to fortify against the cold.

Philadelphia Pepper Pot

George Washington's cook must have had a little French in him. The recipe he created was very like *tripe à la mode de Caen.* There are some differences very likely attributable to the circumstances. He simmered his in a pot, instead of baking it in the oven; used cayenne pepper instead of allspice; added some bell peppers and potatoes to the pot; then finished the dish with cream.

- 3 pounds honeycomb tripe (prepared as described in Basic Prep I, pages 254–55)
- 1 veal knuckle with some meat on it
- 1 tablespoon salt
- 2 large onions, chopped
- 1 bay leaf
- 1 stalk celery
- 2 leeks, split and well rinsed
- 2 sprigs parsley
- 1 sprig fresh thyme
- 4 quarts water
- 1 teaspoon freshly ground black pepper
- Dash hot red pepper (cayenne)
- 1 or 2 dried red chilies, crushed
- 4 cups diced potatoes
- 1 bell pepper, seeded and diced
- 2 tablespoons chopped parsley
- ⅓ cup flour
- 1 cup milk
- 5 tablespoons butter

≈

1. Cut the tripe into ½-inch squares and set aside.
2. Place the veal knuckle, 1 teaspoon of the salt, and the onions, bay leaf, celery, leeks, parsley, thyme, and water in a large stockpot. Bring to a boil and skim off any scum that rises to the top. Simmer, covered, for 2 hours. Strain and reserve the stock. Remove any meat from the bone and dice it.
3. Put the veal back in the pot with the stock. Add the tripe, the remaining salt, and the pepper, cayenne, and chilies. Cover and simmer for 1½ hours longer.
4. Add the potatoes, bell pepper, and parsley. Cook another 20 minutes, until the potatoes are tender.
5. Blend the flour and milk together; gradually add it to the soup mixture, bring to the simmer, and stir until thickened slightly. Add the butter and stir. Serve very hot in large bowls with plenty of crusty bread.

Serves 8 to 10.

Pickled Tripe

2 pounds honeycomb tripe (prepared as described in Basic Prep I and II, pages 254–55)
1 cup reserved stock from Basic Prep II
2 cloves garlic, minced
½ cup cider vinegar
Juice of 1 lemon
2 onions, sliced thin

A jar of Pickled Tripe in the refrigerator is great to have on hand for hors d'oeuvre, to add to salads, or for an interesting first course. The tripe will keep, refrigerated, for several weeks. The pickled tripe that you may find in your supermarket is not fully cooked, so don't try to eat it as is. It is, however, a good product to use in making this recipe.

≈

1. Slice the tripe into thin strips about 3 inches long.

2. Make a brine. Mix 1 cup of the broth in which the tripe was cooked, the garlic, vinegar, and lemon juice. Place the tripe strips in a glass dish and cover with the brine; add the sliced onions and refrigerate. Let the tripe soak in the brine for 2 or 3 days, stirring occasionally. Serve as an hors d'oeuvre or as a salad on a bed of greens with a vinaigrette dressing.

Serves 6 to 8.

Tripe Fried in Batter

2 pounds honeycomb tripe (prepared as described in Basic Prep I and II, pages 254–55)
1 egg
1 cup milk
1¼ cups flour
½ teaspoon salt
Lard or vegetable oil for frying

This may be the best way with tripe for first time "tripers." Serve with mashed potatoes, steamed vegetables, and a salad.

≈

1. Cut the tripe into pieces about the size of an oyster.

2. Combine the egg, milk, flour, and salt to make a smooth batter. Dip the tripe in the batter and brown on both sides in hot fat.

Serves 6 to 8.

VARIATIONS

Tripe Fried in Bread Crumbs Instead of making a batter, simply dust the tripe with flour, dip in beaten egg, then coat with bread crumbs seasoned with salt and pepper, and fry in hot oil.

Broiled Tripe Cut the precooked tripe into bite-sized pieces, dust them with flour seasoned with salt and pepper, and dip them in melted butter. Broil for 3 or 4 minutes, then turn and continue broiling for another few minutes until nicely browned. Serve with a tartar sauce or salsa.

Sautéed Tripe with Mushrooms and Onions Cut the precooked tripe into thin strips and sauté them in 2 or 3 tablespoons of butter along with 1 onion, sliced thin, and 1 cup of sliced fresh mushrooms. When the onion is tender, stir in ¼ cup of the reserved broth in which the tripe was cooked and continue cooking to form a nice sauce coating the tripe. Serve with a rice pilaf or on slices of toasted French bread.

HEART

When the Indians of the Great Plains of America hunted the bison, legend claims, the heart of the animal was the trophy that went to the warrior who brought home the beast. Or maybe even to the big chief, since the heart was considered to be the source of strength, courage, and wisdom, and everybody knows that any big chief (or even a small, brave warrior) needs all of that kind of stuff he can get.

But legend and myths are made of fragile stuff, and the heart no longer holds the place of honor it once enjoyed. You may have a hard time getting the young warriors around your house to try it at all.

The hearts of beef, veal, lamb, and pork all are good food if you treat them right. The recommended cooking procedure given in most recipe books is some kind of moist-heat cooking, but the hearts of young animals—veal, lamb, or even small beef hearts—are tender enough to be cooked with dry heat. Try trimming up a few lamb hearts, cutting them into cubes, and using them in place of more expensive lamb in your favorite recipe for shish kabob.

Heart in Brandy Mustard Sauce

- 1 pound beef or calf heart, sliced thin
- 2 tablespoons prepared mustard, smooth or grainy
- 4 tablespoons flour
- 4 tablespoons butter
- Salt and pepper to taste
- Brandy (approximately 2 tablespoons)

This dish goes wonderfully well served with Barley Pilaf (page 193) and a hearty red wine.

≈

1. Spread each slice of heart with a little mustard and dust with flour.
2. Melt the butter in a heavy skillet. Add the slices of heart and brown quickly over fairly high heat, turning once. Season with salt and pepper. Cover, reduce the heat, and cook for 5 more minutes.
3. Before serving, splash on a bit of brandy. Stand back, ignite, and let the flames burn out.

Serves 4.

Stuffed Beef Heart

Our favorite heart recipe from down on the farm is Aunt Gert's Stuffed Beef Heart.

- 1 beef heart (or 2 veal or 6 lamb hearts)
- 1 teaspoon salt
- ½ teaspoon black pepper
- 2 cups of Aunt Gert's Onion Stuffing (recipe follows) or your favorite
- 2 tablespoons cooking oil
- Water to cover
- Brandy (approximately 2 tablespoons)
- 1 tablespoon arrowroot dissolved in ⅓ cup water

≈

1. Rinse the heart or hearts. Trim away any hard arteries and ligaments inside, and any excess fat from the outside. Season with salt and pepper. Fill the heart with the prepared stuffing and close the opening with small skewers.

2. In a large heavy saucepan brown the meat on all sides in the hot oil; add water to cover, then cover the pot and simmer slowly for 2 to 3 hours, until tender.

3. Remove the heart and slice it. Arrange the slices on a warm serving platter. Turn what's left in the pan into a delicious sauce by adding a splash of brandy over low heat to deglaze the pan, then thickening with the arrowroot mixture. Spoon some sauce over the slices and pass the rest in a gravy boat.

Serves 4.

Aunt Gert's Onion Stuffing

This recipe is one from my Great-Aunt Gert.

- ½ onion, finely chopped
- ¼ cup cooking oil
- 2 cups soft bread crumbs
- 1 teaspoon salt
- ¼ teaspoon black pepper

≈

Gently cook the onion in hot oil until limp and transparent. Add the bread crumbs, salt, and pepper. Mix well and stuff lightly into the heart. Don't pack too tightly, because the dressing will expand.

Makes approximately 2 cups.

SWEETBREADS

Throughout history, sweetbreads have been among the most cherished of all the odds 'n' ends and innards of our meat-eating culture. The first edition of *Larousse Gastronomique,* published in 1938, contained over forty recipes for their preparation. They were found on elegant banquet menus and in country kitchens throughout America. Fannie Farmer had about ten recipes for sweetbreads in the first edition of her famous cookbook. James Beard, the Dean of American Cooking and a fan of all that offal stuff, included fifteen recipes for sweetbreads in his book *James Beard's American Cookery,* published as recently as 1972.

In recent years, sweetbreads seem to have become exclusively restaurant fare. They are what I'm apt to order whenever I see them on the menu. But there are so many things to be done with sweetbreads, and they are so good, we need to get them back in the home kitchen. Ask your butcher to order some for you!

Sweetbreads are expensive little goodies, the most expensive by far of all the offal. Because they're expensive, it is important to know about what you are buying. For the same reason, it is important to know the tricks of pre-preparation that will assure you that the quality you paid for will be apparent in the finished dish.

Selection

Sweetbreads are glands, and there are two different kinds found in beef, veal, and lamb. (Lamb sweetbreads are, so I have been told, the most delicious sweetbreads there are. Unfortunately, in the United States they aren't: they are not commercially marketed here. So, unless you work in a lamb-packing plant or head for Europe, where they are available, you'll have to settle for sweetbreads from veal or beef.)

The two different glands used as sweetbreads are the thymus and pancreas. The thymus is an elongated gland found in the neck of young animals, such as calves and lambs. As the animal matures, the thymus gland shrinks away, becoming almost nonexistent in full-grown beef or mutton. The pancreas glands—or "belly sweetbreads," as they are called—are round in shape and do not shrink as the animal matures. Rather, they grow larger, tougher, and much less desirable.

Veal sweetbreads are usually sold in "pairs," which means you get both the thymus and the pancreas glands from a single calf. The best quality will be a creamy, grayish pink in color; they will be firm and plump and weigh approximately one pound per pair.

Beef sweetbreads are darker in color. They will not be sold in pairs, since the thymus gland does not exist in mature cattle, and they should be considerably cheaper in price than "paired" veal sweetbreads. So be careful. Don't pay a premium price for sweetbreads labeled veal that are in fact beef. Check the color, and check for pairing. If you're lucky, you'll find a market that sells Delft Blue Provimi brand sweetbreads. They are by far the best I've found.

Basic Sweetbreads Preparation

Most recipes tell you to soak sweetbreads in several changes of cold water and then blanch (parboil) them. Soaking is necessary for beef sweetbreads to remove any blood, but good-quality veal sweetbreads don't need to go through that step.

To blanch them, put them in a pan, cover with cold water, and add a dash of salt and a splash of vinegar. Bring to a gentle boil, reduce the heat, and simmer for 5 to 15 minutes, depending on how you plan to use them. If your recipe calls for long simmering in some kind of sauce, 5 minutes of blanching is enough. If they are to be sauced and served without any further simmering, blanch them for 10 to 15 minutes.

After blanching, drain and plunge them into cold water, which makes it easier to peel off the covering membrane. The membrane on veal sweetbreads is often so delicate that it need not be removed, but removing the membrane from beef sweetbreads is a must.

Many cooks, and this butcher, recommend pressing sweetbreads under weights in the refrigerator for an hour or so after blanching. It improves the texture greatly. Sweetbreads that have not been pressed are often rubbery.

All this may seem like a lot of trouble—blanching, peeling, and pressing, even before you begin—but it's worth it. There is no more delicate, mouthwatering morsel of meat in the world than well-prepared sweetbreads.

Frank's Sweetbreads Vin Blanc

1½ to 2 pounds sweetbreads, blanched 10 to 15 minutes (see Basic Sweetbreads Preparation, page 265)
1¼ cups flour
3 tablespoons butter
½ cup white wine
Salt and pepper to taste
A few sprigs parsley, chopped

Twenty years ago, Jim Beard introduced me to a little restaurant called Frank's on 14th Street between Ninth and Tenth Avenues in New York's Greenwich Village, right in the heart of the city's wholesale-meat district. In addition to great steaks, George Molinari—whose maternal grandfather founded the place in 1912—does wonderful things with offal and all the odds 'n' ends.

I get to Frank's whenever I visit New York and most always have the Sweetbreads Vin Blanc. George gave me his recipe and I can now make them in my kitchen. They are super-simple and oh so good!

≈

1. Slice the sweetbreads into ¼-inch-thick slices. Dust with the flour and sauté them in the butter over moderate heat until nicely browned.

2. Add the white wine and cook, stirring, until the sauce thickens slightly. Season to taste with salt and pepper, sprinkle on the chopped parsley, and serve.

NOTE: When you get to New York, stop in at Frank's, but it isn't where it was. In October of 1994, they suffered a loss due to fire and as a result have moved around the corner, to 85 Tenth Avenue.

Serves 4 to 6.

Sweetbreads with Country Ham and Cheese

Here is a great way to use some of the leftovers from a holiday ham. If you have no leftover ham, prosciutto works wonderfully well.

- 1½ to 2 pounds sweetbreads, blanched 10 to 15 minutes (see Basic Sweetbreads Preparation, page 265)
- ½ pound ham or prosciutto, thinly sliced
- 1 cup grated Monterey Jack cheese
- ½ teaspoon salt
- ¼ teaspoon freshly ground black pepper
- ¼ teaspoon freshly grated nutmeg

≈

1. Slice the sweetbreads crosswise into ¼-inch-thick slices. Layer them in a shallow buttered baking dish.
2. Top the sweetbreads with a layer of ham, then with the grated cheese. Season with the salt and pepper and nutmeg. Bake in a preheated 450-degree oven for 15 minutes, until the cheese is melted and bubbling. Serve on toasted French-bread slices.

Serves 4 to 6.

Braised Sweetbreads

This recipe can be served with elegance in fancy pastry shells or very simply over toast, mashed potatoes, fried cornmeal mush, or polenta, depending on the ethnic heritage of your guest list.

- 1½ to 2 pounds sweetbreads, blanched 10 to 15 minutes (see Basic Sweetbreads Preparation, page 265)
- 1 medium onion, chopped
- 1 carrot, peeled and chopped
- 1 rib celery, sliced thin
- 3 tablespoons butter

≈

1. Cut the sweetbreads into ½-inch-thick slices.
2. Sauté the onion, carrot, and celery in the butter until tender.
3. Season the sweetbread slices with salt and pepper and dust them generously with flour. Add them to the skillet along with the vegetables and cook over moderate heat until golden brown.

(recipe continues)

Braised Sweetbreads *(cont.)*

- Salt and pepper to taste
- Flour
- 1 cup beef or chicken stock
- ¼ cup wine (red, white, or Madeira; French, Italian, or other, depending on your ethnic preference)
- 2 tablespoons chopped parsley

4. Add the stock and your choice of wine. Stir to blend everything together. Cover and simmer gently for 10 to 12 minutes. Adjust the seasonings if needed, sprinkle with chopped parsley, and serve.

Serves 4 to 6.

Sweetbread Sauté

- 1 pound sweetbreads, blanched 10 to 15 minutes (see Basic Sweetbreads Preparation, page 265)
- ½ cup fine bread crumbs
- ½ teaspoon salt
- ¼ teaspoon white pepper
- ½ teaspoon powdered ginger
- 1 egg, beaten
- 2 to 3 tablespoons butter

This recipe is, I think, my favorite for sweetbreads. It's fast, and the delicate flavor of the sweetbreads is not disguised. My wife and I have it often when we dine alone.

≈

1. Cut the sweetbreads into ½-inch-thick slices.
2. Combine the bread crumbs with the seasonings. Roll the sweetbreads in the crumbs, dip them in the egg, and roll them once again in the crumbs. Cook gently in butter over medium heat until lightly brown.

Serves 2 generously.

Braised Sweetbreads with Mushrooms

Wild mushrooms were once reserved only for those who knew what they were looking for and went into the woods when the weather was right to find them. Now many are available fresh or dried in most American supermarkets. There are wood ears, shiitake, porcini, chanterelles, and more. And of course there are the regular cultivated mushrooms. They all are delicious with sweetbreads. Use any of them or a combination in this recipe.

- 1½ to 2 pounds sweetbreads, blanched 10 to 15 minutes (see Basic Sweetbreads Preparation, page 265)
- Flour for dredging
- 3 tablespoons butter
- 2 shallots, finely chopped
- 2 cloves garlic, minced
- ¼ cup dry white wine
- 1½ cups chicken broth
- 2 tablespoons chopped fresh tarragon or ½ teaspoon dried
- Salt and freshly ground black pepper
- ¼ pound mushrooms, any kind, cut into small pieces (if you are using dry mushrooms, they need to be soaked in warm water for 30 minutes before being added to the sauce)

≈

1. Cut the sweetbreads into bite-sized pieces.
2. Dredge the sweetbreads in the flour and shake off any excess.
3. Melt the butter in a good-sized skillet over moderate heat, add the sweetbreads, and cook, stirring, until they are browned slightly.
4. Add the shallots and garlic and cook, stirring, for another minute.
5. Pour in the white wine and chicken broth and continue to stir, scraping up and incorporating any bits from the bottom of the pan. Add the tarragon, salt, and pepper. Cover and simmer gently for 10 to 12 minutes.
6. Add the mushrooms and continue cooking for another 4 to 5 minutes. Adjust the seasonings and serve with either a pasta or a pilaf.

Serves 4 to 6.

BRAINS

Of all the offal, brains, it seems, are the hardest for most people to accept. I confess they are not my favorite, and I know it's more psychological than gastronomic. My wife loves them. Her favorite breakfast dish is Brains and Scrambled Eggs. As a girl she enjoyed fried-brain sandwiches as her school lunch until too many young classmates with wrinkled noses commented, "Yuk!"

Selection

Brains should be bought and prepared when absolutely fresh. They are very perishable and do not freeze well, so cook them the day you buy them. Look for brains that are plump and moist with a pinkish-gray sheen to them. Avoid any that look shriveled and dry.

Although they are different in texture and flavor, brains and sweetbreads can be used interchangeably in most recipes. Most people who like brains will like sweetbreads, although I can attest that the reverse is not always the case.

Basic Brains Preparation

Like sweetbreads, brains need to be soaked and blanched before use in any recipe. Soak in cool water for an hour. Pull off any covering membranes.

Put 1 quart of water in a saucepan, add 2 tablespoons of vinegar or lemon juice, 1 bay leaf, ½ cup coarsely chopped onion, 1 teaspoon salt, and 1 teaspoon coarsely crushed peppercorns. Bring to a boil, reduce heat, and simmer for 15 minutes. Add the brains to the stock and simmer slowly for 10 minutes. When the parboiling is completed, either plunge the brains into cold water for immediate use or let them cool in the liquid and refrigerate in the liquid until ready to proceed.

Fried Bacon and Brains

1½ to 2 pounds prepared brains (see Basic Brains Preparation, above)

Aunt Gert used to make this with pork brains at "hog-killin' time." Pork brains tend to be a little mushy. The cornmeal coating improves the texture, and the crisp bacon is a nice addition. Veal brains are even better prepared this way.

≈

1. Cut the brains into ¾-inch slices.

2. In a heavy skillet (Aunt Gert used cast iron), fry the bacon until crisp. Remove the bacon and drain the slices on paper towels. Save the drippings in the pan.

3. Season the brains with salt and pepper, then dust them generously with cornmeal. Fry the brains in the rendered bacon fat until browned on both sides. Remove them to a warm serving platter and keep warm.

4. Pour off the bacon fat and deglaze the pan with the lemon juice and wine. Add a dollop of butter and stir until it melts. Pour the sauce over the brains. Crumble the bacon over the top and sprinkle on the parsley or chives.

Serves 4.

- 1½ to 2 pounds prepared brains (see Basic Brains Preparation, page 270)
- 4 to 6 slices of good country bacon
- Salt and pepper to taste
- ¾ cup yellow cornmeal
- 2 tablespoons fresh lemon juice
- ¼ cup dry white wine
- 1 tablespoon butter
- 2 tablespoons chopped parsley or chives

Brains and Scrambled Eggs

This is one of my wife's favorite ways with brains. Any brains can be used, but Neva prefers veal.

- ½ to ¾ pound prepared brains (see Basic Brains Preparation, page 270)
- 2 tablespoons finely chopped parsley
- 2 tablespoons chopped chives
- Dash hot red pepper (cayenne)
- Salt and freshly ground pepper to taste
- 3 tablespoons butter
- 6 eggs
- 3 tablespoons cream
- Cooked bacon slices (optional)

≈

1. Pat the brains dry and cut them into small dice. Combine the brains with the chopped parsley, chives, cayenne, salt, and pepper.

2. Cook the mixture in the butter over moderate heat, turning often, until lightly browned.

3. Whip the eggs and cream with a wire whisk and pour over the cooked ingredients. Reduce the heat to low and stir gently, folding the eggs and brains together until the eggs are set. Place on a heated platter and serve with crisp bacon, if desired.

Serves 4.

Fried Brains with a Mustard Crumb Coating

- Oil for frying
- 1½ to 2 pounds prepared veal brains (see Basic Brains Preparation, page 270)
- Salt and pepper to taste
- ¼ cup mustard (of the many different styles available, use your favorite)
- 1 egg, lightly beaten
- 2 cups fresh bread crumbs
- Lemon quarters

This recipe is based on one given to me by a lady who knows good food: my editor, Judith Jones. It works best here to rinse the brains in cold water after the basic preparation and refrigerate them for at least 30 minutes or overnight with a heavy plate on top as a weight. This firms the texture and prepares the brains for the final, very quick cooking process.

≈

1. Pour ½ inch of oil into a large skillet. Heat it slowly.
2. Season the brains with salt and pepper and smear mustard liberally on both sides. Dip the brains into the egg, then roll in the bread crumbs.
3. When the oil is hot, transfer the brains carefully to the skillet and fry over medium-high heat for about 2 minutes on each side. Serve immediately, garnished with lemon quarters.

Serves 4.

Brain Fritters

- 1½ to 2 pounds prepared brains (see Basic Brains Preparation, page 270)
- 2 tablespoons butter
- 1 tablespoon flour
- ¼ cup whole milk
- Salt and freshly ground pepper to taste
- ¼ teaspoon freshly grated nutmeg

Jana Allen was one of the food editors at the San Francisco *Chronicle* when I first started writing a weekly column on meat in 1972. In 1974, she and Margaret Gin wrote a marvelous little book called *Innards and Other Variety Meats.* My copy is dog-eared, and one of the pages that show the most use has a version of this recipe. Here is my adaptation.

≈

1. Finely chop the prepared brains and set aside. Melt the butter in a saucepan, then add the flour, blend, and

cook for 2 to 3 minutes. Add the milk and blend into a smooth sauce. Season with salt, pepper, and nutmeg. Transfer to a large bowl.

2. Add the brains to the bowl. Stir in the egg white and enough bread crumbs to form a thick mass. Shape into balls about the size of a walnut. In a large skillet heat the vegetable oil to 375 degrees. Fry the fritters until golden brown. Drain on paper towels.

- 1 egg white, beaten
- ½ cup (or more) fine bread crumbs
- ½ cup vegetable oil for frying

Serves 4.

ROCKY MOUNTAIN OYSTERS

I first tasted Rocky Mountain oysters at Bercham's Bar on the Winnebago Indian Reservation in Winnebago, Nebraska, just across the river and down the road from where I learned the butcher trade, in Sioux City, Iowa. They were, they are, delicious!

"What," some of you may be asking, "are Rocky Mountain oysters?" Well, you see, they're a . . . well, uh, they're a sort of a freshwater shellfish from the Colorado Rockies. No! That's not true! They are, quite bluntly, bulls' balls: the testicles of the male bovine animal, most often those of calves taken at castrating time, although the testicles of mature bulls are also used. Those were the ones I first tasted at that bar in Winnebago.

In sheep country, lamb testicles, called "fries," are also served as Rocky Mountain oysters. I tasted those only recently, at the Hi-Country Lamb Cook-Off in Greeley, Colorado. In my estimation, they're the best of the bunch, but, then, I have yet to taste turkey oysters. Yes! Tom-turkey testicles are also highly prized, and according to my friend Sam Arnold, a gastronomic historian who is something of an authority on this subject (among many others), turkey "surprises," as they are known in the trade, are the tastiest of all!

Rocky Mountain oysters, no matter the source, have a membrane covering the gland that must be removed. It is much easier to remove that membrane and to slice the fries if they are frozen to the point of being frosty. Bull, calf, or lamb testicles are usually sliced into ¼-to-½-inch-thick slices for frying. Bull fries are sometimes run through the meat tenderizer at the market. That isn't necessary with calf or lamb testicles. I doubt that turkey fries even need to be sliced. They can simply be skinned, stuck on a toothpick, deep-fried, and served as an hors d'oeuvre. According to Sam Arnold, that's the best way to eat any Rocky Mountain oyster. "At castration time on the range," Sam recalls, "the fries were simply impaled on a stick and roasted over the campfire till cooked." Thanks, Sam. I'll have mine sliced and fried and served with a horseradish sauce.

Some people soak the beef testicles in salt water for a couple of hours to soften the strong flavor. Calf or lamb fries, and I'm certain turkey too, will not need soaking. Cooking Rocky Mountain oysters, whatever the species, is a simple process, once the necessary skinning and slicing are done. The fries, either sliced or whole, are dusted with seasoned flour, dipped in egg or milk, then rolled in flour or crumbs and deep-fried in 400-degree fat until just golden brown. Overcooking will toughen them.

Rocky Mountain oysters are not an item that you are apt to find in the meat case of your average local supermarket. There is, as I am sure you understand, a somewhat limited supply. Most calf testicles are taken at calving time on the ranch rather than in a USDA-inspected meat plant and are therefore not allowed to be sold. You have to know a cowboy!

Rocky Mountain Oysters

12 medium or 24 small mountain oysters
6 eggs
3 cups cracker crumbs, seasoned to taste with salt and pepper
Oil for frying

As soon as the last male calf was castrated and branded on the last day of the roundup, some of the cowpokes would clean and peel the "oysters," then take them up to the ranch house soaking in cold water. An hour or two later, the ranch wife would bring out a platter of fried mountain oysters along with the other dishes—beans, salad, and such—to feed the hands. Just being able to feast on this delicacy, some say, made the work of the roundup well worthwhile.

≈

1. If using medium-sized oysters, cut into smaller pieces. Beat the eggs until just blended. Dip the oysters in egg and roll in the seasoned cracker crumbs.

2. Fry over high heat until browned. Place on a cookie sheet and bake in a preheated 350-degree oven for 20 minutes. Season to taste.

Serves 4 to 6.

HEADCHEESE

From the time I was twelve, working with my dad at the Council Oak Store in Sioux City, Iowa, one of my favorite luncheon meats has been headcheese. Two, three, four times a day during my 4-to-6-p.m. after-school work at the market, I would "lift" a slice of headcheese from the deli case, roll it around a spoonful of potato salad (also lifted from the deli case, but, since Mom had made it, somehow it seemed a lesser crime), slip into the back room, and enjoy my snack.

Headcheese is a good old-fashioned home-style product that was developed, I'm sure, as a means of using all of the variety meats that resulted from home slaughter at hog-killin' time. Everything "except the squeal" could and did go into it: heart, tongue, feet, and other meats, but the head for sure.

Grandma's Headcheese

This is a recipe from Grandma's old cookbook—*The Allen Cookbook*—to give you an idea of how it was made.

> *Clean head thoroughly, removing hair and scruff; skin out snout and lower jaw and remove jaw bones. Cut head in two pieces. The tongue, heart and feet properly cleaned may also be included if desired. Cook until meat falls from bones. Cool, remove all bones, run through chopper. Season with salt, pepper, sage and the strained broth in with the meat that was cooked. Mix and place in earthen vessel, weigh down. When very cold, cut in slices. Serve for luncheon or supper.*

Or slice ¼ inch thick and serve with a good vinaigrette as a first course.

Most of you, I'm sure, are not quite up to all of that, even if you had easy access to a hog's head. But you can make a very good headcheese in your own kitchen with meat that is readily available in any supermarket.

Headless Headcheese

- 3 pounds fresh pork picnic shoulder, bone-in
- 2 pork tongues or 1 veal tongue
- 2 pigs' feet, split
- 1 large onion, stuck with 3 or 4 cloves
- 1 bay leaf
- ½ teaspoon dried sage
- ½ teaspoon dried thyme
- 1 teaspoon salt
- 1 teaspoon freshly ground black pepper

This recipe resulted from a trip to New York, where I had a marvelous headcheese first course at a restaurant called La Tulipe. When I got home and tried to duplicate the dish, I couldn't find a pig's head. This comes close.

Headcheese keeps wrapped in the refrigerator for up to a week, or frozen (preferably in large pieces) for a month or more.

≈

1. Put everything in a large, heavy pot, cover with water, bring to a boil, reduce the heat, and simmer for 1½ hours. Remove the pork shoulder and the tongue. Continue simmering the pigs' feet for an additional hour to develop a rich gelatinous broth.

2. Allow the pork shoulder and tongue to cool so that they can be handled. Then remove all the skin, bones, and gristle. Cut the meat into ½-to-¾-inch cubes and set aside. Reserve any small pieces and trimmings.

3. Remove the pigs' feet from the broth, allow to cool, and remove the bones. Grind, or finely chop, the meat and skin from the pigs' feet along with the reserved trimmings and small pieces of tongue and pork shoulder.

4. Mix the cubes of pork shoulder and tongue with the finely chopped meat. Add enough of the strained broth to cover. Return the mixture to the heat and bring to a boil. This reheating serves to mix the natural gelatin from the pigs' feet thoroughly through the mixture, so that when the headcheese is chilled it will slice without crumbling.

5. Pour into containers of desired size and shape; loaf pans work well. Chill till firm, place weights over the headcheese, and refrigerate for 24 hours.

Makes about 5 pounds.

VARIATIONS

The possible variations on headcheese are almost endless. Different seasonings can be added at the beginning of the reheating step. Try a bit of marjoram, coriander, and/or cloves. Mix in a few small button mushrooms that have been blanched and drained. Add julienned strips of carrots, or asparagus spears. Add ½ cup or so of cider vinegar to the broth, toss in a few green olives, and you have a sour headcheese, or "souse." Use your imagination!

• One-half-inch-thick slices served on lettuce and topped with a vinaigrette dressing make a marvelous first course.

• Cut headcheese into cubes and toss them into a green salad, or stick toothpicks in the cubes to serve with cocktails.

• Cut a few slices and serve with potato salad for a great summer lunch.

PIGS' FEET

There comes a time in every boy's life when, as they say in the TV commercial, "he knows he's a man." I think that time came in my young life one Saturday night when my dad tossed an extra beer into the pigs'-feet barrel. Now, don't laugh . . .

Dad used to keep a fifty-gallon barrel at least half full of pickled pigs' feet in the cooler of the little market where he taught me the trade. Every Saturday night at about six o'clock or so, he would go over to the grocery side of the market, buy a couple of beers, and drop them into the pigs'-feet barrel to chill.

Then, after the store closed at 9 p.m., while we cleaned up the shop, he and Gene (his "second man") would drink a cold beer and have a couple of pigs' feet while I had an orange soda. Pigs' feet don't go very well with orange soda.

One Saturday night, my dad dropped three beers in the brine and opened one for me at nine o'clock. I think I felt as big that night as I've ever felt, and I've loved pickled pigs' feet ever since.

You can buy pickled pigs' feet in jars, but I've yet to find a jar that can compare to the pigs' feet you pickle yourself in a barrel in the cooler or a big crock in the refrigerator.

Fresh pigs' feet are readily available and quite inexpensive in most markets, but if they're not in your butcher's meat case, ring the bell and ask if he will order some for you. You may be surprised at what the butcher will do for you if you will only ask.

Basic Pigs'-Feet Preparation

Select the largest pigs' feet that you can find (the larger ones usually have more of the meaty pork hock left on). Have the butcher split the feet for you. You can do this yourself after they are cooked, but it is a big saving in time and trouble if you have him do it on the electric saw.

Wrap each foot, either whole or in 2 split halves, in a couple of layers of cheesecloth and tie securely. This prevents the feet from falling apart in the long, slow parboiling process required for pigs' feet. Put the feet in a large pot with enough salted water to cover. Use 1 teaspoon of salt for each quart of water. Add a stalk or two of celery, an onion stuck with a couple of cloves, a carrot, 6 or 8 black peppercorns, a bay leaf or two, and, if you like, 6 or 8 allspice berries. Bring to a boil, reduce heat, and simmer for 3 hours. Let the pigs' feet cool in their own cooking liquid until cool enough to handle. Remove cheesecloth and proceed. You may want to strain and reserve some of the cooking liquid to use for sauces and gravies.

Pickled Pigs' Feet

- **4 to 6 pigs' feet (see Basic Pigs'-Feet Preparation, above), liquid reserved**
- **1 large onion, thinly sliced**
- **2 cups reserved cooking liquid**

These keep well in the refrigerator for months; freezing is not necessary. They are wonderful to have on hand during the hot summer months just for snacking, or for picnics, tailgate parties, and the like.

≈

1. Cut the pigs' feet into random-sized pieces and put the pieces in jars or a covered crock.

2. Bring the liquid to a boil. Add all of the remaining ingredients and simmer for about 5 minutes. Pour the liquid over the pigs' feet and let cool. It's important that the liquid (brine) completely cover the pigs' feet. So, if you're using a crock in which the feet may float to the top, it's a good idea to weight the feet with a heavy plate. Refrigerate, covered, for at least 24 hours to allow the flavors to blend. The feet will keep for 2 or 3 months refrigerated. Will satisfy a few on a hot summer afternoon of yard work, or up to 8 under less strenuous conditions.

Serves 6 to 8.

- 2 cups white vinegar
- 1 or 2 bay leaves
- 1 teaspoon whole black peppercorns
- 4 whole allspice berries
- 5 cloves garlic, peeled and split
- 1 or more dried red chilies (optional)

Pigs' Feet and Sauerkraut

There are dozens of things to be done to pigs' feet besides pickling. Here is a family favorite.

≈

- 6 pigs' feet, split and prepared (see Basic Pigs'-Feet Preparation, page 278)
- 2 quarts sauerkraut, rinsed and drained
- 6 or 8 small potatoes, peeled and sliced
- 1 tart apple, peeled and sliced
- 1 onion, sliced
- 1 tablespoon caraway seeds
- Dry white wine

1. Place a third of the split feet in the bottom of a heavy casserole. Put a third of the sauerkraut on top, followed by a third of the potatoes. Repeat with alternate layers of pigs' feet, sauerkraut, and potatoes, finishing off with a single layer of apples and onions. Top with a sprinkling of caraway seeds.

2. Add wine to cover and bake, covered, in a preheated 325-degree oven until the potatoes are tender, 30 to 45 minutes.

Serves 6 to 8.

Pigs' Feet St. Mènehould

4 pigs' feet, split and prepared (see Basic Pigs'-Feet Preparation, page 278)
¼ cup Dijon mustard
1 cup dried bread crumbs
8 tablespoons (1 stick) butter

This is a classic way with pigs' feet that comes to us from France. Traditionally the pigs' feet were simmered so long that even the bones could be eaten. This version cooks long enough for the meat to be tender. Don't eat the bones.

≈

1. When cool enough to handle, remove the cheesecloth and pick out all of the bones from each foot.
2. Brush each boneless foot liberally with mustard and coat with bread crumbs.
3. Fry in the butter until nicely browned on all sides and serve with more mustard, dill pickles, and a cold beer.

Serves 4 to 6.

TAIL OF THE OX

Oxtails don't come from oxen anymore, if indeed they ever did. (Oxen are the adult castrated males that pulled wagons and plows in the old days.) Oxtails come from the same steers and heifers that our steaks come from, and to my mind they have more lip-smackin' flavor than any other cut in the meat case, when it comes to really good stew.

Oxtails are a mess to eat, so it's best to enjoy them with family or very good friends. Each joint in the tail is a vertebra that contains sweet, tasty meat, and a gelatinlike substance so delicious it defies description. You must suck it out from the tiny crevices where it hides. Wonderful!

"Finger-Lickin'" Stew

Oxtails make a great stew, but you have to eat it with your fingers. The cartilage between the joints makes for a rich broth, which I like just as it is. If you want a thicker sauce, add the arrowroot mixture and simmer the stew, stirring, for two minutes before adding the potatoes and carrots. Serve with plenty of crusty bread to mop up the sauce.

- 2 tablespoons butter
- 1 cup chopped onion
- 3 cloves garlic, peeled and crushed
- 2 teaspoons salt
- 3½ to 4 pounds oxtails, cut into sections by cutting through the cartilage between the joints with a large kitchen knife
- 2 tablespoons flour
- 2 tablespoons vegetable oil
- 6 cups beef stock or water
- ¼ teaspoon freshly ground black pepper
- 1 teaspoon crushed dried thyme
- 1 bay leaf
- 2 tablespoons tomato paste
- 1 tablespoon arrowroot dissolved in ¼ cup cold water (optional)
- 4 medium potatoes, peeled and quartered
- 4 medium carrots, peeled and quartered

≈

1. In a large Dutch oven, melt the butter. Cook the onion and garlic over moderately low heat, stirring often, until soft but not brown. Set aside.
2. Salt the oxtails and dust them with the flour. In the same Dutch oven, heat oil until sizzling. Add the oxtails and cook them, turning frequently with tongs, until they are nicely browned on all sides.
3. Add the onion and garlic, the beef stock, pepper, thyme, bay leaf, and tomato paste. Bring to a boil, lower the heat, and let the stew simmer, covered, for 2½ to 3 hours, until the meat is very tender. Skim off and discard the excess fat a few minutes before serving. Stir in the arrowroot mixture, if desired.
4. As the stew nears the end of its cooking time, cook the potatoes and carrots separately in boiling salted water. Add them to the stew just before serving.

Serves 4.

Grandma Aki's Oxtails

1 large or 2 small oxtails (2½ to 3 pounds), cut into sections by cutting through the cartilage between the joints with a large kitchen knife
Water to cover for parboiling plus 2 quarts for cooking
3 or 4 cloves star anise*
1 stick cinnamon
¼ teaspoon red-pepper flakes
3 tablespoons brown sugar
3 tablespoons soy sauce

* Star anise (pods, not powder) can be found in Asian and gourmet food shops.

This delicious oxtail dish comes not from my Midwestern side of the family but from my wife's Hawaiian grandmother. They raise a lot of cattle in Hawaii, too.

≈

1. Put the oxtails in a good-sized pot, cover with water, and bring to a boil over high heat. Reduce the heat and simmer for about 5 minutes, so that scum that can cloud the finished sauce rises to the surface. Drain the oxtails in a colander and rinse them and the pot with water.

2. Return the oxtails to the pot and add the 2 quarts of water, the star anise, and the cinnamon. Cover the pot and bring to a boil, reduce the heat, and simmer gently for 1 hour.

3. Add the pepper flakes, brown sugar, and soy sauce, cover, and continue simmering for 2 more hours, until the meat is tender and almost falling from the bone. Remove the oxtails to a serving platter. Turn the heat to high. Boil the sauce 4 to 5 minutes, until it has reduced by a third. The brown sugar causes the sauce to thicken to a rich, shiny gravy. Pour the sauce over the oxtails and enjoy. Don't try to be neat! Serve with rice or pilaf.

Serves 4.

Oxtail Soup

This is a hearty soup, great for family and friends.

≈

1 oxtail (approximately 2 pounds), cut into sections by cutting through the cartilage between the joints with a large kitchen knife
2 tablespoons cooking oil or beef drippings
1 tablespoon salt
½ teaspoon black pepper
¼ teaspoon dried rosemary
¼ teaspoon dried marjoram
¼ teaspoon dried sage
2 quarts beef stock or water
1 medium onion, chopped
1 or 2 carrots, sliced thin
1 stalk celery, sliced thin
½ cup sauerkraut, rinsed and drained
1 medium tomato, peeled and chopped
Hot red pepper (cayenne) (optional)

1. Brown the oxtail in the cooking oil or beef drippings in a heavy skillet. Add the seasonings and beef stock. Cover and simmer for 3½ hours.

2. Add the vegetables, cover, and simmer for 30 minutes more. Add additional salt and some cayenne if needed. (A touch of hot pepper is good if you like a bit of heat to wake up your taste buds.) Skim off any excess fat.

Serves 6 to 8.

≈

SAUSAGE

You may brag about your breakfast foods you eat at break of day,
Your crisp, delightful shavings and your stack of last year's hay,
Your toasted flakes of rye and corn that fairly swim in cream,
Or rave about a sawdust mash, an epicurean dream.
But none of these appeals to me, though all of them I've tried—
The breakfast that I liked the best was sausage mother fried.

These lines from Edgar Guest's poem called "Sausage" bring back a flood of memories from my childhood. "Old country sausage," the kind that he described, was the sausage that my grandma made at "hog-killin' time." All the trimmings from the pig—"everything but the squeal"—were ground up, seasoned up, made into patties, and fried up, then "put down" in lard in a crock in the cave to be refried for breakfasts for months to come.

Sausage is unquestionably one of the oldest forms of meat preservation. Every meat-eating culture where there were grandmothers developed sausage as a means of preserving meat.

Many of those early sausage makers became so adept in the spicing and processing of sausages of distinctive types that the fame of their products spread throughout all Europe, and ultimately to America. A sausage that originated in Frankfurt am Main, Germany, became known as the frankfurter sausage, and is known to us today as the hot dog. Another product, produced in Bologna, Italy,

A procession of butchers carrying a giant sausage, Nuremberg, 1658.

became bologna sausage. Rome became famous for its romano; Genoa for Genoa salami; Berlin for berliner; Braunschweig (Brunswick, Germany) for its braunschweiger; Gotha for its gothaer; Gothenburg (Sweden) for göteborg; Lyons (France) for Lyons sausage; and Arles (France) for Arles sausage—to mention only a few.

Emigrants from Europe brought their knowledge of sausage making and their preferences for different types with them when they came to America. Thus Old World products were duplicated in the United States in response to the demand from immigrants and their descendants and varying with the climate in the region of America where they settled.

The sausage Grandma made on the farm in Nebraska at hog-killin' time can, I'm quite sure, be traced to her English heritage. The boudin and andouille of Cajun and Creole cooking of southern Louisiana can be traced to the French who settled there. The Germans and the Danish who settled much of Minnesota and Wisconsin brought with them the best of the *wurst*—bockwurst, bratwurst, leberwurst, and countless others. The settlers from Sweden had their husholls-medvurst—potato sausage—which has become a Christmas tradition in the

Farm women rinsing sausage casings.

Swedish communities of America. In the Southwest, the Spanish heritage is deliciously preserved in various types of chorizo sausage.

Today's supermarket meat cases are loaded with countless varieties of sausage that had their beginnings in country kitchens all over the world. There are Italian sausages in a variety of styles, German bratwurst, Danish bockworst, Spanish chorizo, and hundreds of others with origins from around the world. All provide great eating that will put you in touch with your heritage, whatever it is. The best sausages, though, I think, are the ones you make in your own kitchen.

Why, you might ask, make your own sausage when there are so many wonderful varieties available? There are a couple of reasons. First, it saves money! Sausage need not be made from an expensive cut of meat. Traditionally it was—and is today—made from the scraps and leftovers of the meat-cutting process. I make it a habit to save any lean trimmings of beef, pork, lamb, and veal that come through my kitchen. I keep each in a separate ziplock bag in the freezer until my wife says: "Honey, would you please stuff some sausage? The freezer's full of stuff!"

The main reason, however, for making your own sausage is quite simply that it is a lot of fun! Making sausage has become a hobby around our house.

Types of Sausage

The meat industry generally divides sausage products into five basic categories:

Fresh sausage is made from fresh, uncured meat cuts, principally pork but also beef, veal, poultry, or some combination thereof. This type of sausage must be kept under refrigeration and must be thoroughly cooked before eating. Some examples are: fresh pork sausage, fresh chorizo, fresh Italian sausage, and country-style pork sausage.

Fresh smoked sausages are made from fresh and/or cured meats and are lightly smoked. They are not thoroughly cooked, however, and must be fully cooked before eating. All such products should be kept refrigerated prior to preparation. Examples are: mettworst, kielbasa (or Polish sausage), smoked Italian sausage, and Cajun andouille sausage.

Cooked sausage is made basically from fresh meats, although occasionally some cured meats are used. These are thoroughly cooked in the sausage-making process and come to the consumer ready to serve. They are usually served cold. Examples: liver sausage, cotto salami, thüringer, and most of those products labeled "luncheon meats."

Cooked smoked sausage is prepared from fresh meats that are both cooked and smoked in the process. Some of the most popular sausage products fall into this category—hot dogs and bologna, for example. Sausage in this category is ready-to-eat, and those in the larger-diameter casings are traditionally served cold—bologna and mortadella, for example. Smaller sausages, like the hot dogs, are best reheated in some way before serving.

Finally, *dry and semi-dry sausages* are made from beef, pork, or a combination of the two in a complicated and carefully controlled fermentation-and-drying process. They will keep for long periods of time, in many cases without refrigeration, and require no cooking. Examples: Italian dry salami, pepperoni, landjaeger, and cervelat. This category of sausage requires at least a master's if not a Ph.D. in sausage making, and is not recommended for the beginning sausage maker. Recipes for such sausages are not covered herein. The closest we come is Easy Beef Salami (page 305).

FRESH SAUSAGE

Making Fresh Sausage

Fresh sausage is the simplest for the home sausage maker. All that is required is a few pounds of meat, some herbs and spices, a meat grinder, a "hank" or a "half-doll" of hog casings, and lots of imagination. Actually, the hog casings are optional. Back in the days before refrigerators and freezers, country cooks, my grandmother among them, would make sausage at hog-killin' time and simply form the meat into patties, which were then fried and layered in a crock. The fat from the frying was poured over the sausage to cover, and the crock was set on a shelf in the "storm cellar." For a hearty country breakfast, the required number of patties were taken from the crock and reheated. The remainder were left in the crock, preserved in fat for later use. That's a little primitive for today's cooks. With modern refrigerators and freezers, we can put fresh sausage "down" in a much simpler fashion, in the refrigerator for several days or in the freezer for several months.

Though stuffing sausage in casings is optional for most homemade sausage, I have included sausage-stuffing tubes and casings among the necessary equipment. It's part of the fun and it gives you professional-looking sausages that hold together nicely.

Meat Grinder

My father, and my grandfather, used a hand-crank meat grinder, and it's still the best for home sausage making. There are attachments available to turn your electric home mixer into a meat grinder. Some even have sausage-stuffing attachments, but my experience has been that these don't have the capacity for very effective sausage making. The motors on such machines are not powerful enough to grind the meat without overheating it, and it is important in making sausage that the meat not be allowed to overheat.

Buy the biggest hand-cranked meat grinder you can find. One with a four-by-five-inch hopper (opening where you stuff in the meat) will work much better for sausage making than a three- or four-inch model, and you'll not work as hard making sausage. Be sure you buy a model with a removable ring that allows for changing the grinder plates from coarse to fine. You'll need that versatility in preparing different types of sausage. Also, such a grinder can be used for stuffing sausage with the simple addition of a stuffing tube, which is held in place by the ring.

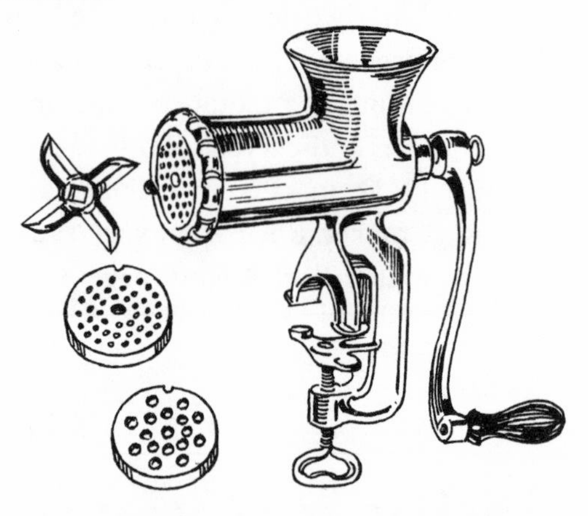

Most grinders come equipped with a medium grinder plate. But for sausage making it is advisable to invest in a variety of plates, to allow you to make sausage of fine, medium-fine, medium, medium-coarse, and coarse grinds, as called for in various recipes.

Casings

Now that you have bought a meat grinder and a stuffing tube, what you need is something to stuff your sausage into—casings. There is a variety of synthetic casings used in commercial sausage kitchens, but by far the best and most readily available for home use are natural hog casings. Hog casings come either in a ready-to-use, preflushed form, packed in a brine solution, or in a dry salt pack.

If you plan to make lots of sausage, all at one time, the preflushed kind are great, but they are perishable. Dry salt-pack casings will keep for years under refrigeration and are therefore much more practical for home use. Hog casings are available in bundles called "hanks." A "hank" is a hundred yards, enough casings to hold eighty to ninety pounds of meat. Hog casings can also be purchased in some parts of the country in what is called a "half-doll," which is ideal for home use—seven and a half yards, enough for ten pounds of sausage. Check with your butcher, or look under "butcher supplies" in your telephone directory, for a source for casings.

A bit now about how to handle these casings when stuffing sausage.

First, remove from your hank or half-doll the length of casing you need for the amount of sausage you have to stuff. Put the rest back in the refrigerator for another time. Rinse the casings under running water to remove the excess salt, then put them in a bowl, cover with water, and let them sit for an hour or longer to soften.

Next, open one end of the casing, slip it over the faucet, and run a gentle stream of water through its entire length. As you do, straighten the casing to free any knots or twists and check for holes. If you find a hole, simply cut the damaged area out and treat the two remaining pieces as separate casings.

After rinsing the casings, you're ready to stuff. It's a good idea to leave a small amount of water in the casing as you thread it on the stuffing tube. Water acts as a lubricant and makes it easier to slip the casings over the tube; it also helps them slip easily off as you stuff them. Use plenty of water.

When you have a length of casing threaded on the stuffing tube, tie a knot in the end, then prick a hole in the end of the casing to let the air escape as you start the stuffing process. Although most instructions for making sausage links at home tell you to tie each link with string as it emerges from the stuffing tube, don't! Stuff the entire length of casing first, then twist into links.

Start at one end of the length of sausage; measure off the size link you want and pinch the casing to squeeze the meat out; then measure off another link and pinch the casing with your other hand. Then twirl the sausage as if you were turning a tiny jump rope. A couple of twirls and you have a link. Measure off another link and repeat the twirling. There really is no need to tie each link with string.

Sausage-Making Tips

Before you stuff the sausage meat into casings, you should always taste it first and adjust the seasoning if necessary. To do so, just fry a teaspoon of the sausage mixture until it is well browned and cooked through. Now taste it critically and add more salt or other seasoning, if needed. You want your sausages to be spicy, not bland.

When a recipe calls for grinding meat, put cubes of the meat in the freezer for a short time to chill well. Chilled meat grinds much better than room-temperature meat, which can quickly turn to mush.

Breakfast Pork Sausage

This recipe can easily be varied to suit your individual taste for breakfast sausage. Some folks prefer to eliminate the sage. You may want to grind the meat a second time to achieve a finer texture.

2 pounds boneless pork shoulder, coarsely ground
2 teaspoons salt
1½ teaspoons dried sage
1 teaspoon black pepper
½ teaspoon dried marjoram
½ teaspoon dried savory
¼ teaspoon freshly grated nutmeg
½ cup cold milk
Hog casings (narrow), soaked and rinsed

≈

Combine the ground pork, seasonings, and milk; mix thoroughly, using your hands to knead the mixture. Fill the casings, twisting into 4-inch links. If air pockets develop, pierce the casing with a fine needle. Immediately refrigerate sausages to be used within 2 days. Freeze the remainder.

Makes approximately 20 to 24 links.

Garlic Sausage

These are great simply served up on a hot-dog bun with mustard and onions. They are also good sliced after cooking and included in stir-fry dishes and casseroles.

- 2 pounds boneless pork butt, coarsely ground
- 1 pound boneless beef chuck, coarsely ground
- ½ cup finely chopped onion
- 4 garlic cloves, crushed
- 1 tablespoon prepared mustard
- 2 teaspoons salt
- 2 teaspoons dried marjoram
- 1 teaspoon dried sage
- 1 teaspoon black pepper
- ½ teaspoon thyme
- ½ teaspoon grated nutmeg
- ¼ cup cold water
- Hog casings (narrow), soaked and rinsed

≈

1. In a meat grinder, grind the meats, onion, garlic, mustard, and salt together, using the fine blade. Add the remaining spices and water; mix thoroughly, using your hands to knead the mixture.

2. Fill the casings loosely, twisting into 5-inch links. If air pockets develop, pierce the casing with a fine needle. Immediately refrigerate sausage to be used within 2 days. Freeze the remainder.

Makes approximately 30 to 36 links.

sausage stuffer

Swedish Potato Sausage

- 2 pounds coarsely ground beef
- 2 pounds coarsely ground pork
- 2 pounds potatoes
- 2 medium onions, grated
- 1 tablespoon salt
- 2 teaspoons dry mustard
- 1 teaspoon white pepper
- ½ teaspoon ground allspice
- ½ teaspoon dried marjoram
- Hog casings (narrow), soaked and rinsed

Potato sausages are a Swedish Christmas tradition, but you needn't wait for the holidays to enjoy them. This is a very mild sausage that goes well with poached eggs for brunch.

≈

1. Mix the ground meats together.
2. Peel and grate the potatoes and squeeze them dry to help keep them from turning dark. Add the potatoes and all the seasonings to the meat and mix thoroughly. Nothing can beat using your hands to get the seasonings well mixed into the meat, so don't try to be neat. Just dig in. Fill the casings loosely and twist into approximately 4-inch links.

Makes approximately 45 to 50 links.

Bratwurst

- 1 pound chilled boneless pork shoulder
- ½ pound chilled boneless veal
- 1½ teaspoons salt
- 1 teaspoon black pepper
- ½ teaspoon freshly grated nutmeg
- ½ teaspoon mace
- ½ cup water or beer
- Hog casings (wide), soaked and rinsed

Beer and bratwurst are a tradition in Wisconsin. In Sheboygan there is an annual Bratwurst Festival where thousands of "brats" are simmered in beer, then grilled and served on a roll with sautéed onions and mustard, and washed down with more beer. Brats and beer go together. You may want to substitute beer for the water in this recipe.

≈

Cut the meat into 1-inch cubes and grind twice through the fine plate of your meat grinder. Mix all of the seasonings in the water. Pour over the meat and mix well with your hands. Stuff into hog casings and twist into 4- or 5-inch lengths. Refrigerate. Use within 2 or 3 days, or freeze.

Makes approximately 10 to 12 links.

VARIATION

Curried Bratwurst

There are dozens of variations of bratwurst sausage made in different countries around the globe. This is a somewhat spicier "brat." I know not from which country it comes, but it is a favorite with us.

Use the ingredients and follow the directions from the preceding Bratwurst recipe, but eliminate the pepper, nutmeg, and mace, and add the ingredients listed here.

- 1 to 2 teaspoons curry powder
- 1 teaspoon ground coriander
- 1 teaspoon white pepper
- ½ teaspoon dry mustard
- ¼ teaspoon ground ginger

≈

To broil or grill: Place the sausages in water, cover, lower the heat, and simmer (do not boil) for 15 minutes. Drain. Broil 3 inches from the heat, or grill on a rack over medium coals, turning frequently to brown evenly.

To cook in beer and fry: Place the sausage in a cold skillet. Add 1 can of beer and 1 can of cold water and bring to a boil. Remove from the heat and let stand 10 minutes. Drain. Fry in butter for 10 minutes, turning frequently to brown evenly.

Makes approximately 10 to 12 links.

Italian-Style Sausage

The recipe that follows makes a fairly mild-flavored sausage. If you prefer something a bit hotter, replace some of the black pepper with red-pepper flakes. And if Italian to you isn't Italian without garlic, add a teaspoon of finely chopped garlic to the recipe.

- 2 teaspoons salt
- 1 teaspoon black pepper
- ½ teaspoon crushed anise seed
- 1 teaspoon finely chopped garlic (optional)

≈

1. Mix the seasonings and sprinkle over the cubes of meat. Toss the meat well. Sprinkle on the wine and toss

(recipe continues)

Italian-Style Sausage *(cont.)*

- 1 tablespoon paprika
- 2 pounds fresh pork shoulder, cut into ½-inch cubes
- 1 or 2 tablespoons white wine
- Hog casings (wide), soaked and rinsed

again. Set in the freezer to chill well before grinding. The meat grinds much better if it is well chilled.

2. Grind the meat through the coarse or medium plate of your grinder, stuff it into the hog casings, and twist into 4- or 5-inch lengths. Refrigerate. Use within 2 or 3 days, or freeze.

Makes 14 to 16 links.

Chorizo

- 2 pounds coarsely ground lean pork
- ¼ pound finely ground pork fat
- 2 tablespoons paprika
- 2 tablespoons chili powder
- 1 teaspoon coarsely ground black pepper
- 1 teaspoon dried oregano
- 1 teaspoon cumin
- ½ teaspoon cinnamon
- ½ teaspoon ground cloves
- ¼ teaspoon coriander seed
- ¼ teaspoon ground ginger
- 6 whole garlic cloves, crushed
- ½ cup cider vinegar
- ½ cup sherry or brandy
- Hog casings (wide), soaked and rinsed

Chorizo sausage is made in every nation where Spanish is spoken—even a little bit. This Mexican-style chorizo is a deliciously spicy version that picks up some of its zip from spending time in a "pickle," or "cure." It is best served in casseroles, stews, and stir-fries, where it can lend its rich flavor to other foods.

≈

1. Mix the pork and the fat thoroughly. Add the rest of the ingredients and mix together, using your hands, making sure to distribute the vinegar evenly in the mixture. Put the mixture in an earthenware crock or glass jar in a cool place (50 to 60 degrees) and allow the sausage to cure for at least 24 hours or, preferably, for 2 or 3 days.

2. Stuff into the hog casings and twist into 4-inch links. Refrigerate. If you wish to keep the sausages for an extended time, freeze them. This sausage must be *cooked well* before eating.

Makes 14 to 16 links.

Boudin

Here is a traditional recipe for boudin from the collection of Keith E. Courrege, a Cajun friend of mine from New Iberia, Louisiana.

- 2 pounds pork
- ½ pound pork liver
- Salt and pepper to taste
- 1 large onion, chopped
- 2 bunches green onions, chopped
- 1 bunch parsley, chopped
- 6 cups cooked rice
- Sausage casings, soaked in cold water

≈

1. Simmer the pork, liver, and seasonings in water to cover, until the meat falls apart, approximately 30 to 45 minutes. Remove the meat and reserve the broth.

2. Grind the meat, onion, green onions, and parsley (reserving about ½ cup of green-onion tops and parsley). Mix ground-meat mixture with the reserved ½ cup of green onions and parsley, the rice, and enough broth to make a moist dressing. Stuff into casings, using a sausage stuffer.

Makes 16 to 20 links.

Moroccan Lamb Sausage

Pork is not the only meat for sausage making. For lamb lovers, here is a recipe that is sure to please. I got it from a friend, Narsai David, one of the most knowledgeable "foodies" I know.

If you don't have lamb trimmings in the freezer, you can use any cut of lamb. Ask your butcher to bone-out a shoulder or leg of lamb for you, or, better still, ask if he has some lean lamb trimmings he would like to "find a home for." He may even sell them to you at a bargain price.

This is a coarse-textured sausage, spicy but not hot. The currants, cinnamon, and pomegranate juice give the sausage just a touch of sweetness. The sausages are great on the grill.

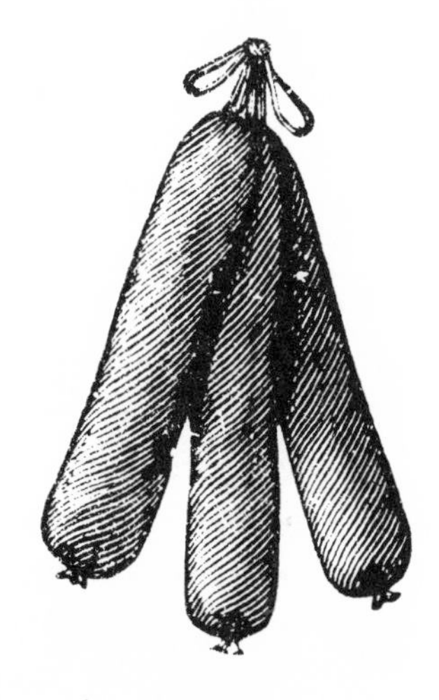

≈

Moroccan Lamb Sausage *(cont.)*

- 3 pounds chilled lean lamb trimmings
- 1 tablespoon minced garlic
- 1 tablespoon salt
- 1½ teaspoons curry powder
- 1½ teaspoons coarse-ground black pepper
- ½ teaspoon cinnamon
- ½ teaspoon dried thyme
- ½ cup currants
- ½ cup pomegranate juice*
- Hog casings for stuffing, soaked and rinsed

* Available at Middle Eastern or specialty markets.

1. Grind the lamb trimmings once through a meat grinder's fine plate. Mix together all the remaining ingredients, pour over the meat, and mix well with your hands.
2. Stuff the meat mixture into casings and twist into 5-inch lengths.

VARIATION

Assyrian Lamb Sausage Assyrian sausage is a mild, flavorful sausage that goes very well with lentils or in a barley casserole. Follow the ingredients and instructions for the Moroccan Lamb Sausage, eliminating the curry powder, cinnamon, thyme, and currants, and adding 1 tablespoon finely chopped fresh basil and 1 teaspoon minced fresh tarragon.

Makes approximately 20 links.

FRESH SMOKED SAUSAGE

Aunt Gert had a smokehouse on the old "Homeplace" when I was a boy. It was a small building about six feet by eight feet that sat out behind the cob shed. There was a little fire box down the hill a few feet toward the creek, where smoldering hickory, maple, or corn cobs kept a steady stream of rich smoke pouring through the flue that connected it to the smokehouse itself. The smells that came from the building along about November every year were fantastic! Hams, bacon, and sausage soaking up that rich smoke and sending off a fragrance that gave out great promise for their flavor. Fond memories of those days come to mind every time I open up a package of good bacon or sausage that has that rich color and great aroma of smoke.

If you are really "into" smoked meats, sausage included, you may want to build a smokehouse like Aunt Gert's, but it isn't necessary. Actually, there are several different ways of smoking meat, depending on the desired result, and you may have everything you need to make some great smoked treats right in your kitchen.

There are a number of small smokers on the market that work well for things like smoked fish, beef jerky, small sausage links, and poultry. Luhr-Jensen and Sons, Inc., in Hood River, Oregon, makes one they call the "Little Chief Smoker" that I have used and enjoyed for years. Water smokers are readily available at any store that sells barbecue equipment.

The simplest and least expensive smokehouse I've ever seen was made out of an old wooden barrel. A hole was dug in the earth to permit the building of a good-size fire. After the wood had been burned down to red-hot coals, sawdust or damp wood chips were put on top to create a good smoke. Over the hole were placed boards with an opening for the smoke to pass into the barrel. The barrel, with the bottom knocked out, was placed over the opening.

The meat and sausage to be smoked were hung on strips of wood from the top of the barrel, with more boards, placed on the strips, to make the smokehouse cover. The strips of wood held the cover an inch or so above the barrel, causing a draft to draw the smoke up and around the meat.

Even without a smokehouse, a smoked flavor can still be accomplished in some meat and sausage products through the use of liquid smoke.

What is liquid smoke, anyway? It sounds like a contradiction in terms, like warm ice. Actually, liquid smoke is real honest–to–Aunt Gert hickory, maple, maybe even corn-cob smoke condensed into a liquid form, just as steam can be condensed into water. It has some advantages over smoke in a gaseous form, in that after condensation it can be filtered and some of the undesirable elements removed. It is also much cleaner—take it from a kid who cleaned the gunk out of Aunt Gert's smokehouse a time or two.

Liquid smoke is natural smoke, condensed and purified. It is available in most grocery stores. In recipes for sausage products such as hot dogs, breakfast sausage, Polish sausage, etc., liquid smoke can be added directly to the mixture. Start out with a quarter-teaspoon of liquid smoke per pound of meat. Dilute it with some of the water or other liquid in the recipe to aid the uniform distribution of the smoke flavor, then mix it in just before stuffing.

Any of the "fresh sausage" described previously can be turned into "fresh smoked sausage" with the addition of liquid smoke.

Polish Sausage

4½ pounds lean beef
1½ pounds lean pork
½ cup flour (buckwheat, rye, or whole wheat)
3 tablespoons salt
1½ tablespoons black pepper
2 tablespoons dried sage
1 tablespoon mustard seeds
1½ to 2 teaspoons liquid smoke
Hog casings, rinsed and cleaned

This Polish-sausage recipe came from a sausage-maker friend in Wisconsin. He has a smokehouse, and the liquid smoke is my substitution for that.

≈

1. Chop the meat into ¼-inch pieces, or grind it once through the coarse plate of your meat grinder. Sift the flour, salt, pepper, and sage together; sprinkle the mixture over the meat. Add the mustard seeds and liquid smoke and mix thoroughly with your hands.

2. Regrind the mixture, stuff into hog casings (approximately 1¼ inches in diameter) and twist into links 4 to 5 inches long. "Mett sausage" may be made with the same formula, stuffing the casings into 12-inch lengths and tying the ends together to form a ring. The casings can be stuffed after the meat is reground, using a hand

stuffing tube, or while the meat is being reground, using a stuffing-tube attachment on the front of the grinder.

3. Precook the smoked sausage in water at a simmering temperature (180 degrees) for 10 minutes, or until they float. Immerse the cooked sausages in cold water to cool quickly, then hang them in a well-ventilated spot to dry. Store the sausage in the refrigerator.

Polish sausage may be served hot—fried, broiled, grilled—or in soups and casseroles. Or they can be served cold after cooking—sliced thin in salads or for hors d'oeuvres. For the latter, they are absolutely delicious pickled.

Makes approximately 6 pounds.

VARIATION

Pickled Polish Sausage

This is a great dish to serve at a poker party, accompanied by hard-cooked eggs and cold beer.

- 2 pounds Polish sausage
- 1 large onion
- 2 cups water
- 2 cups white-wine vinegar
- 2 tablespoons sugar
- 2 teaspoons salt
- 1 heaping teaspoon whole black peppercorns
- 1 level teaspoon whole allspice

≈

1. Slice the Polish sausage on the diagonal into ½-inch-thick slices. Cut the onion into thin slices and separate the slices into rings. Alternate layers of Polish sausage and onion rings in a 2-quart jar or crock.

2. Make a brine by combining all of the remaining ingredients in a good-sized saucepan. Bring the liquid to a boil, stirring to dissolve the sugar and salt. Reduce the heat and simmer for 10 minutes to blend the flavors well. Let the liquid cool to lukewarm.

3. Pour the brine, a little at a time, over the sausage and onions. Make sure that a few of the peppercorns and allspice are mixed throughout, and that the sausage and onions are completely covered with the brine. Cover the jar or crock and refrigerate for at least 3 days. Pickled Polish Sausage will keep refrigerated for several weeks—unless you have a poker party.

Portuguese Sausage

2 pounds lean pork
¼ cup cold water
1 tablespoon cider vinegar
8 cloves garlic, minced
2 Hawaiian red peppers, minced, or ½ teaspoon dry red-pepper flakes
1 teaspoon salt
½ teaspoon black pepper
⅛ teaspoon paprika
½ teaspoon liquid smoke
Hog casings, cleaned and rinsed

Some variation of Portuguese sausage can be found wherever Portuguese people settled in this country. I discovered Portuguese sausage on my honeymoon in Hawaii. It is a favorite there in the morning, served with fried eggs and rice. Here's a recipe from my wife's cousin in Hawaii; she's part Portuguese.

≈

1. Chop the pork into ¼-inch cubes and grind through the coarse plate of your meat grinder. Combine all remaining ingredients in a bowl and stir to dissolve the salt and mix thoroughly. Pour the seasoning mixture over the ground pork and mix with your hands to blend the spices through the meat. Refrigerate for 2 days, mixing again occasionally to ensure an even distribution of spices.

2. Stuff into hog casings (approximately 1¼ inches in diameter) and twist into links that are 8 to 10 inches long. Hang the links in a well-ventilated spot for a half-hour or so to dry before refrigerating. Store the sausage under refrigeration for up to 5 days, or freeze for longer storage.

3. To cook: Slice the links on the diagonal into approximately ½-inch-thick slices and fry. Serve with fried or scrambled eggs. If hog casings are difficult to find, the sausage is equally good simply formed into patties and fried.

Serves 8 to 10.

COOKED AND COOKED SMOKED SAUSAGE

Most of the products that you find in your supermarket deli case under the general heading of "luncheon meats"—bologna, pimento loaf, liver sausage, braunschweiger, and all of the products labeled "hot dogs," "franks," "wieners," etc.—fall into the categories of "cooked" or "cooked and smoked" sausage products.

Since they are made to be consumed without further cooking, many—if not most—of the products in this group require NITRATES. Now, don't panic!

Somehow it has become the suspicion of many, maybe even most, Americans that the modern food industry is out to kill us with a lot of new and unnecessary chemicals that were not needed and were not used back in Aunt Gert's day.

Nothing could be further from the truth. Aunt Gert used chemicals too. They just didn't have the unpronounceable names they have today. She cured hams and bacon with saltpeter, and so did all other ham-and-bacon makers and their fathers, mothers, aunts, and uncles before them, from Aunt Gert's day back to the dim reaches of time. Saltpeter is, you see, sodium or potassium nitrate, and it has been used in the curing of meat since man began curing meats.

You can, should you get really serious about sausage making, make cooked and cooked smoked sausage in your own kitchen. Many books have been written on the subject. Most of us, however, myself included, enjoy these sausage products best when we buy them from the butcher, or, better yet, at the ball park. Here is where we find America's favorite sausage—the hot dog.

Hot Dogs

Call them "hot dogs," "wieners," "frankfurters," "franks," or "furters," they are without question America's favorite sausage product. It is estimated that over fifty million hot dogs are eaten in the United States every day. That's approximately eighty hot dogs per person per year, or better than eighteen billion hot dogs!

Hot dogs come in a variety of sizes and styles. There are all-beef hot dogs, hot dogs that "plump" when you cook them, kosher hot dogs, turkey hot dogs, chicken hot dogs, hot dogs with cheese in them. They come ten, eight, and four in a package; some are made a "foot long," and most these days are unfortunately "skinless." But you have never truly tasted a truly great hot dog until you've tasted an old-fashioned "sheep-casing" frank, preferably right out of the smokehouse—a classic treat!

Skinless hot dogs are made by stuffing the meat mixture into inedible air-and-smoke-permeated cellulose casings. In a large packing plant, the whole operation is automated. The hot dogs are never touched by human hands. As the emulsion flows though the stuffing horn into the casings, the filled strands are automatically linked into hot dogs of exact size. The strand of links is then put on a continuous-line conveyor system that moves the hot dogs through the smokehouse, where, under controlled temperature and humidity, they are smoked and fully cooked.

When they emerge from the smokehouse, they go into a "wiener skinner," which peels off the cellulose casing to yield a "skinless" hot dog. Now, I like hot dogs and I don't mean to imply that there is anything wrong with "skinless" ones, but in my opinion even the best of them pale when compared with a good "old-fashioned" hot dog.

"Old-fashioned" or "regular" hot dogs, as they are sometimes called, are usually a more expensive product, but worth the extra few cents. Old-fashioned hot dogs are stuffed into natural casings, usually sheep casings, and the casing remains on the sausage, locking in the wonderful juices and flavors of the meat until you bite into it. Then it bursts with goodness, unlike any sausage without a skin.

Producing old-fashioned hot dogs is a more expensive, more labor-intensive process. Much of the work must be done by hand—the old-fashioned way. Casings must be stuffed using hand-operated equipment; the sausage must be twisted by hand into links. They are the kind of hot dog more likely to be produced not by the big processors but, rather, by the smaller independent packers, or even old-fashioned butchers in little mom-and-pop stores.

There are a number of special ways that the all-American hot dog is traditionally served in different parts of America. In Chicago, a city that truly loves the hot dog, more hot dogs are sold at Chicago's O'Hare International Airport than at any other single location in the world; there the traditional hot dog is served on a poppy-seed bun, garnished with yellow mustard, dark-green relish, chopped raw onion, and tomato slices, topped with a dash of celery salt.

In Kansas City, the Reuben dog is a specialty served with sauerkraut and melted Swiss cheese on a sesame-seed roll. In New York City, vendors offer customers stewed onions with their hot dogs; in Coney Island, sauerkraut is optional.

In Boston, Cleveland, and Los Angeles, chili dogs are popular served with chopped onions and grated cheese. A specialty found in Columbus, Ohio, is "pigs in a blanket," hot dogs split down the middle, filled with water chestnuts, wrapped in bacon, and covered with melted cheese.

No matter how you serve hot dogs, I urge you to seek out the "old-fashioned" kind. At their best, they are better than any sausage Grandma ever made.

History of the Hot Dog

Frankfurt am Main, Germany, is traditionally credited with originating the frankfurter. However, this claim is disputed by those who assert that the popular sausage—known as a "dachshund" or "little-dog" sausage—was created in the late 1600s by a butcher living in Coburg, Germany. According to this report, the butcher, Johann Georg Lahner, later traveled to Frankfurt to promote his new product.

The people from Vienna (Wien), Austria, point to the term "wiener" to prove their claim as the birthplace of the hot dog.

Also in doubt is who first served dachshund sausages with rolls. One report says a German immigrant sold them, along with milk rolls and

Hot Dogs (continued)

sauerkraut, from a pushcart in New York City's Bowery during the 1860s. In 1871, Charles Feltman, a German butcher, opened up the first Coney Island hot-dog stand, and sold 3,684 dachshund sausages in milk rolls during his first year in business.

The term "hot dog" was coined in 1901 at the New York Polo Grounds. One cold April day, concessionaire Harry Stevens (his company is still in business) was losing money with ice cream and ice-cold soda. So he sent his salesmen out to buy up all the dachshund sausages they could find and an equal number of rolls. In less than an hour, his vendors were hawking hot dogs from portable hot-water tanks with "They're red hot! Get your dachshund sausages while they're red hot!" In the press box, cartoonist Tad Dorgan was nearing his deadline and desperate for an idea. Hearing the vendors, he hastily drew a cartoon of barking dachshund sausages nestled warmly in rolls. Not sure how to spell "dachshund," he simply wrote "hot dog!" The cartoon was a sensation—and the term "hot dog" was born.

DRY AND SEMI-DRY SAUSAGE—MAKE YOUR OWN SALAMI

San Francisco is famous for, among a long list of other gastronomic things, its very special Italian dry salami. Stores all over the country carry Gallo, Cariani, and other of the famous brands made only in San Francisco because that's the only place such sausage can be made—there's something in the air, they say.

But you can make an awfully good salami in your own kitchen. It won't be Italian dry salami, San Francisco–style, covered with a white powdery mold, but it will be good. It is surprisingly easy to make, keeps well, and, as an added bonus, is quite inexpensive. You make it out of hamburger, plain old lean ground beef.

The following recipe is one that my family enjoys. You can use that for starters, but you can also vary the seasonings to suit your own personal flavor preferences. Leave out the liquid smoke if you like, or go lighter or heavier on the peppers. Use white wine instead of red, and mustard seed, oregano, and sweet basil in place of the chili powder, pepper, and cumin. Substitute whole black peppercorns for the red pepper. Use your imagination!

Easy Beef Salami

This recipe calls for the use of curing salt. It is important to use a curing salt that is called a "complete cure"—that is, a mixture of salt, sugar, sodium nitrate, and/or sodium nitrite in the proper proportions for home use. There are several companies around the country that make a "complete cure." Probably the best known to home sausage makers is Morton's Salt Company's Tender Quick. Another old company that has been making a curing salt for home curing since Aunt Gert was a girl is B. Heller and Company. Their product is called Complete Cure with Sugar. Whatever you do, be sure to get a "complete cure." Many curing salts are much too high in nitrate/nitrite for home use.

You will need about half a yard of red nylon net, which

Easy Beef Salami *(cont.)*

- **3 tablespoons curing salt**
- **4 tablespoons dry red wine**
- **2 tablespoons liquid smoke**
- **5 pounds lean ground beef**
- **1½ teaspoons garlic powder**
- **2 tablespoons chili powder**
- **2 tablespoons hot red-pepper flakes**
- **1¼ teaspoons ground cumin**
- **2 tablespoons brown sugar**

is available in any yard-goods store and is quite inexpensive. Netting allows the sausage to dry in the cooking process, and the drying acts as a preservative. Aluminum foil could be used instead, but since the aluminum foil holds in the juices, the sausage will be less dry and will not keep as long in the refrigerator.

The reason that the recipe calls for low heat (225 degrees) for a relatively long cooking time is to aid in the drying process. If aluminum foil is used, increase the oven temperature to 325 degrees and reduce the cooking time to two hours.

≈

1. To help blend the curing salt well into the meat, first mix the cure with the red wine and liquid smoke. Cover the bowl and refrigerate for 24 hours.

2. Mix together the wine-smoke mixture with the remaining ingredients in a large bowl. Dip in with both hands and blend thoroughly. It is important that the ingredients, particularly the curing salt, be blended well. Mix again 2 or 3 times during the next 24 hours to help the spices permeate the meat, and the curing salt to do its job of flavoring and producing a nice color.

3. Divide the meat into 4 equal portions and roll each into a log-shaped roll 2 to 3 inches in diameter and 6 to 8 inches in length. Roll each in nylon netting and tie the ends securely with string.

4. Bake in a preheated 225-degree oven for 4 hours, rolling the salamis back and forth from time to time so they don't flatten out on one side.

5. After baking, allow the sausage to cool and remove the netting. Dry thoroughly with paper towels. Wrap with aluminum foil and refrigerate. Use within a week or two, or freeze.

6. To serve: These sausage rolls are delicious served cold, sliced thin, with crackers and beer, but for a real treat, slice some into ¼-to-½-inch-thick slices, sauté them in a bit of butter, and serve with a good hot German-style potato salad.

Makes 4 sausages.

RECIPES USING SAUSAGE

Pasta with Italian Sausage, Peas, and Fried Sage

This light pasta dish featuring Italian sausage is ideal for cooks on the run—it cooks up in less than twenty minutes. For a colorful change, substitute for the peas blanched or frozen broccoli, snap peas, green beans, or carrots, or a combination of any of these.

- 18 ounces mild or hot Italian sausages, removed from their casings
- 20 to 30 whole fresh sage leaves
- ¼ cup olive oil
- 2 teaspoons minced garlic
- 1 10-ounce package frozen peas, thawed and drained
- 1 pound dried pasta of your choice, such as linguine or spaghetti
- Grated Parmesan cheese

≈

1. In a medium skillet, sauté the sausage over medium-high heat, crumbling with a fork, for about 6 to 7 minutes, until most of the fat is rendered. Drain and reserve the sausage; set aside.
2. In a clean skillet, fry the sage leaves in hot olive oil for about 1 minute, or until crisp. Add the garlic and the peas and cook, stirring, for 1 or 2 minutes, until the peas are just cooked.
3. In a large saucepan, cook the pasta according to the package directions. Add the reserved sausage to the sage leaves, garlic, and peas and toss with the drained pasta and Parmesan cheese.

Serves 4 to 6.

Smoky Sausage and Apple Salad

1 medium red delicious apple, halved, cored, and thinly sliced
1 quart well-cleaned mixed greens (Boston, Bibb, or leaf lettuce)
½ medium red onion, thinly sliced lengthwise
3 tablespoons olive oil
6 ounces lean, coarse-textured smoked sausage, chopped
1 teaspoon honey
2 teaspoons sweet-hot mustard
3 tablespoons cider or red-wine vinegar
Salt and pepper to taste

Highly smoked, coarse-textured sausages, such as Polish, andouille, or smoked country sausage, and crunchy, sweet apples add a savory note to this wilted-lettuce salad. For variety, try substituting spinach leaves, Swiss chard, collard greens, or watercress for the lettuce.

≈

1. In a large salad bowl, place the apple, greens, and onion.

2. Heat the oil in a medium skillet over medium-high heat and fry the sausage for about 5 minutes, until it is nicely browned and all the fat is rendered.

3. Whisk the remaining ingredients into the hot fat. Immediately pour the hot dressing over the salad and toss well. Add salt and pepper to taste and serve at once.

Makes 4 servings.

Sausage-Stuffed Baguette

A perfect do-ahead hors d'oeuvre which can be baked just before serving, this delicious Sausage-Stuffed Baguette also makes a tasty sandwich which can be served for lunch or dinner. The crusty bread is the perfect match for the warm sage-sausage filling inside.

- 1 pound bulk sage pork sausage
- ¼ pound smoked ham, diced
- 1 cup ricotta cheese
- 1 10-ounce package frozen spinach, thawed, liquid squeezed out
- 1 egg, lightly beaten
- ¼ cup thinly sliced green onion
- ¼ teaspoon black pepper or to taste
- 2 22-inch baguettes or 6 8-inch French dinner rolls

≈

1. In a medium skillet, fry the sausage over medium heat, breaking it up into small pieces with a fork. Fry for about 5 minutes or until the fat is rendered and the sausage is no longer pink. Drain all the fat and place the sausage in a mixing bowl.
2. Add the ham, ricotta, spinach, egg, green onion, and pepper to the sausage, and mix well.
3. Slice the bread in half lengthwise and hollow out each half with a fork or knife. Fill each half with the sausage mixture and press the halves together. Wrap the bread in aluminum foil, leaving the top open so the bread can get crusty.
4. Bake on a cookie sheet in a preheated 375-degree oven for 25 to 30 minutes (sausage mixture should be at 160 degrees). Cool for 5 minutes. Slice with a serrated knife into 1-to-1½-inch rounds for hors d'oeuvres or 6-to-8-inch slices for sandwiches. Follow the same procedure if using dinner rolls.

Makes 35 to 40 hors d'oeuvres or 6 sandwiches.

Mexican Sausage-Noodle Casserole

≈

- 1 pound chorizo, cut into 2-inch pieces
- 6 ounces vermicelli, broken into quarters
- 4 whole tomatoes, peeled and cut up
- 1½ cups chicken broth
- 1 onion, cut up
- 2 cloves garlic, minced
- 1 teaspoon salt
- ½ teaspoon black pepper
- ½ teaspoon dried oregano
- 1 tablespoon sugar
- ¼ teaspoon dried red-pepper flakes
- 3 tablespoons grated jack or Cheddar cheese
- 1 small can chopped green chilies

1. Brown the sausage. Drain, set aside, and reserve about 2 tablespoons of the sausage oil. Brown pieces of vermicelli in the oil.

2. In a blender, blend the tomatoes, chicken broth, onion, garlic, salt, pepper, oregano, sugar, and red pepper. Pour the mixture over the vermicelli. Arrange the chorizo on the top. Cover and simmer over medium-low heat for 10 to 12 minutes, until the vermicelli is tender. Garnish with cheese and green chilies.

Serves 6 to 8.

Chorizo, Eggplant, and Red Pepper Stir-Fry

A delicious, quick, and easy dish to serve over pasta or rice, garnished with chopped green onions.

≈

- 1 pound chorizo, cut into thick slices
- 1 large eggplant, cut into 1-inch cubes
- 2 tablespoons olive oil

1. Fry the sausage until brown, remove from the pan, and set aside to drain on paper towels. Fry the eggplant in

the sausage fat and olive oil until soft, about 10 minutes.

2. Add the peppers and onion and cook for 5 minutes. Add the garlic and wine and cook an additional 5 minutes. Season with salt and pepper.

3. Return the sausages to the pan and cook for 1 minute.

4. Serve over rice or pasta; garnish with chopped green onions.

Serves 4 to 6.

2 red bell peppers, seeded and cut into strips
1 red onion, thinly sliced
3 cloves garlic, minced
¼ cup white wine, dry sherry, or vermouth
Salt and pepper to taste
Cooked pasta or rice
¼ cup finely chopped green onions

Country French White Beans and Sausage

This is a savory stick-to-your-ribs dish that is quick and easy and very nutritious.

≈

Vegetable cooking spray
1 medium onion, halved and sliced
1 clove garlic, crushed
8 ounces fresh Italian sausage
8 ounces fully cooked smoked sausage, sliced diagonally
1 15-ounce can cannellini beans (white kidney beans), drained and rinsed
1 15-ounce can garbanzo beans (chick peas), drained and rinsed
1 14½-ounce can stewed tomatoes, undrained
2 tablespoons dry white wine (optional)
1 tablespoon brown sugar
½ teaspoon crushed dried rosemary
½ teaspoon dried oregano leaves
½ teaspoon dried thyme
Minced parsley

1. Spray a large saucepan or Dutch oven with the vegetable cooking spray. Add the onion and garlic; cook and stir until tender. Remove the Italian sausage from its casing, crumble, and add to the onion and garlic.

Cook and stir for 3 minutes. Add the smoked sausage and cook for 3 to 5 minutes. Pour off and discard the drippings.

2. Stir in the beans, tomatoes, wine (if desired), brown sugar, rosemary, oregano, and thyme; gently mix. Cover and simmer 5 minutes; uncover and cook over medium-low heat 5 to 10 minutes to blend the flavors. Garnish with minced parsley.

Serves 6.

Italian Sausage Casserole

Served with polenta, a crisp salad, crusty bread, and hearty red wine, this is a great dish for simple entertaining. It can be assembled ahead and baked when guests arrive.

≈

- 1 cup flour
- 2 large eggplants, peeled, cut crosswise into ½-inch slices
- 8 small zucchini, cut lengthwise into ½-inch slices
- 3 tablespoons olive oil
- 5 large onions, sliced
- 6 garlic cloves, minced
- 6 green peppers, seeded and cut into small pieces
- 1 cup chopped fresh parsley
- 2 teaspoons dried oregano
- 2 teaspoons dried thyme
- 2 teaspoons dried basil
- Salt and pepper to taste
- 8 large ripe tomatoes cut in strips, or 2 large cans of tomatoes, drained and cut into strips
- 12 to 14 Italian-Style Sausages (see page 293)

1. Put the flour in a bag and toss the eggplant and zucchini lightly to coat. Cook them in the olive oil until just barely tender. Remove and drain on paper towels.

2. Sauté the onions, garlic, and green peppers in the same pan until just tender. Sprinkle with the herbs and salt and pepper to taste. Layer the zucchini and eggplant,

the onions, garlic, and peppers, and the tomatoes in a large casserole dish. Cover and bake in a preheated 350-degree oven for 30 minutes.

3. In the meantime, poach the sausages in water for 8 to 10 minutes. Slice the links diagonally into ½-inch-thick slices and sauté them, in the same pan used for the vegetables, for about 2 to 3 minutes, turning often.

4. When the vegetables have baked for 30 minutes, add the cooked sausages and mix them in thoroughly, leaving enough slices to garnish the top of the casserole. Return to the oven and bake, uncovered, for 20 minutes.

Serves 10 to 12.

POTTED MEATS—PÂTÉS, TERRINES, AND RILLETTES

Grandma called them "potted meats." The more sophisticated among you call them pâtés, terrines, or rillettes. Whatever you call them, they can be a delightful addition. They can be made from all manner of meat. "Take some meat, fish, poultry, game and/or liver, cut or mince it and mix with fat and spices, put it in a small dish lined with pastry or bacon, cook it slowly in the oven and then it is perfect." So said Thomas van der Noot of his pâté in *En Notable Boecxken van Cokeregen* (a cookbook from about 1510).

The term "pâté" is used rather loosely these days. Originally a pâté, whatever it was made from, was baked in a pastry crust. The same ingredients without the crust, baked in a pottery dish, were called a "terrine." Put them in little ramekins, top them with lard or butter, and call them "rillettes." These days the terms are often used interchangeably: with or without a crust, the lard, or butter, the dish is usually referred to as pâté.

Country Liver Pâté

- 1½ pounds beef or pork liver
- ½ cup whipping cream
- ½ pound ground pork fat
- 1½ pounds ground pork
- 1 large onion, chopped
- 1 tablespoon butter
- 2 cloves garlic, crushed
- 2 tablespoons chopped parsley
- 1 teaspoon dried basil or 1 tablespoon chopped fresh
- 1 teaspoon dried thyme or 1 tablespoon chopped fresh
- 2 eggs
- 1 tablespoon salt
- 1 teaspoon black pepper
- 1 tablespoon flour
- ⅓ cup brandy
- 3 thin slices pork fat
- 3 medium bay leaves

Yvonne Boulleray, a charming little French lady with thirty-five years of professional French cookery to her credit, served me this pâté years ago at her little house in the Sonoma Valley in California. It has become a favorite at our house.

≈

1. Grind the liver through the fine (¼-inch) plate of your meat grinder or use a food processor. Let the liver stand in the cream for 1 hour. Meanwhile, add the pork fat to the pork and mix well. Sauté the onion in the butter for 5 minutes. Add the garlic, parsley, basil, and thyme. Remove the pan from the heat.

2. Add the liver and cream to the meat, along with the eggs, salt, pepper, flour, and brandy. Mix all the ingredients well; an electric mixer will help.

3. Place the 3 slices of pork fat in the bottom of a 6-cup tureen or a 9-by-5-by-3-inch loaf pan. Pour in the meat mixture. Place the bay leaves on top. Seal the casserole with foil. Cover tightly. Place the casserole in a pan that has boiling water coming halfway up the side of the dish. Bake for 1 to 1½ hours at 350 degrees, until the blade of a knife inserted in the center comes out clean. Alternatively, insert a meat thermometer into the center; the pâté is done when the internal temperature reaches 160 degrees.

4. The pâté may be served straight from the cooking dish. If you do this, remove the foil 20 minutes before the end of the cooking time so that the top can brown appetizingly. Cool for an hour. Then cover with foil and weight it gently with a few small cans of vegetables or soups. The pâté will taste better the next day.

Makes approximately 16 to 18 servings.

Pork and Spinach Pâté

This makes a pretty pâté for a first course at a dinner party, or a main course at a summer luncheon.

≈

1 pound boneless pork, untrimmed (leave the fat!)
½ pound boneless veal
1 cup chopped onion
3 cloves garlic, minced
1 tablespoon butter
1½ cups chopped fresh spinach
3 tablespoons brandy
1 egg
1 teaspoon dried basil
1 teaspoon dried rosemary
½ teaspoon dried thyme
1½ teaspoons salt
½ teaspoon crushed fennel seeds
½ teaspoon pepper
6 slices bacon
3 hard-cooked eggs
Sour gherkins (or cornichons)
Pickled onions

1. Cut the meat into small pieces and chop fine in food processor or meat grinder. Sauté the onion and garlic in butter. Add the spinach and cook for a minute. Put the spinach mixture in a bowl and stir in the chopped meat. Add brandy, 1 egg, and seasonings. Mix well.

2. Arrange the bacon across the bottom and 1 side of an 8½-by-4½-inch loaf pan, letting the slices hang over the edge. Put half of meat mixture into the pan. Arrange the hard-cooked eggs (peeled) lengthwise down the center of the meat, pressing down slightly. Put the remaining meat on the top and wrap the bacon across the top.

3. Preheat the oven to 350 degrees. Cover the pan with aluminum foil. Set it in a baking pan that has hot water reaching halfway up the side of the loaf pan. Bake for 1¼ hours, until the meat juices run clear. Let stand uncovered for 30 minutes. Pour off the fat. Cover and put weights on top and refrigerate for 24 hours.

4. To serve: Remove from pan and trim off excess fat. Cut into ½-inch slices and serve with gherkins and onions.

Serves approximately 10 to 12.

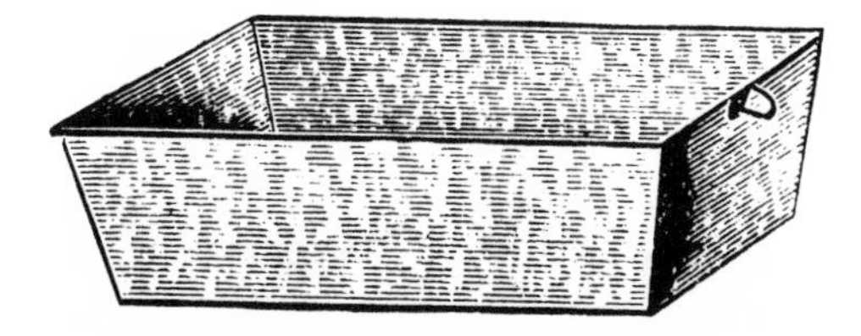

Country Ham and Honey Pâté

2 pounds country ham
1 pound lean fresh bacon (side pork)*
2 onions, sliced
2 cups port wine
1 pound small fresh mushrooms
½ pound butter
1 cup flour
1 pound fresh pork liver
1 teaspoon salt
¼ cup honey
1 teaspoon allspice
2 or 3 slices smoked bacon (for garnish)

* If fresh side pork is unavailable, smoked bacon can be used. Blanch 4 to 5 minutes.

This recipe alone is reason enough to order a good country ham from Jesse Brown (see page 131). There is no better way with a little leftover country ham.

≈

1. In a large, heavy covered pot, simmer over low heat the ham, side pork, and onions in port wine for 40 minutes.

2. Meanwhile, sauté the mushrooms in butter until tender, about 5 or 6 minutes. Remove the mushrooms from the pan and set aside. Add the flour to the butter in the pan and cook, stirring, over low heat to make a rich brown roux. Set aside.

3. Grind the liver through the fine plate of your meat grinder (or use a food processor). Mix in the salt and stir until the liver takes on a sticky texture. This helps bind the pâté together. Set aside.

4. When the ham, pork, and onions are done, allow to cool slightly. When cool enough to handle, remove the ham and cut into cubes. Put the side pork and onions through the coarse plate of the meat grinder or chop them coarsely by hand. Put the roux back on the stove over low heat and pour in the warm port wine to make a sauce.

5. Put everything together in a large bowl: the liver, the ham cubes, the coarse-chopped bacon and onions, the whole mushrooms (if they are too big, cut them in half), the sauce, the honey, and the allspice. Mix well and pour into a terrine. Garnish with a few slices of smoked bacon.

6. Set the terrine in a pan of water and bake in a 350-degree oven for 45 minutes to an hour, until the blade of a knife inserted in the center comes out clean. Cool slightly, then cover with a towel or aluminum foil and put weights on top. Refrigerate for 12 hours before using. Will keep in the refrigerator for 2 or 3 weeks.

Serves 24 to 32.

Pork and Mushroom Terrine

Take advantage of some of the wonderful fresh or dried mushrooms that we have available to add even more interest to this terrine. If you use dried, they should be soaked first in warm water to cover.

- 1 medium onion
- ½ pound mushrooms
- 2 tablespoons butter
- 1 teaspoon dried mixed herbs or ¼ teaspoon each rosemary, oregano, thyme, and basil
- 2 teaspoons Dijon mustard
- ⅓ cup fresh bread crumbs
- ½ pound chilled sliced bacon
- ½ pound chilled pork liver (calf's, beef, or chicken liver can be substituted if pork liver is unavailable)
- Salt and pepper to taste
- 2 tablespoons shelled pistachio nuts
- A 1-pound pork tenderloin

≈

1. Finely chop the onion and mushrooms. Sauté in the butter until the onion is beginning to soften and all excess moisture has cooked away. Stir in the herbs, mustard, and bread crumbs. Set aside to cool.
2. Chop half of the bacon and all the liver and stir into the cool mushroom mixture. Season with salt and pepper.
3. Place the pistachio nuts in boiling water for a few seconds only, then ease off the skins. Cut each pistachio in half lengthwise.
4. Cut the pork tenderloin into ¼-inch strips lengthwise, and flatten them between sheets of waxed paper with a rolling pin.
5. Line a 6-cup terrine (a deep earthenware bowl) with the remaining strips of bacon. Arrange a layer of pork tenderloin. Cover that with a layer of mushroom-onion mixture. Sprinkle on some of the pistachios. Repeat the layers, ending with a layer of pork-tenderloin strips.
6. Cover the dish tightly with aluminum foil. Place the terrine in a roasting pan or baking dish and pour enough water in the pan to come halfway up the side.
7. Bake the terrine in a preheated 350-degree oven for about an hour, or until the juices run clear when the top of the terrine is pierced with a knife blade.
8. Remove the foil and pour off and discard any juices. Replace the foil, weight with small cans of soup, and refrigerate for a couple days before serving.

Serves 6 to 8.

Beef Rillettes

- 1 pound leftover roast beef, chopped
- ¼ cup beer
- ¼ teaspoon ground cloves
- ¼ teaspoon fresh-ground black pepper
- 2 to 3 anchovy fillets, chopped
- 2 tablespoons butter, softened
- 2 to 3 tablespoons butter, melted

Rillettes—or potted meats, as Grandma called them—are cooked meat, poultry, or fish that has been pounded or shredded into fibers, mixed with lard or butter, then preserved in little stoneware, porcelain, or glass crocks. Covered with a thin layer of fat, either butter or lard, rillettes will keep refrigerated for weeks. They also freeze well.

Purists in the food field will insist that rillettes be made from scratch with fresh meat cooked specifically for the purpose. But, as you may have noticed, I am not a purist, particularly when it comes to saving money and time. There are wonderful things to be done with leftover meats that can be done in the name of rillettes.

This is a great way to turn any leftover roast beef from a holiday dinner into hors d'oeuvres for a New Year's buffet.

≈

1. Put all the ingredients except the butter in a heavy pot; cover and simmer for 10 to 15 minutes to heat through and blend flavors.

2. Pour the contents of the pot into the bowl of your food processor and process by using a pulsing action. Do not puree; you want a mixture with a coarse texture. Stir in the softened butter.

3. Pour the mixture into 3 or 4 small crocks or ramekins. Refrigerate to cool. Pour a thin film of melted butter over each rillette. Refrigerate, covered, until the butter sets, or overnight. Rillettes will keep for several days. Serve with thin toast.

Serves 10 to 12 as hors d'oeuvres.

VARIATIONS

Pork Rillettes Use leftover pork roast and ¼ cup chicken stock instead of the beer. Season with 1 teaspoon chopped parsley, ¼ teaspoon grated nutmeg, ⅓ cup finely minced onion, and ¼ teaspoon powdered mace. Salt and pepper to taste. Process in the food processor and proceed as above. If the roast pork has a fair amount of fat, the softened butter may not be necessary—use your own judgment.

Ham and Cheese Rillettes Combine 1 cup chopped cooked ham, 2 chopped hard-cooked eggs, 1 3-ounce package cream cheese, 1 teaspoon Dijon mustard, 2 or 3 finely chopped mushrooms, and 1 or 2 tablespoons finely chopped onion. Process in a food processor, pack into small crocks, and cover with melted butter. Refrigerate, covered, overnight. This is excellent served with warm buttermilk biscuits as a buffet item.

Appendix
Sources of Country Hams

≈

Burger Ozark Country Cured Hams, Inc.
Hwy. 87 S.
RR 3, Box 3248
California, MO 65018
(314) 796-3134
fax (314) 796-3137
(800) 624-5426

Clifty Farms/TN Valley Ham Co.
P.O. Box 1146
Paris, TN 38242
(901) 642-9740
fax (901) 642-7129
(800) 486-4267

Johnston County Country Hams
204 N. Bright Leaf Blvd.
Smithfield, NC 27577
(919) 934-8054
fax (919) 934-1091
(800) 543-4267

Marion's Ham House
P.O. Box 536
Glade Valley, NC 28627
(800) 289-2123

Mom 'n Pop's Smokehouse
P.O. Box 399
Claremont, NC 28610
fax (704) 459-5405
(800) 222-9771

S. Wallace Edwards & Sons, Inc.
P.O. Box 25
Surry, VA 23883
(804) 294-3121
fax (804) 294-5378
(800) 222-4267

Scott Hams
1301 Scott Rd.
Greenville, KY 42345
(502) 338-3402
fax (502) 338-6643

Stadlers Country Hams, Inc.
P.O. Box 397
Elon College, NC 27244-0397
(910) 584-1396
fax (910) 584-9483
(800) 262-1795

Tripp Country Hams
P.O. Box 527
Brownville, TN 38012
(901) 772-2130
fax (901) 772-6798

V. W. Joyner & Co.
P.O. Box 387
Smithfield, VA 23430
(804) 357-2161
fax (804) 357-0184
(800) 628-2242

Wayco Ham Co.
P.O. Box 841
Goldsboro, NC 27533
(919) 735-3962
fax (919) 734-4080
(800) 962-2614

Finchville Farms
P.O. Box 56
Finchville, KY 40022
(502) 834-7952
fax (502) 834-7095
(800) 678-1521

Hickory Mountain Farms
P.O. Box 445
Siler City, NC 27344
(919) 742-2144
fax (919) 742-4806
(800) 472-3132

Index

≈

Page numbers in *italics* refer to illustrations.

A Note About the Author

Merle Ellis was born and grew up in Sioux City, Iowa, where he apprenticed in his father's meat market. He started writing about meat in 1973 in the San Francisco *Chronicle* with a weekly column entitled "The Butcher." He was for years a frequent guest on *The Dinah Shore Show, Good Morning America,* and numerous other television shows. His syndicated newspaper column and television series have made him America's best-known butcher. His best-selling previous book, *Cutting Up in the Kitchen,* is now in its eighteenth printing. He and his wife, Neva (whose Hawaiian heritage lends an Asian accent to some of Merle's contemporary recipes), live in Tiburon, California.

A Note on the Type

The text of this book was set in Plantin, a typeface first cut in 1913 by the Monotype Corporation of London. Though the face bears the name of the great Christopher Plantin (ca. 1520–1589), who in the latter part of the sixteenth century owned, in Antwerp, the largest printing and publishing firm in Europe, it is a rather free adaptation of designs by Claude Garamond made for that firm. With its strong, simple lines, Plantin is a no-nonsense face of exceptional legibility.

Composed by North Market Street Graphics,
Lancaster, Pennsylvania
Printed and bound by Courier Book Companies,
Westford, Massachusetts
Designed by Virginia Tan

KNOPF COOKS AMERICAN

The series of cookbooks that celebrates the culinary heritage of America, telling different aspects of our story through recipes interspersed with historical lore, personal reflections, and the recollections of old-timers.

ALREADY PUBLISHED:

Biscuits, Spoonbread, and Sweet Potato Pie by Bill Neal

Hot Links & Country Flavors by Bruce Aidells and Denis Kelly

Barbecued Ribs, Smoked Butts, and Other Great Feeds by Jeanne Voltz

We Called It Macaroni by Nancy Verde Barr

The West Coast Cook Book by Helen Evans Brown

Pleasures of the Good Earth by Edward Giobbi

The Brooklyn Cookbook by Lyn Stallworth and Rod Kennedy, Jr.

Dungeness Crabs and Blackberry Cobblers by Janie Hibler

Preserving Today by Jeanne Lesem

Blue Corn and Chocolate by Elisabeth Rozin

Real Beer & Good Eats by Bruce Aidells and Denis Kelly

The Florida Cookbook by Jeanne Voltz and Caroline Stuart

Jewish Cooking in America by Joan Nathan

Savoring the Seasons of the Northern Heartland by Beth Dooley and Lucia Watson

"Our food tells us where we came from and who we are . . ."